POLITICAL AND INCORRECT

Tavleen Singh is the author of four books, *Kashmir: A Tragedy of Errors*; *Lollipop Street: Why India Will Survive Her Politicians*; *Political and Incorrect: The Real India, Warts and All* and *Durbar*. She writes four weekly political columns—in English for the *Indian Express* and for syndication, and in Hindi for *Amar Ujala* and *Jansatta*.

POLITICAL AND INCORRECT

THE REAL INDIA, WARTS AND ALL

Tavleen Singh

HarperCollins *Publishers* India

THE EXPRESS GROUP

THE EXPRESS GROUP BOOK SERIES

First published in hardback in India by
HarperCollins *Publishers* in 2008

Building 10, Tower A, 4th Floor, DLF Cyber II,
Gurugram Haryana - 122002, India
www.harpercollins.co.in
First published in paperback in 2014

The columns in page 134 to 213 appeared in India Today

4 6 8 10 9 7 5

ISBN: 978-93-5136-258-6

Typeset in 10.5/13 Sabon Roman at
SÜRYA
Printed and bound at
MicroPrints India, New Delhi

CONTENTS

FOREWORD

The pages of the *Indian Express* have hosted India's finest columnists over 75 years. But Tavleen Singh, whose Fifth Column has just completed 20 years (unbroken except for a short period) is in so many ways the quintessential Express columnist: bold, in your face, argumentative and opinionated. Also she is not one to mince or waste words. She makes her point briefly—a skill I adore as an editor, and envy as a writer. She is also a most professional columnist. Her piece arrives on time, on the appointed day, always, no explanation, no excuses. So she is an editor's delight in more ways than one.

But, as a fellow—and equally argumentative journalist—I have always enjoyed sparring with her. That, in fact, is exactly what happened to our first conversation almost a quarter century ago. We had both chosen to travel by overnight train—Frontier Mail—to Amritsar, something sane people never did during those peak years of terrorism. Sure enough, the train was empty. Tavleen and I had a coupe to ourselves and we spent hours fighting over what was wrong with Punjab—then under Bhindranwale's shadow—and how Indira Gandhi could fix it. Sure enough, nobody lost the argument and we have maintained that record since, over many issues, from politics and economics to foreign policy. But on one point, there can be no argument. Tavleen is a wonderful writer-journalist, a jewel in the crown of this newspaper. And this collection, that tracks India's revolution through the era of one Mrs Gandhi to another, is a must read for anybody with a stake in the country's politics and governance.

SHEKHAR GUPTA
Editor-in-Chief, The Indian Express Group

ACKNOWLEDGEMENTS

I would like to thank Nandini Mehta for giving me the chance to write a political column at a time when women were considered incapable of doing such things. I would like to thank Shekhar Gupta and Aroon Purie for making this book possible and for never interfering in anything I wrote. I would like to thank Ambreen Khan, Rakesh Dewal, Doreen Khakusuma and Pankaj Bhutani for their help in digging up material from archives that existed before computers came along. I would like to thank Krishan Chopra and Minakshi Thakur for all their help.

For giving me the title of the book I would like to thank my son, Aatish Taseer, who was seven years old when the first Fifth Column appeared in the *Indian Express*, and for valuable advice and criticism over these past twenty years I would like to thank Ajit Gulabchand.

INTRODUCTION

When I sat down to put this compilation together and looked back consciously to the decade in which I began writing a political column for the *Indian Express*, I remembered how different India was in 1987. Forty years of socialism had left us with more than half our people living in absolute poverty, no middle class to speak of, pre-modern infrastructure and a shabby, defeated sort of country. If we had something to be proud of it was only that we had survived as a democracy. India has changed immeasurably since then and the most important change in my view is that modern technology and revolutionary changes in communications enable India to be presented to Indians as never before.

As an illustration of how much India has changed I give you a story from 1987 of starvation deaths in Orissa. They occurred in Koraput and Kalahandi and because children dying of hunger was routine in this part of India the story barely made a paragraph in the national newspapers. It was only because I wrote for a British newspaper for whom starvation deaths were unusual and shocking enough to make front page news that I went to investigate. There were no roads connecting Koraput to the villages from which the deaths were being reported so the only way to get there was on foot. Hours of walking up steep dirt trails brought me to villages totally bereft of food because the rains had failed that year destroying the area's primitive single-crop economy. Children were dying after weeks of being fed on only a watery gruel made of some kind of birdseed. They lay with distended bellies and glassy eyes dying slowly on the floors of mud huts in which there was nothing.

The response of the Orissa government was to set up 'khichdi' kitchens miles away in the nearest town and only for children under the age of five. With typical government insensitivity children older than five were turned away so their younger siblings took their meal of lentils and rice home to share with the whole family. The point of this story is that this could not happen in today's India. Children still die of hunger even in supposedly rich states like Maharashtra but not without television crews descending to record what is happening and forcing government into action. Television has been in my view the single most important engine of change in India followed closely by the cellphone. It is because of technology rather than better governance that it has been possible for India's villages to leapfrog from the eighteenth century to the edge of the twenty-first.

The eighties was India's last decade of unbending socialism. Our version of socialism gave us neither the achievements in healthcare, education and employment of other socialist countries nor the energy and enterprise that comes with free markets. We had political freedom and free elections but the state's control over the economy was totalitarian. In the name of protecting the interests of what officials called the 'weaker sections of society' the state actively discouraged the private sector and frowned upon prosperity. The result was unrelenting, pervasive, dreadful poverty which the state supposedly alleviated through grandiose schemes.

Central planning and its arm the public sector were the economic idea of the eighties with the Ambassador car as the shoddy symbol of what India could produce. Government factories produced everything from matchsticks and edible oil to bread and milk. It was a time of grim shortages but even when the state failed to produce what people needed private enterprise was discouraged. In the limited area of economic activity in which Indian entrepreneurs were allowed to function the state controlled licences and quotas. Businessmen could be fined for exceeding their quotas or producing without a licence. The economy stagnated and the poor remained poor and mostly illiterate.

Politically there was a different kind of mess. Grave policy mistakes had led to secessionist movements in most of India's border states. Up north in Punjab and Kashmir, secessionist movements turned into armed struggles. In the northeast, states like Assam, Mizoram and Nagaland remained victims of similar movements that began much earlier. The southern states were under siege because of Indian policies that allowed Tamil separatist groups from Sri Lanka to use India as a hinterland for their struggle.

So embroiled was India in its internal problems that it lost touch with what was going on in the rest of the world. While East Asia was taking full advantage of Western technology and computerization to start catching up with the First World, India remained mired in deprivation. The average Indian lived without reliable supplies of such basic necessities as clean water, electricity, education and healthcare. These problems still exist but there is awareness, hope and the aspiration for a better life even in remote villages now.

It was in the nineties that real change began when India came to the brink of defaulting on international loans. This forced economic reforms that ended the infamous licence-quota-permit raj. Change also happened because technology made some controls impossible. Satellite television could not be stopped when it arrived in the early nineties. The Indian state fought back by trying to control the growth of Indian channels but failed. Private television channels have proliferated in all of India's languages despite government efforts to contain their spread. The arrival of the cellphone a few years later made the state's inability to provide sufficient telephone lines irrelevant. Today, it is hard to find a village in India where the cellphone has not reached and where there isn't at least one television set. The spread of personal computers is not yet that extensive but there is hardly a town left in which internet is not available and it is becoming increasingly available in rural India.

India has changed incalculably. In the early eighties, I remember going to a village in Bihar's Palamu district where bonded labourers in a village less than ten kilometres from Daltonganj had never been to the town. I remember another village barely a hundred kilometres from Udaipur in which I met adivasi families who did not know that India was no longer ruled by the British. This kind of isolation and ignorance is hard to find in today's India.

The twenty-first century has brought an awareness of the need to replace India's dilapidated infrastructure. Our ports, railways and airports remain pre-modern but there is at least the awareness of the need for them to change. The need to build highways has been recognized but India remains one of the few countries left in the world that does not have a modern access-controlled motorway.

As much as there has been dramatic change there has been a dramatic absence of change in areas of vital need. India remains a country that has failed to meet the basic requirements of its people like power, clean water, roads and sanitary living conditions. One reason for this abysmal state of affairs is that there has been almost no change in methods of governance. Computerization has arrived but government offices across the country continue to reek of decaying files and remain mired in procedures of governance so convoluted that only Indian officials can understand them. They plead that they are victims of the 'system' but nobody takes responsibility for having made the system or changing it.

Things will change when the Indian politician changes for the better but the twenty-first century has brought a change for the worse. The idealists and Gandhians that the freedom movement bequeathed us have been replaced by an aggressive new breed of grassroots political leaders whose main reason for being in public life is usually self-aggrandizement. Parliamentary constituencies have come to be treated as personal fiefdoms with political parties handing them down from one generation to the next. Politics has become such a profitable career option that criminals give up crime to contest for election.

If despite these failings there is a sense of optimism in twenty-first century India it is because civil society is now more confident and mature making the role of the state less important. But, without some improvement in governance India will be unable to win the war against poverty. Half of India's citizens continue to live on less than Rs. 20 a day and nearly half of India's children are malnourished. These are problems that cannot be solved unless governance improves and, alas, there are few signs of this happening. This book is a chronicle of change in India in the past twenty years as seen through the prism of a column that revels in being politically incorrect.

FIRST DECADE
(1987–1997)

OFF WITH THEIR HEADS

13 December 1987

Shortly after the public sacking of Foreign Secretary A.P. Venkateswaran earlier this year, I was summoned for a private chat by a former high official of the ministry of external affairs. Like many other once exalted mandarins he now works in some obscure political capacity and one of his tasks is to keep a beady eye on adverse changes in the prime minister's image. It was in an attempt to rectify the damage brought about by the public sacking that I was summoned. We talked for a while of this and that and took many sips of hot sweet instant coffee before he said, 'Well, what are people saying? Do they say the prime minister was wrong to have done what he did?' I confirmed that this was basically what people were saying and more. It did not look good, I pointed out warming to the theme, for democratically elected leaders to go around behaving like spoilt princes and Venkat was a highly respected civil servant and so on. A look of impatience crossed the face of the former high official and he interrupted me to say, 'It's only people who do not understand the prime minister who talk like this. Anyone who knows him would know that there are many things that would have irritated the prime minister about someone like Venkat. After all the prime minister is a man of some style and sophistication and Venkat had this habit of sitting with his leg crossed over his knee. This used to upset the prime minister.'

So it was 'off with his head' for Venkat and then it was 'off with his head' for the police commissioner. He also offended the prime minister's sense of style. The prime minister forgave Ved Marwah for being unable to prevent innocent people being shot at birthday parties and while they were offering prayers to the Goddess Durga. He even forgave him for having been unable to prevent some idiot taking a potshot at him from behind bushes that should have been checked but when it comes to style and decorum no lapse is permissible.

Ved Marwah's version of events is not known since he has chosen to remain absolutely silent. But according to the stories that have trickled down through 'reliable sources' what happened was a serious breach of protocol, style and decorum.

The arrival of the Russian prime minister had gone perfectly...soft November sunshine, Sonia looking ravishing in brightly coloured silk and RG at his elegant best in a dark Nehru jacket. If it had not been for the police commissioner trying to take shortcuts and giving lifts to ministers who should have been in their own cars the Russian prime minister would have gone home convinced that India was the most stylish country in the world.

What happened was as follows. Natwar Singh, our minister of state for external affairs, decided to hitch a ride to Rashtrapati Bhavan in the police commissioner's car and urged him to try and get there before the Russian prime minister's motorcade arrived, so they took a shortcut and arrived just as the motorcade was streaming into the president's house. They backed slightly to stay out of the way and in his panic the driver reversed into the bumper of Mr Bhajan Lal's car, which was also trying to take a shortcut. The minister's Black Cat commandos, who have been trained to leap into action the minute a car dares to touch theirs, jumped out and took positions before realizing that they were aiming at the police commissioner.

Meanwhile, the Russian prime minister's bodyguards, also trained to shoot unidentified armed men in the vicinity of their prime minister, nearly leapt into action themselves. Then someone spotted the police commissioner. There was no shootout. The day was saved and surely all could have been explained to the Russians and apologies profusely tendered. But no, Marwah had to go because his little shortcut embarrassed our prime minister in front of the Russians and these things matter to him.

ALL SOUND, NO LIGHT

20 December 1987

On a cold clear night not long ago I took myself off to the Old Fort to witness a son et lumiere on Indira Gandhi. I went not out of a desire to remember our late prime minister but because I was curious about why Indira Gandhi's story was being told against the backdrop of a monument that had never had anything to do with her life. Had some idiot in the ministry of information confused the Purana Qila (old fort) with the Red Fort, from whose ramparts the late prime minister unfurled the national flag thirteen times on Independence Day?

I have to report sadly that neither curiosity nor patriotism drew Delhi's other citizens to the event. There were so few people that I thought the show had been cancelled. Then as I waited uncertainly between the empty VIP enclosure and the nearly empty citizens enclosure a group of persons with blankets thrown over their shoulders and packets of peanuts in their hands suddenly arrived. There were at this point songs about family planning filling the air—something about how even the sky had only two children, the sun and the moon, and how they lighted up the world. The words made the youths laugh their heads off. The family planning song was replaced by a patriotic one, which I thought must mean that the show had begun but it had not. The organizers were waiting for more people to arrive but apart from more youths with peanut packets and a few children who started turning somersaults in the VIP enclosure nobody came. After delaying things for about half an hour the show began.

It began with sound rather than light and it began badly. For ten minutes all that we got were credits announced in one of those boring Films Division documentary voices. Then just when I thought my peanut-munching comrades in the plebs enclosure were about to throw their packets at the voice, a spotlight came on and focused on two women dressed in Rajasthani skirts and a man who looked like one of the president's bodyguards. They sang 'come gather round and hear the story of Indira, this daughter of India, and of our great country.'

Of our great country there was little said other than some praise of our secularism and our varied folk dances, but of the Nehru family much was said and it was said in the soap opera genre. A soap opera of such appalling quality that I am convinced the Opposition parties have somehow taken over the ministry of information and engineered a dark and devious plot to sabotage the memory of our dear departed prime minister. Two departed prime ministers actually. Let me give you a sample of a dialogue between Motilal and Jawaharlal Nehru when father comes to visit son in jail. 'Father, how are you?' 'Just as a moti (pearl) should be. And you Jawahar?' 'Just as a Jawahar (precious stone) should be.'

As for poor Bharat Ratna Indira, she comes across as a half-crazed hysteric much given to screeching at our villagers that their lives must be like John (sic) of Arc. May I add that the show did have a limited success with the youths in the plebs enclosure. They seemed to think it was meant to be a spoof. They burst into raucous laughter in all the serious parts but when after an hour we had only got as far as the death of Jawaharlal Nehru they left.

The next time the Government of India wants to treat us to a patriotic son et lumiere they should consult Bhagwan Rajneesh, who is now back in business in Poona. I recently visited the ashram in connection with all that AIDS business and, incidentally, must say that I think it shocking that some little doctor in Bombay should be able to get up and state that Rajneesh has AIDS without bothering to verify the facts. It is even more shocking that newspapers should carry the story under headlines like 'Rajneesh has AIDS'. I must be among the very few people who have never been to one of Rajneesh's shows (sorry, discourses) so at the ashram when I got the chance to participate in his morning discourse I leapt at it.

What a show! We were led after being sniffed, body searched and metal detected into an enclosed garden full of trees through which the morning sunlight filtered down in magical colours on to a vast green mosquito net which enclosed the open air Chuang Tzu auditorium. There could not be a more perfect spot for thoughts of mysticism and spirituality and all achieved with sound and light. From where we sat on the green mosaic floor we could see the trees through the mosquito net and watch them change colour with the light. Sound was provided by Bhagwan's personal musicians who mixed flute with guitar and tabla to create the right special effects. So magical was the atmosphere that when Rajneesh floated in looking very well and proceeded to tell dirty jokes about grabbing bank managers by the balls and racist jokes about Jews he managed to pass them off as the thoughts of an enlightened master. A truly impressive son et lumiere.

THE NEW RAJIV

27 December 1987

At a New Year's Eve party last year I met a friend of Rajiv Gandhi. The prime minister was at the time holidaying in the Andaman Islands with Italian family and friends and all was well with the world. The grim shadow of Bofors had yet to lengthen over Camelot and we were still safe in our illusion that India was being ruled by a fairytale prince who could wave a magic wand and give us peace, prosperity and even the twenty-first century. But this friend of RG was worried. He explained that he foresaw troubled times ahead and feared that political difficulties would turn his friend into a politician. 'If he can survive and remain Rajiv Gandhi then we will be all right, but if he succumbs and becomes a politician then I am not so sure.' Well, 1987 did turn out to be a bad year and RG did become a politician but sadly not a very good one. Gone overnight was the starry-eyed young man who had scoured the villages of India looking for poor people to help and corrupt people to punish. Instead we got the hard-headed party leader who could make several trips to Nagaland to announce massive drought relief for a non-existent drought, merely because elections were due there, while children starved to death in Orissa.

A politician's most important weapon is a thick skin and you would have had to be in the Lok Sabha during the debate on the no-confidence motion to have seen that 1987 has given RG enough time to develop one. It was clear from question hour that something special was going to happen in the Lok Sabha because unlike normal days the House was nearly full. Then, shortly before question hour ended the ministers began to file in...K.C. Pant, Narasimha Rao, Buta Singh, Bhajan Lal, Tytler...you name them and they were there. Except for Madhav Rao Scindia, who was marrying his daughter off that day.

Then the prime minister arrived and proceedings began with Madhav Reddy of the Telugu Desam moving the motion. He barely started and the heckling began when he said that the prime minister was hardly ever in the House and this reflected his disdain for Parliament. Congress (I) MPs hissed, booed and hooted, ministers joining in, while the prime minister sat smiling happily until things seemed to be getting totally out of hand, when with a wave of his hand he silenced his supporters. Fortunately he did not stay throughout and when he was not in the House most of his party went with him, so the Opposition got the chance to raise important issues. The drought, the problems with defence deals, the rise in prices, the non-punishment of those involved in the Sikh massacres of 1984 and the worsening communal situation.

When the prime minister returned to make his two-hour reply what did he say? That the Opposition parties were talking rubbish because they were filled with men who had a 'total bankruptcy of thinking, ideas and vision' and were capable only of making 'petty, personal remarks'.

Poor RG. Those who have taught him the art of politics have clearly told him that the only way to deal with reality is to close one's eyes and pretend to be deaf. Had he wanted to see he would have noticed that the real no-confidence motion was being moved not in the Lok Sabha but just outside at the Boat Club, where the Left parties managed to gather half a million people from the Hindi-belt states to protest against his policies. And where in one corner a group of Sikhs fasted in relays to demand that the guilty of 1984 be punished.

REGIMENTAL COLOURS

13 March 1988

I ran for my country. By this I do not mean that I staggered through the streets of Delhi dying of thirst and heat. Us VIPs were not expected to. For us a symbolic jog down Rajpath in the company of the prime minister, half the Cabinet and some glamorous film stars was considered sufficient evidence of devotion to Bharat Mata. How can I begin to tell you what fun it was. The usual cynical commentators have attacked the Freedom Run under nasty headlines like 'Running Away from Reality' and 'Tasteless and Chaotic', but these are people who can never see anything right with Rajiv's India.

I have a serious-minded friend who said she recently went to a village and puzzled villagers gathered around her to demand an explanation for the Freedom Run. 'I tried,' she said 'but when I told them about running to express our sense of determination to face external and internal threats to the country they only got more confused and said surely if these threats exist then we should work together solidly instead of running around.'

What can peasants know of such sophisticated concepts as Running for Freedom? What can they know of the exhilaration of listening to the soundtrack from *Chariots of Fire* as we jogged towards India Gate? To understand the meaning of running for freedom you would have had to see it from our point of vantage in the VIP enclosure.

I nearly never made it because of the usual problems with

security. There was confusion over the passes and the guards outside the VIP enclosure were extra vigilant. They told me politely but firmly that they could not care less whether I was from the press or not, if I could not get another pass (we were one short) then I could forget about trying to get in. Mani Shankar Aiyar, who happened to be sitting at the entrance looking quite fetching in a grey tracksuit, came to the rescue. I thought it was sporting of him to dress for the occasion till I discovered that it was the VIP uniform for the day.

If you were in a grey tracksuit in the VIP enclosure then it meant that you were more than a mere VIP. You were a star, and there were a lot of stars that day. Sharmila Tagore. Tiger Pataudi, Kapil Dev, Sunil Gavaskar, Om Puri, Naseeruddin Shah, Shabana Azmi and Sunil Dutt to name only a few. Zeenat Aman was also there with her husband and was the only star not in a tracksuit possibly on account of some unshed maternal bulges. But if I were giving a prize for sporting spirit it would have gone to H.K.L. Bhagat who looked so utterly out of place in a tracksuit that it really must have taken courage to wear it.

Later Romi Chopra (who along with Suresh Kalmadi is one of the masterminds of the Freedom Run) commented on how wonderful it was to see cabinet ministers in tracksuits, 'Like khadi, tracksuits are a great leveller,' he said and I found it hard to suppress the image of Gandhiji jogging down to Dandi in a grey tracksuit. But then Gandhiji would not have fit in with the spirit of the Freedom Run. Had he been around and had he been allowed inside the VIP enclosure I doubt that he would have understood the new patriotism and the new India. He may have gone on boringly about how the real India lives in the villages and this would have ruined the atmosphere of fun and frolic in our enclosure.

Other than the stars and the politicians, everyone who is anyone in Delhi social circles was also present, and had there been chilled champagne instead of Thums Up it would have been the best party I have ever been to in Delhi. I mentioned this, en passant, to Romi and he said, 'The real champagne is the sight of a hundred thousand people running together down Rajpath.' There were a few bad moments when the massive crowd came to a complete standstill in front of our enclosure and looked as if they were going to break in, but the police came to the rescue and they were hastily moved along. After the plebs had been dispersed came our turn to run and our joy knew no bounds when our young and handsome prime minister (looking really dishy in his grey tracksuit) joined us for some distance. Afterwards, still reeling from the heady spirit of freedom, many of us jogged off to the nearest five star hotel for sustenance. How wonderful to no longer have to pretend to be a socialist to be considered patriotic!

INDIA'S MID-LIFE CRISIS?

10 April 1988

Why is everyone making such a fuss about India's fortieth birthday? The question came from a friend from abroad who was passing through Delhi during the period when much noise was being made about running and marching for the country. He said he could understand celebrations of a fiftieth or a twenty-fifth anniversary but was puzzled about the significance of forty. For human beings, forty is a sad sort of age redolent of mid-life crises of one kind or another so it is hard to think of fortieth birthdays as being occasions for celebration. Yet India's fortieth year of independence is being celebrated with more gusto than any other year so far. Why?

The answer is simple. India's fortieth year happens to coincide with Jawaharlal Nehru's hundredth, so the government thought it would be a wonderful opportunity for everyone to once again be reminded of the sacrifices and achievements of India's leading political family. We who live in Delhi can hardly forget the dynasty, reminded as we are daily by the numerous and diverse institutions that have mushroomed in the city bearing the names Nehru or Gandhi (Indira Nehru Gandhi as opposed to Mahatma). To mention only a few, there is the Indira Gandhi International Airport, the Indira Gandhi Indoor stadium and the Jawaharlal Nehru stadium. There are occasionally other reminders. For a few months in 1985 a giant, ninety-foot, cardboard cut-out of Mrs Gandhi towered over India Gate, but it was removed because it caused unfortunate misunderstandings. It was erected around Dussehra and confused the children who kept demanding to know why there was only one and not three.

For us in Delhi, the sacrifices of the Nehrus and the Gandhis are always foremost in our minds but certain sections of the government were of the view that in the provinces remembrance was getting lax, hence the setting up of what has come to be known as the 40/100 Committee. Prominent Indians of all kinds (politicians, poets, painters, musicians, journalists and film stars) are members of the committee but the actual work is done by a smaller implementation committee that was headed by Amitabh Bachchan.

When he retired from public life Mrs Sheila Dikshit took his place. She is assisted by former Foreign Secretary Romesh Bhandari and the prime minister's close friend Romi Chopra. It is this team that has given us the nationalistic television advertisements and the programmes on the freedom movement designed to revive dead memories.

I saw one recently on the Dandi March and found it particularly poignant because of a line of commentary which said that Gandhiji had undertaken the march because he had been horrified by the callousness of a government that could tax such an 'irreplaceable ingredient' as salt. The commentator described how the average diet of a poor Indian in those days was roti and salt. The writer was perhaps unaware that in Orissa during the worst periods of last year's drought people ate only a gruel of boiled mango seeds. In many villages, people did not have enough money to buy salt, leave alone grain. Considering that it was a salt tax that started a mass movement in India, it is just as well that there is no electricity in that part of Orissa leave alone television sets. In any case nobody would have understood a word of the film since it was in English.

For us of the urban English-speaking elite at whom the film was directed there was a delicious irony in Romesh Bhandari telling us at the end that the new Dandi March (led by RG in saffron peasant turban) was meant to reaffirm our commitment to the poor—'The future of India depends on the future of the poor of India.'

HANGING FIRE

23 October 1988

Ever since the death warrants for Satwant Singh and Kehar Singh were signed Delhi has waited with bated breath to see if the hanging will actually happen. Some Sikh leaders have pleaded for a pardon, arguing that mercy will go a long way to improving Rajiv Gandhi's image in Punjab, especially since we have yet to see justice for the victims of the 1984 massacres.

I have been trying to interview Satwant Singh but without any luck so far so I decided as the next best thing to interview his lawyer, R.S. Sodhi, who is one of the few people allowed to see him regularly in the four years that he has been in solitary confinement in Tihar. During the early stages of the trial held under the highest security in a makeshift courtroom in Tihar some of us managed to exchange a few words with him but this was quickly made impossible. He would be ushered straight into his bullet-proof glass cubicle through which we could only see and not hear him. The impression that remains is of a young quite good-looking man who likes dressing up. On the first day of the trial he arrived wearing a white silk kurta-pyjama, with gold embroidered Punjabi shoes, a blue turban and a saffron scarf around his shoulders. As the days went by he switched to well-cut jeans and shirts which made him look athletic and surprisingly healthy for a man who told the court that he was in agony because of a bullet lodged in his spine.

After the assassination Mrs Gandhi's security guards opened

fire on the two assassins killing Beant Singh and injuring Satwant. According to Mr Sodhi, he now does no exercise at all and instead sits for hours reading the Granth Sahib or meditating. Sometimes he goes into a sort of trance from which he has to be physically shaken out of for meals. I asked if he was showing any signs of remorse, fear or panic, the sort of things one expects from a man awaiting death. 'No. He is very fatalistic and believes that people only die when their time has come.'

His family is allowed to see him once a week but his wife, the woman who insisted on marrying his photograph, is not permitted to see him any more and this is the only thing that saddens him. She was allowed to see him while she was his fiancée but has not been permitted any visits since she decided to become his wife.

He is allowed newspapers in his cell after they have been censored and is said to have observed that all the judges involved in the trial have been given out of turn promotions. He pointed out to his lawyer that Mahesh Chandra was promoted to the High Court, Justice S. Ranganathan to the Supreme Court and Justice M. Thakkar was appointed to the Law Commission after retirement.

According to Sodhi, Satwant now refuses to leave his cell even for the mandatory daily exercise because he finds it humiliating to be dragged around handcuffed. The result is that he can barely walk any more and will have to be taken to his execution in a van. He is no longer in any pain from the bullet in his spine. The jail doctors said it could not be removed because it could cripple him so he pulled it out himself and the pain went. The execution has been temporarily postponed (it should have been last week) till Kehar Singh's mercy petition is decided but this does not affect Satwant who is believed to have said, 'I had no enmity with Mrs Gandhi. She could not have died unless God wanted her to. I will die only when God wants me to.'

TROUBLE IN PARADISE

13 November 1988

It is sad that despite the best efforts of SAARC (South Asian Association for Regional Cooperation) the only way we citizens of South Asia can discover each other's countries is when there is trouble. Currency restrictions, visa problems and suspicions bordering on paranoia make it impossible even for journalists to cross SAARC boundaries unless there is an assassination, a revolution or a coup. So it was the ethnic violence between Tamils and Sinhalese that gave me a chance to visit Sri Lanka and it was last week's attempted coup that took me to the Maldives.

We went courtesy of the MEA (ministry of external affairs) in an Indian Air Force AN 32. It took us seven hours, sitting cramped in a toothpaste tube of a plane, but it was the only way to go since the airport was closed to civilian traffic. When we finally hobbled off, semi-crippled from sitting hunchbacked for so long, it was at an airport that resembled an Indian military base. All around us were tall, strapping soldiers wearing the camouflage battle fatigues of the 15th Independent Para Brigade, and there were howitzers (Bofors?) on wheels and machine guns mounted on jeeps, all of which made us feel we had strayed onto the sets of a battle scene in a Bombay film.

This surreal feeling was heightened by the contrast between our immediate setting and the spectacular beauty just beyond. The sea comes all the way up to the doorway of the VIP arrival lounge and its colours were enough to make me momentarily forget that we were here to cover a coup. On account of the coral or the light or something the colour of the water changes every few yards so it goes from turquoise to deep emerald to purple and dark grey all at the same time and like little dots everywhere are the 1200 islands that constitute the Maldives. An ideal place for an attack by mercenaries because what happens on one island hardly has any effect on the others.

So when Male was invaded by Tamil mercenaries led by a group of disgruntled Maldivians on 3 November, none of the thousands of Western tourists sleeping peacefully in resorts on other islands knew anything about it. Some found out when they tried to go into Male several hours later. Others only when the Indian Air Force planes arrived late at night.

For all its surreal quality it was a serious coup. In Male we saw walls smashed by rockets and buildings pock-marked with bullet holes. Some of Male's citizens had began to venture tentatively into its unpaved streets and they told of hearing the shooting at dawn and innocent people being shot dead. The power supply was cut so there was no radio or television for nearly twenty-four hours and nothing to do but hide in their houses and peer out at the fighting in the empty streets. Male is about the size of one of Delhi's large government buildings so nearly everyone had a ringside seat and the nightmare only ended when our troops arrived and the mercenaries fled.

So far, it is hard to meet anyone who is not rapturous about the role played by the Indian army and navy but how long will it be before the citizens of Male begin to resent the sight of Indian soldiers swaggering through their narrow streets? Our government would like the troops to return as soon as possible but the Maldives has no army, only a militia of 2000 men to handle defence, policing, customs and security. If there is one idea whose time has come it is a SAARC task force instead of this proliferation of IPKFs (Indian Peace Keeping Force).

There are lessons we can learn from the Maldives. I recommend that our ministry of tourism send a team here immediately to learn how the Maldives has become in tourism terms the most successful country in the region. Tourism is increasing annually at a phenomenal twenty-five per cent a year and yet the Maldives islands remain unspoilt and unbelievably beautiful. Male is a place of whitewashed houses and spotless streets in which bicycles are the main form of transport. And as for the resorts...words fail me. There are now nearly seventy resort islands and we spent the night in one of the newest, the Kurumba Village resort. To describe it as a hotel would be inaccurate. It is more like the most perfect village you could ever see with little whitewashed bungalows covered in bougainvillea and gardens sloping down to the sea.

When we met President Gayoom at a press conference someone asked whether he feared that the attempted coup would have a bad effect on tourism. He replied that on the contrary he believed that so much international publicity could only be for the good. He could not be more right and if at next month's SAARC summit our leaders can work out some currency relaxations he may find that tourism from India alone could occupy many an island.

THE RETURN OF THE BHUTTO LEGEND

27 November 1988

I arrived in Lahore on the night of Nawaz Sharif's last rally of the campaign. The night before it had been Benazir's turn and everyone was still talking about the unbelievable welcome she received. The city waited till dawn to hear her speak. It took all night for her to drive in from Gujranwala because of the thousands who lined the route. They lay down in front of her Pajero (a Japanese landrover that has become a political status symbol since she started using one), they danced in the streets, and when she finally spoke many wept. 'Lahore,' she said, 'raushniyon ka shehar hai' (Lahore is a city of lights), quoting Faiz Ahmed Faiz's famous poem, 'Lahore zindadilon ka shehar hai...' (Lahore is a city of people whose hearts are alive). 'Lahore Benazir Bhutto ka shehar hai.'

Nawaz Sharif, as incumbent caretaker chief minister, did everything in his power to match her rally. Several hundred thousand rupees were spent on a fireworks display, which changed the colour of the sky and turned buildings into props for fiery waterfalls that poured down drowning out the speeches of lesser leaders who spoke before him. Through the noise of the fireworks, the head of the Jamaat-e-Islami, Qazi Hussain Ahmed, could be heard making an even more ambitious version of his now famous campaign speech. 'We shall first conquer Kabul,' he said, 'and then together we will conquer Delhi and the green flag will fly once more from the ramparts of the Red Fort.' Zia-ul-Haq's son, Ejaz-ul-Haq, was present as the representative of the 'Ziaism' that the Islami Jamhoori Ittehad (IJI) stands for. Women were not allowed anywhere near the stage in the name of the version of Islam that the party favours. A strange mixture of maulvi Islam, state power and militarism. The filthiest anti-women slogans were shouted during the procession in which Nawaz Sharif, pasty-faced and balding, was carried on the roof of a truck.

The slogans were not well received. When the IJI candidate in whose constituency Hira Mandi, the city's famous red light district falls made a speech in which he said he was not asking for votes only for two rooms, one for the mother and the other for the daughter, an old prostitute leaned down from her balcony and answered, 'We have two rooms. When are you bringing your mother and daughter?'

The crowds were large at Nawaz Sharif's rally and the procession was impressive. Nawaz Sharif has a following but it is restricted to urban lower middle class youths filled with rage and religious zeal. They are the children of military rule to whom democracy means nothing and state power everything.

In Sindh Nawaz Sharif is just another name. We left Karachi at 2 a.m. to try and catch Benazir in Larkana before she cast her vote. We took the super highway to Hyderabad and then travelled endlessly through the rugged dung-coloured countryside of interior Sindh. It was a long way to Larkana and the desperate poverty of Sindh's villages was a shock after the prosperity of Pakistan's cities. Sindh is as poor as Bihar and with less hope because the land is still in the hands of powerful feudal lords many of whom support Benazir. We drove for hundreds of kilometres without seeing a tractor or a village with 'pucca' houses. But everywhere on the little mud houses and the mosques and the thatched shacks, there was the red, black and green People's Party flag. The roads were patrolled by soldiers with machine guns mounted on jeeps and there were military checkpoints everywhere but nobody seemed afraid to show who they were voting for.

In Sindh was Zulfikar Ali Bhutto's election. Benazir went out of her way to make this point by visiting his grave immediately after casting her vote. He is buried a few kilometres from Larkana in the little village of Garhi Khudabux which but for a brand new mosque and the Bhuttos' ancestral graveyard is just like any other mud-coloured Sindhi village. A giant cardboard cut-out of Bhutto in a white robe dominates the burial site. His small wooden grave is draped in a People's Party flag and covered with rose petals. Benazir had just left when we arrived. The only other person there was was an old grey-bearded maulvi who read silently from the Koran. He turned out to be the Bhutto family's personal priest, the maulvi who read the nikah for Baby Sahib as she is still called here. There are other graves. Bhutto's ancestors buried under white marble headstones and that of his son Shahnawaz but it is his presence alone that you feel. Ten years have passed but in Garhi Khudabux you feel the horror of his execution as if it happened yesterday.

I finally caught up with Benazir in the narrow dirt streets of a village a few kilometers from Garhi Khudabux where she had gone to check if polling was free and fair. After driving for several kilometres in the dusty wake of her Pajero I got a chance to talk to her in a rest house where she stopped for lunch. She seemed tense and preoccupied and complained about the number of people who had not been able to vote because of not having identity cards. To all questions she said that she would rather talk in the evening when it was all over.

Late that night after it became clear that the PPP (Pakistan People's Party) was in the lead she came out and talked to the army of foreign correspondents who had descended on Al-Murtaza, the Bhutto home in Larkana, but it was on the drive back to Karachi through the dacoit-ridden interior of Sindh that I really got a sense of what this election meant. Even before the results were announced it seemed clear to everyone that Bhutto had won. All along the route there were crowds celebrating a victory that had not yet happened.

In Karachi, the next day when television results showed a PPP victory, even if not a clear majority, and the defeat of such protégés of martial law as Junejo and Jatoi, it was as if the lid had suddenly been taken off Pakistan and the whole country exploded into the streets. Cries of 'Jiye Bhutto' mixed with the war cry of the Mohajir Quomi Movement (MQM) 'Jiye Mohajir' as thousands of MQM supporters joined PPP partisans to dance and sing in the streets till the early hours of the morning. This in a country where because of Zia's Islam singing and dancing has been banned for several years. It is hard to compare the atmosphere to anything in India simply because no election or political event has ever generated this sort of emotional outpouring.

So while politicians debated the meaning of an unclear majority and journalists pondered over the possibilities of Benazir not being made prime minister the people simply danced in the streets. Soldiers still stood behind machine guns at street corners and roundabouts but did nothing to stop the celebrations.

In Karachi most of the people in the streets were MQM supporters among whom were hundreds of women wearing orange, green and white bangles on their arms. Their party colours. The MQM is more a movement for the rights of the Mohajirs or refugees who went from India after Partition than a political party. The 'Mohajirs' have remained a separate ethnic group unable to assimilate into either Punjab or Sindh.

Karachi is their city as the election results showed. Altaf Hussain, the young leader who founded the MQM, started his political career in the Jamaat-e-Islami but is now believed to be bitterly opposed to it. His meteoric rise to fame (the movement only began in 1983) is attributed not just to the 'Mohajir' identity crisis. He is said to be a brilliant orator capable of making the whole of Karachi stop or start at his command. He lives in a simple house in a crowded lower middle class locality which the day after the results literally burst at the seams with jubilant supporters. Houses were lighted up and there was no question that middle class Mohajir Karachi belonged to Altaf Hussain.

Benazir lives in a more posh part of the city. Number 70 Clifton, the Bhutto family home, has been abandoned for a new home called Bilawal House after her son. Getting to see her meant fighting through huge crowds that gathered outside the black wrought-iron gates. Every evening groups of foreign correspondents would descend on Bilawal House only to be seated in an office outside the main house and asked to wait for a chance to see her. It did not come often because she was 'holding meetings with party leaders'. The meetings seemed to continue all day and all night but on my last night in Karachi, the day after the provincial assembly elections, she emerged for a hastily arranged press conference.

She wore a green salwar-kurta with a white dupatta covering her head and for a few seconds after she walked in there was a moment of stunned silence. Afterwards, we agreed that she had never looked quite so radiant and beautiful. But there was something else as well: a quiet confidence as if she was already the prime minister.

She said that she had no doubt that she would be asked to form the government and there was no question of the PPP going into Opposition since it had proved that it was the single largest party. And no, she was not disappointed at not having a clear majority 'because look at the obstacles that there were, look at what we were up against'. Then with a hint of tears in her eyes she said, 'In the end this election is a tribute to the people of Pakistan. To their spirit which nothing was able to break.'

COURTING KANSHI RAM

25 December 1988

The real victor of Allahabad is finally beginning to show his hand. While V.P. Singh was feted and fussed over and built up as the alternative prime minister for having won this crucial by-election Kanshi Ram vanished into his lair to lick his wounds. It is now becoming clear that far from worrying about his defeat he was calculating the significance of his unsung victory. By picking up 19.2 per cent of the vote (only five per cent less than the Congress (I) as he likes to point out) he proved to both the Opposition and the ruling party that they could not do without him in Uttar Pradesh so he sat back and waited for them to come to him on bended knees. And come they did. The Congress (I) opened negotiations as far back as the first week of July, according to Kanshi Ram, and the Opposition followed shortly afterwards so that today he can safely be described as the most courted man in Delhi's political circles.

He is not an easy man to court or even reach since he spends most of his time travelling. And when in Delhi resides in a part of the city that is so crowded and such a maze of narrow, cluttered, apparently unnamed streets that only the most intrepid residents of New Delhi dare to make the trip. I like to think of myself as intrepid but nearly gave up on account of the number of times I was on the point of being trampled to death by all manner of vehicle and pedestrian. Even the traffic police appear to have given up on this part of

Regarpura, and if you are caught in a traffic jam you could be stuck all day. When I finally made it to Kanshi Ram's street I was a broken woman and had he not positioned one of his minions on the road I may well have driven on and waited to do this interview once he moved into one of those palatial bungalows in Lutyens' Delhi.

The leader of the Bahujan Samaj Party and the new Harijan messiah works out of an office that is little more than a hole in the wall at the top of a flight of stone steps. Piles of dusty newspapers litter the floor and pictures of Kanshi Ram are everywhere.That he is well connected can be gauged from the handwritten list of telephone numbers on his desk. Under 'personalities' he has Giani Zail Singh, Menaka Gandhi and Swami Agnivesh along with the numbers of every major political party in Delhi. He was late for our appointment so I had time to study the neat list of numbers and to chat to one of his subordinates about his future plans. These involve travelling to Uttar Pradesh, Punjab, Bengal, back to Uttar Pradesh and then Bihar. 'Long tour,' said the subordinate, 'he will not be coming to Delhi for some time.'

Kanshi Ram confirmed this when he arrived and explained that he was trying to keep away from politicians and press people in order to decide whether he should go with the ruling party or the Opposition. He is a soft-spoken man with the manner of a government clerk rather than a political leader but he talks and thinks big. 'The next election cannot be held without consulting Kanshi Ram because in Uttar Pradesh the Congress (I) cannot win a single seat without my consent.' He then reels off electoral arithmetic. 'In the Hindi belt out of the 226 seats that there are the Bahujan Samaj Party will decide what happens in 126 seats. I am not saying we can win all these but we can make sure that the Congress (I) loses.' Then he goes into the categories of seats they have worked out—A, B, C and D—and calculates that even in the D category the BSP will pick up at least 50,000 votes.

This is not just hot air, he emphasizes, but assessments based on serious groundwork. When he goes on tour he does not just go into a new area and address a few public meetings. He first lays the ground for the BSP to become a force. This is done by holding a series of meetings through which a core of at least 1500 committed workers are recruited and instructed in the party's ideology and strategy. These 'cadres' are then made the backbone of the movement in the state Kanshi Ram is preparing to enter. Their training involves hours of group discussions and lessons in strategy. Since Allahabad the BSP has concentrated on spreading its influence in states outside the Hindi belt with West Bengal being the latest.

With so much going for him why would he want to do a deal with the Congress (I)? 'Because it is a question of choosing between the lesser of the two evils,' he replies. 'Our struggle is against brahminism and I have been saying so far that the Congress (I) is the biggest representative of brahminism but now I feel there is a greater danger from the feudalism and the neo-feudalism that can be seen in the Opposition.' Kanshi Ram's sympathy for the ruling party also comes from his view of it as a crumbling institution of brahminism unlikely to withstand the onslaught of the forces of 'feudalism and neo-feudalism'. He sees the Congress (I) facing defeat in the next general election. He deduces this through a process of simple arithmetic. In Uttar Pradesh in 1984 when his party contested their first elections the Opposition parties did not manage to get more than two per cent of the vote each but when they united for the battle of Allahabad they managed to get fifty-two per cent of the vote. This he sees as an ominous sign. He is worried about the attitude of parties like the AGP (Asom Gana Parishad) in the east and the DMK in the south as well as the Janata Dal which he considers a party of 'rotten rajas who have played havoc with humanity'.

It is Devi Lal whom he considers the ringleader of everything rotten in the Opposition. 'Devi Lal is the worst brahminical and neo-feudal force and it is my topmost duty to smash him. What is all this talk of Ajgar, can you tell me? Who is this Ajgar (also the name of a serpent) planning to swallow, can you tell me? It has an alliance with the brahmins and the baniyas through the BJP so that leaves only the scheduled castes and scheduled tribes for this Ajgar to swallow does not it?' When I last met Kanshi Ram in Allahabad his strongest abuse was reserved for the ruling party and its brahminism and I reminded him of this. Will his supporters not be confused by his sudden desire to cooperate with the Congress (I)? No, he replies, his Harijan support comes not from disappointment with the Congress (I) but because of a feeling that brahminism needs to be destroyed. He pulls out a ballpoint pen and holds it vertically to demonstrate that brahminism is a vertical structure in which there is no question of equality for the bottom end and says that the BSP's philosophy is that the structure should be horizontal with every caste being given an equal chance. The enemy is not the Congress (I) but anyone who thinks vertically and not horizontally.

KEHAR'S LAST HOUR

15 January 1989

Even as we waited outside Tihar Jail in the rain that morning the questions continued to be asked. Was Kehar Singh innocent after all? Was justice really done? Did being related to an assassin, having an unheard conversation with him, and visiting a gurudwara with him amount to conspiracy? They would not let us near the jail's main entrance. We were stopped at a barricade near the outer walls from where we could neither see nor hear what went on inside so there was lots of time to ask questions and worry about Kehar Singh's possible innocence. A hanging is a grim enough occasion and the idea of an innocent man going to the gallows makes it much more difficult. This seemed to be on everyone's conscience that morning as if we were responsible in some way. Some of us had seen him during the trial—a small, grey-bearded man with the eyes of a frightened rabbit. He would stare at us from behind the bullet-proof glass cage in which he sat with Satwant and Balbir as if he did not quite understand what was happening. He had the drooping shoulders and obsequious manner of a lower level government clerk and it was hard to think of him as someone who could have secretly plotted anything as grand as the assassination of a prime minister.

Jansatta that morning carried a profile of him put together from conversations with his colleagues in the government department in which he worked. They said he was an unambitious, unremarkable sort of man who liked sitting in the sun during lunch break and chatting about everyday problems. There was a description in the story of him sitting on one of those broken office chairs on the roof of the building sunning himself and eating his lunch and as we stood in the rain it was this image that kept flashing through my head.

At 8 a.m. his wife and sons who were also waiting at the barricade with us shouted 'Jo boley so nihal, Sat Sri Akal'. It was over. A strange change came over the waiting newsmen. Suddenly, in seconds, the Kehar Singh story became a thing of the past and everyone began to talk of other things—the cold, the rain, the chances of getting a cup of tea, anything at all other than Kehar Singh. There was no point any more in debating his innocence. This has been the general reaction in Delhi. Forget about whether he was innocent or not because there is no point now in remembering. For a couple of days after the hangings there was tension in the city. A fear of reprisals, a fear that November 1984 might be repeated. When this did not happen and everyone remained calm there was a sense of relief at an ugly chapter having closed.

In Punjab it is likely to be the beginning of an ugly new chapter because among the Sikhs there is a sense that justice has yet again not been done. It is this sense of injustice that is the root of the Punjab problem. So even a moderate Sikh politician like Surjit Singh Barnala talks of his 'heart being heavy with the thoughts of what happened to Satwant and Kehar' and there is already talk of the Sikh religion's two new martyrs.

THE GUCCI GANDHIANS

28 March 1989

It is that time of year when even the most privileged corner of privileged Delhi gets a taste of what it's like to live in the rest of India. Despite our best efforts to steal power from the peasants in neighbouring states power cuts happen daily and without warning, causing incalculable damage in these days of computers. Unless you live in lesser parts of the city the power comes back after an hour or so but by then your story could simply vanish off the screen as could vital statistics or important political secrets if you happen to be a minister. As for water even in Race Course Road shortages are not unknown and municipality tankers have to make regular visits to keep VVIP baths flowing. Then there is the problem that the little water that is available is best not trusted at this time of year what with last summer's cholera outbreak and the gastroenteritis (officially denied) epidemic that is currently raging.

The heat gets to the Press as well and a single major power cut in Delhi makes page one first lead where 24-hour power cuts elsewhere merit barely a paragraph. The English dailies get especially agitated about such things as can be judged from a story in one of our sister newspapers last week entitled 'Battling the Sun's Fury at Zoo'. The story was particularly sympathetic to the tigers who had 'to take turns at the artificially cooled enclave while some of them have to find a cool corner in the shade'. Conditions in the Delhi zoo are much better than in the slums and resettlement colonies but we who write in elitist languages have elitist concerns.

Speaking of which I have to sadly inform you that this wretched panchayati raj business has led to the complete decimation of the Gucci Gandhians who had become such a popular and important part of political life in the capital.

At the recent AICC (I) session and at other Congress (I) events lately I have searched in vain for what had come to be known in political circles as the prime minister's Doon School set. This was a loosely applied term because many of those included went to lesser public schools. The Bachchan brothers went to some school in Nainital and nobody knows if Satish Sharma went to school at all but they were counted in the Doon School set because it has become a metaphor for those who come from backgrounds of privilege.

Before our prime minister decided to sacrifice flying and his happy family life for the sake of the country Doon School types treated politics as a dirty business and preferred to keep away. Rajiv injected the right degree of 'cleanliness' into the political atmosphere to attract a new breed of politician. They spoke English rather than native tongues, went to elitist schools and wore the softest superior quality white khadi as opposed to the coarse variety favoured by less privileged politicians. Their sartorial elegance was legendary, expensive and widely imitated by those who sought to create the impression that they also belonged in the 'inner circle'. Cartier watches, Mont Blanc pens and Gucci Kolhapuris (loafers) became commonplace. And, increasing numbers of young politicians found admittance to formerly closed Delhi drawing rooms.

Their contribution to Indian history other than in sartorial and social terms was limited. There was the idea to have copycat Doon Schools (Navodaya Vidyalayas) dot the countryside for the benefit of those who could not afford the real thing. There was the emphasis on computerization and the twenty-first century. What else, what else? The culture festivals, Sam Pitroda, the freedom runs, the Dandi March, the 40/100 excitement, Coca-Cola and Pepsi.

Not bad from an urban middle class point of view but not

enough to get more than fifty seats in Parliament, so out the Gucci Gandhians went and we are back to what is euphemistically described as 'the traditional Congressman'. But, behind the new homegrown smokescreen many a Doon School product lurks. Mani Shankar Aiyar, Vishwajeet Singh (both directly involved in the Panchayati Bill), Suman Dubey and Ronen Sen. Who knows but the Gucci Gandhians may survive after all.

*

Women members of the Congress Party returned from the last Mahila Congress (I) meeting in Bhubaneshwar frothing at the mouth. They are angry not just because the meeting was a farce with everyone sight-seeing when they should have been debating important political resolutions but also because of the importance given by the prime minister's staff to a certain high society lady.

Several women MPs were keen to get on the prime minister's flight back to Delhi in the hope of snatching a few words with him about 'political matters'. They were informed that this would not be possible on account of a shortage of space but one or two who did manage to get on noticed to their amazement that on board was an exceptionally attractive lady who had no political reason to be there other than her friendship with certain important members of the prime minister's office. This is not the first time this kind of thing has happened hence the fury. Delhi society ladies regularly get included in the prime minister's press parties and foreign tours by passing themselves off as journalists or political workers and generally the route of entry is through some bureaucrat in the PMO.

The link that the Gucci Gandhians established between Delhi drawing rooms and the corridors of power is blamed for this. It has led to a proliferation of ladies who would make Pamela Singh look angelic and these ladies now form a vital link between politics and business. They flit easily between high-powered political parties and high-powered business parties peddling gossip and influence and whatever else is required. The more ambitious encourage stories about their (alleged?) affairs with men in high places and casually drop remarks like 'Oh, I have to rush because the car is coming for me from the prime minister's office.'

Well, if senior bureaucrats and politicians can be so susceptible who can grudge these ladies their moment in the sun and the chance to make the deal of a lifetime. Good girls as they say go to heaven. Bad girls go everywhere.

THE GREAT AWAKENING

9 April 1989

Boliye Sriram Janmabhumi Ki Jai! Gau Mata Ki Jai! Bharat Mata Ki Jai! Translated that reads: Long live Ram Janmabhumi; Long live the cow, the mother; and Long live Bharat, the motherland. This interesting list of priorities comes from a saffron-robed ascetic (not NTR) who addresses us from a stage that resembles a large village hut which has on its roof a gigantic bow and arrow made of glinting fairy lights. The speaker is a militant priest by the name of Mahant Avaidhyanathji who is in the vanguard of the movement to convert the Babri Masjid into a temple and we are attending an event at Delhi's Ramlila Grounds to commemorate the birth centenary of the founder of the RSS, Dr Keshav Baliram Hedgewar. This meeting has been covered in some detail in the national press because Atal Bihari Vajpayee went into RSS mode and demanded that the Babri Masjid be 'bulldozed' as happened in Somnath. More about the thoughts of Vajpayee in a minute. First I want to give you the flavour. The flavour is almost more important than Vajpayee's speech because it gives us a glimpse of the writing on a still distant but visible wall.

As someone who is deeply suspicious of priests who play politics and politicians who mix with priests I was fascinated by the line-up on the stage and the decorations on the hut's mud walls. There was almost as much saffron as white khadi and if you put khaki knickers (Balasaheb Deoras, Rajju Bhaiya) in the saffron slot then the only representatives of 'rajniti' were Sikander Bakht and Vajpayee. Even here there was an abridgement after Vajpayee announced proudly that 'I am here not as a politician but as a swayamsewak.' Now for the décor. On one side was painted a youth in traditional RSS khaki knickers standing at a blackboard earnestly giving lessons to a group of villagers under a tree. On the other side was the image of a similar youth giving injections to a group of half-clothed people with feathers in their hair whom I took to be Red Indians but discovered were adivasis (no wonder the RSS finds it hard to get through to our rural masses). Then as a backdrop to this dun-coloured tableau we had an enormous picture of the god Ram, painted in shades of luminous mauve, blue and green, towering over a rendition of the proposed temple in Ayodhya.

Forgive me if I have spent longer than usual over descriptive details but I want to convey as fully as possible the atmosphere of religiosity and Hindu revivalism at the event. Even without speeches the message would have been clear. But speeches there were.

'We have come together...' said Mahant Avaidhyanath, 'for the sake of Hindu unity. There are those who say what problems can Hindus have when they constitute eighty per cent of the population, but let us not forget that this country was enslaved at a time when Hindus constituted a hundred per cent of the population. How did we become slaves when we were at the height of our civilization? Only because we were disunited.'

It was this disunity, he continued, that was the reason why sadhus like him had given up their prayers and meditations and returned to 'real life' to work for Hindu unity. If it was being destroyed it was because of the government and the political parties. 'It is they who have encouraged the Muslims or they should have realized by now that if they want to live here then they should learn to behave.' He explained what he meant by 'good behaviour'. Stop being stubborn over the Ram Janmabhumi temple. How could Hindus accept that temples of

Ram, Krishna and Shiva were still covered in 'signs of Hindu slavery'.

This theme was taken up by the speakers that followed including Sikander Bakht. He talked of the great tolerance of the Hindus who consider Muslims as belonging to their own family despite the humiliations that they had suffered.

Finally we had the inimitable Vajpayee. He came to Ram Janmabhumi through a circuitous, mellowing route of jokes about the prime minister and a strong critique of such Hindu practices as untouchability and sati. To Ayodhya we came via Thailand and Indonesia, 'Did you know that there is an Ayodhya in Thailand, it is the name of their ancient capital, and their kings have Rama before their names and in Indonesia they have Ramlila even if it is a Muslim country. I asked them about this and they said, "We have changed our religion but not our culture".' Then finally came the point. If the central government could tear down a mosque in Somnath and build a temple then why not in Ayodhya? Vajpayee's speech left me flabbergasted. Less than two months ago I interviewed him to find out why he had become a virtual political recluse.

He explained that he had been unwell and in America for treatment but as we talked it came out that he did not like the changes in the Bharatiya Janata Party that the RSS was bringing. The RSS was never happy while he was at the helm of BJP affairs because he tried to guide the party away from issues like cow slaughter, the 'atom bum' and the demand for abolition of Kashmir's special status towards ideas like 'positive secularism' and 'Gandhian socialism'. Now that the RSS has the BJP back on track, Vajpayee said, he was uncomfortable. Had he considered joining another party, I asked, and he replied unforgettably, 'Jayen to jayen kahan?'

So what has happened between then and now? Your guess is as good as mine but perhaps an answer can be found in the writing on that distant wall that I spoke of earlier. The writing says for those who can see that far that the next election is likely to be a fight for the Hindu vote not so much because the BJP wants it that way but because the ruling party appears to be running out of other ideas.

What other explanation can there be for the daily dose of religious revivalism that we get these days on Doordarshan? On Sundays this reaches a climax of sorts and you may find that if you stay tuned after the *Mahabharata* that *Discovery of India* or *Bharat Ek Khoj* is turning into little more than a historical extension of our mythological past. Last Sunday it was devoted entirely to a recitation of mantras. No matter how hard the Congress (I) tries this is one area in which it is unlikely to make much headway against the BJP. Would they be able to support the RSS move to begin work on the foundation of the new temple in Ayodhya at exactly the time that elections are due? Can they write on the walls of Muslim localities, as the RSS does—'Garv se kaho hum Hindu hain'? (Say proudly that we are Hindus).

But what it can do is go for both the Hindu and the secular vote so while there is the religious revivalism on the one hand there is also a successful whisper campaign conducted through the efforts of certain journalists which warns that if the Congress (I) loses this election it is the BJP that will win. The message is simple. If you are going to have a Hindu Rashtra then it may as well be a 'secular' Hindu Rashtra. An ironic choice for the Congress party to offer in the year of Nehru's centenary but perhaps there are unknown cosmic factors involved that arise from it also being the birth centenary of Hedgewar.

A WOMAN WRONGED

19 August 1990

Bilawal House when Benazir Bhutto first moved into it two years ago used to be an ordinary suburban villa of the sprawling whitewashed kind we see so much of in south Delhi. Today it is a fort. High walls with iron spikes and lookout posts ring the house and the only way in is through iron gates guarded by personal bodyguards from Sindh who look more like bandoleers than soldiers. They let nobody in. Not even the handful of people who come from Sindh to catch a glimpse of their leader.

The press (and especially the foreign press) are allowed in and members of her central executive committee who have come for a meeting which lasts three days and ends in resolutions full of bravado that further conceal the truth from Pakistan's former prime minister.

When she finally sees us the impromptu press conference resembles a 'darshan'. She wants not so much to answer questions as rail and rant against the perfidy of those who think Pakistan's destiny should be decided 'by kingmakers sitting in drawing rooms'. She speaks Urdu like Rajiv Gandhi does Hindi so it sounds more like English mixed with a few Urdu words. When she gets angry she switches completely to English. She speaks with the sort of accent that comes from years of being taught how to round your vowels by Catholic nuns. When she wants to talk about the injustice done to her she uses her hands a lot and because she is beautiful and young, you get a sense of theatre or cinema. And here is the fairytale princess on the verge of losing her kingdom to the wicked villain. At the end of the press conference you know that Benazir sees it that way.

Reality intruded now and then like when the correspondent of *Paris-Match* asked his question. 'About corruption,' he said, 'could you just tell us one thing. Was your husband richer twenty months ago or is he richer now?' There was a moment of deathly silence. Her face turned red. 'My husband is an honourable man,' she shouted, 'and his business has suffered. He is in the construction business and he suffered first because nobody wanted to give a plot of land to a man who was married to the leader of the Opposition and he suffered later because of the questions that could arise since he was married to the prime minister.'

We catch an elusive glimpse of Benazir as she really is, merely another politician who has made the mistake of placing the interests of her family above those of her country. In India this is a common failing among politicians that becomes fatal only in prime ministers. And then they do not like to discuss it.

Nobody dares tell Benazir about the activities of her spouse. Asif Zardari is hated as much as the Queen of Nepal and for the same reason. He is blamed for misusing his position. Karachi seethes with gossip. He is accused of everything from extortion to murder. There are people in Benazir's inner court who admit privately that many of the charges stick but nobody dares tell her. 'He is her blind spot,' they whisper. 'There is nothing that anyone can do about it.'

So if there are elections on 21 October and she becomes prime minister again this is a mistake that is likely to be repeated. She and Asif remain a package deal. It is a big package that they say includes his father, friends, cronies and flunkeys. It is a Sindhi feudal trait, I was told, he would lose face if someone came to him and asked for something that he could not do.

The good news is Benazir appears to be aware of the other

corrupt practices that surround her government. She knows that many of her legislators got away with murder because as leader of a minority government she needed every last vote to keep her in power. The people's interests had to take second place. Vast sums meant for development disappeared even in her own Karachi constituency of Lyari.

There seems also to be the realization that the past twenty months have taken her very far away from the people and this is a mistake. In Karachi ordinary citizens say 'We never saw her. We would know when she was here because Thursday evening the streets would be filled with policemen and then these black cars would flash by towards Bilawal House.'

Like our own Rajiv Benazir appears to have relied totally on the magic of the family name. She has problems, though, that Indian leaders do not face. The biggest of these is that Pakistan as a country has yet to understand the meaning of democracy. Too many Pakistanis think of democracy as a magic wand, a panacea. In Lyari they tell you of schools that never got built, electricity that never came and water supply that remains an unreliable trickle and wonder what is the use of democracy if it cannot get us these things. When I asked if they had existed in Zia's day they said, of course not, but the whole point about democracy was that it should have improved their lives wasn't it?

Then there is Islam. In the streets of Karachi I meet people who tell me they dislike Benazir because she criticized Islam. What did she say? She described some punishments in the shariat as inhuman. It's not easy to be the modern, progressive leader if your own countrymen believe other things to be more important. No matter how much she covers her head in good Islamic style and no matter how much she describes Kashmir as a holy war as a modern political leader she needs to point out that there are things more important than religion. But how do you say this in a country that was born only because of religion?

WHEN THE SAINTS COME MARCHING IN

14 April 1991

The Bharatiya Janata Party has been saying that the main issue in the coming general election is 'pseudo-secularism'. Last week it gave us a taste of 'real secularism' at its mammoth rally at Delhi's Boat Club. It was technically a VHP (Vishwa Hindu Parishad) rally but the only politicians on the stage belonged to the BJP, so there is little point in pretending that the BJP and the VHP are unrelated.

It is important to recognize the relationship because once the election begins the VHP and the BJP will deliberately have separate rallies so that the election code, which forbids the use of religion in politics, does not cause trouble for them. The Boat Club rally was the biggest in recent times—perhaps even the biggest ever—and on the stage sat all manner of 'saints'. Some had coconuts balanced on their heads, some had dreadlocks, and there were those with elegantly cropped hairstyles. There was the delectable Uma Bharti seated beside her fiery sister-sadhvi Rithambara.

The word 'appeasement' has been ringing in our ears since the rathyatra. When you talk to BJP leaders like L.K. Advani they tell you what they are fighting is the kind of secularism that amounts to discrimination against Hinduism. Surely then their own secularism should provide room on the stage for at least a single Muslim priest? And at the dharamsansad (religious parliament) that preceded the rally could they not have squeezed in at least one Imam? On the contrary there were pamphlets distributed at the rally with titles like 'Islamization of Secularism' and 'Loktantra ki hatya dharamnirpekshta dwara' (democracy's murder by secularism) which had on the cover an arm shoving a dagger through a ballot box with the words 'Pakistan Supporters and Anti-national Elements' on it. The prose contained in the pamphlets made it clear to even the most dense of readers that the BJP's saffron secularism was definitely anti-Muslim. And that, I fear, is going to become the main issue in the election. Do we want an India in which political matters are decided by priests or one in which priests of every variety are kept strictly within the confines of temples and mosques? That is the issue.

In better times this kind of issue would never even have come to the fore in the way it has. Hinduism has always been a religion that did not believe in the kind of proselytization that makes other religions such a nuisance. But the VHP is determined to reduce it to the level of the rest and to a large extent they have succeeded. They have also succeeded—and this is more dangerous—in mixing religion with politics on a national scale so that if the BJP ever came to power in Delhi it would have no authority, for instance, to tell the Akali Dal in Punjab that its MPs and MLAs could not march into legislative assemblies with swords dangling around their waists. Nor would it have the right to tell Kashmir's militant leaders that they cannot force Islamic laws down the throat of the local populace because if we are going to have a Hindu Delhi then there will be a Muslim Srinagar and a Christian Mizoram.

If the Boat Club rally is anything to go by then we will be marching backwards into medievalism, obscurantism and sheer lunacy for such a long way that it will take us another fifty years to discover that the world has moved on. What our political leaders need to be asking themselves is why this has happened. Much as the VHP and organizations of similar ilk would like to take credit for the 'jan jagran' (people's awareness) campaigns that they sponsored they are not entirely to be blamed or credited. In India it is easy to use religion to motivate people. Pilgrimages are still virtually the only form of tourism. Even the poorest of the poor travel for religious reasons. The massive attendance at the Kumbh Mela speaks for itself. So just as it is no great feat for the Akali Dal to get Sikhs to vote in the name of Waheguru it is no great feat for the BJP to get Hindus to do so in the name of Ram.

There is a popular view among Delhi's liberal intellectuals that the average Indian voter is some kind of extraordinary creature who always gets it right. Every election brings in its wake political comment that raves about the 'wisdom' of the masses. This is patronizing rubbish. The average Indian voter is no smarter or stupider than you or I so if the BJP's volatile mix of religion and politics can appeal to those who inhabit Delhi's drawing rooms (and it does) why shouldn't it appeal to those who smoke hookahs on village chaupals? If the BJP doubles its strength in Parliament, as it hopes to, it will be due to the failure of the so-called secular parties. To take on aggressive communalism you need at least one political party that is genuinely secular. This we do not have.

THE UNMAKING OF A HERO

21 April 1991

Was it really only fifteen months ago that V.P. Singh was seen as a knight in shining armour? A crusader of such dazzling moral authority that he could single-handedly take on the mighty Congress party and defeat it at the polls? Fifteen months is a long time in politics because that is all it has taken for our Prince Charming to turn into a pumpkin.

There may still be those who believe that the Janata Dal is capable of rising like a phoenix and that V.P. Singh could become the prime minister again but even this steadily diminishing group accepts that this time around there is no shining armour. No knight. We do not hear the word corruption, the word Bofors has disappeared from the campaign and although V.P. continues to try and cling to the moral high ground with talk of 'equity and social justice' everyone sees it as just election talk.

V.P. Singh goes into this election with his saintly image in tatters and the Janata Dal goes in as a party on the verge of splitting. If it is being held together for the moment it is only because of election glue. There is a wide consensus that, afterwards, and particularly if there is defeat ahead the party has had it.

Everyone blames V.P. for what has gone wrong though it was only a few months ago that there were other scapegoats. He was good at appearing like the injured innocent, helpless victim before the villainy of Devi Lal and the machinations of

Chandra Shekhar. Even then there were those who felt that he was weak-kneed and indecisive but these were minor flaws when seen against the backdrop of Chautala's ever-grinning visage. It has only been since the scapegoats departed for greener pastures that people in the Janata Dal have begun to analyse V.P.'s own leadership and style of functioning and the conclusions do not reflect well on him.

V.P. emerges as a leader so much in the mould of the Gandhis that it is hard to understand why he felt it necessary to leave the Congress (I). If comparisons are to be made then he could be said to resemble Indira Gandhi more than Rajiv. It could even be said that he took the worst qualities of both. From Mrs Gandhi he appears to have learned the technique of making unilateral decisions and imposing them on the party, *a la* Mandal. He learned from her the importance of populism and of remaining aloof from the rest of the party. From Rajiv he appears to have learned the need for a coterie.

Even before Mandal started the coterie was already beginning to create difficulties. The coterie is still very much in operation and even among his loyalists there is resentment over Raja Saheb always seeming to have more time for people like Sompal and Santosh Bharatiya. These two gentlemen are considered leading members of the coterie. Bharatiya began his career as a small-time journalist in Lucknow who endeared himself to V.P. Singh by chauffeuring him around when times were bad. Sompal, whose origins are also obscure, appears to have wormed his way to the top by helping Rani Saheba out in the kitchen. In the words of one loyalist, 'He would always be hanging around in the kitchen bringing tea and pakodas, that sort of thing. Hardly the right qualifications for the Rajya Sabha.'

Bharatiya and Sompal act as V.P. Singh's emissaries and are said to be involved in the business of fund collecting, often resorting to petty levels of collection. An example that Arif Mohammed Khan gives is of a planned trip to Bombay for which Rs. 10,000 was collected from him for press facilities. The trip got cancelled but Bharatiya kept the money. Fund collection was a tricky business because of V.P. Singh's sermons against taking money from industrialists.

The leader of the dissidents, Arun Nehru, is happy these days to express his differences openly. When I went to see him last week he was relaxed and determined to stay away from the coming election. He also seemed determined not to leave the Janata Dal. He dismissed rumours of his joining the Congress (I) as a 'disinformation campaign' by Bharatiya and Sompal.

He said differences with V.P. Singh began over Meham and Chautala. 'We felt that it was not a party affair but one of national importance. That is why our view was that if Vishwanath wanted to show real moral ascendancy he should have taken a stand instead of trying to do deals with Devi Lal.' The deals involved bringing Sanjay Singh and Ranjit Singh (Devi Lal's son) to the Rajya Sabha and sending K.K. Deepak off as an ambassador.

When the deals did not work Devi Lal sulked and threw tantrums that ended in his departure but V.P. Singh's gloss had peeled by then. So when he announced his Mandal plan on 7 August nobody believed there was anything sincere about the decision.

There was nothing in V.P. Singh's long record in public life to show that he had special feelings for the backward castes. He never did anything for them when he was chief minister of UP nor in the many years that he served as a cabinet minister. Even as prime minister there were no special OBC appointments or announcements until Devi Lal's kisan rally.

Nehru is frank about his differences with V.P. Singh being because of caste and religion. 'After all if you are going to spend three hours sitting with the Imam of Jama Masjid, who is known to promote Muslim fundamentalism, then how can you speak against Hindu fundamentalism?'

In his view V.P. Singh is lying when he says he is not interested in power. He points out that if this were true he should have agreed to the formation of a national government under Jyoti Basu when the Mandal violence began.

If V.P. Singh's problems were restricted to those who are openly against him it would have been alright, but it's hard to find anyone in the Janata Dal these days who approves of the leader or his policies. Unless he can come up with a decisive victory in the election it looks like bad times ahead.

THERE'S NOTHING WRONG WITH A LUST FOR POWER, BUT...

19 May 1991

Us political pundits have spent most of the past ten days pondering over reasons why. What possessed Sitaram Kesri to do what he did? Was there a game plan? Was there method in the madness? Was it the shadow of Bofors, was it Quattrocchi, or the mysteriously murdered doctor? After much pondering, parleying and analysis at the highest levels of political punditry the consensus is that Kesri did what he did because he wanted to become the prime minister. 'Nothing,' said one of the United Front's senior political pundits, 'but a naked lust for power. This eighty-two-year-old man knows he has little time left and so if he is to be prime minister it has to happen now. A lust for power, that's what it was, nothing more.'

He found it hard to keep the sneer out of his voice as if Kesri had no business to have a lust for power. This is an interesting reflection on what we still expect of our political leaders. We expect them to be saints, social workers, junior clones of the Mahatma himself. So, when they show 'a naked lust for power' our sense of morality is offended. Have we not grown up enough as a democracy to know that politics is often about a lust for power?

Kesri can be accused of many things. Irresponsibility, bad timing, haste, misjudgement, insufficient planning, but can we hold against him his 'lust for power'? Why shouldn't he want to become prime minister? What we need to demand from them is not high moral standards but governance. We should throw them out when they do not provide schools, roads, hospitals and we should keep a close watch on whether the money they are supposed to be spending on these things isn't slipping quietly into their own pockets. But, please let us stop expecting our political leaders to be saints. They are not and nor should they be. When Gandhiji donned Mahatma robes, or at least allowed them to be thrust upon him, he understood that his fight was not about power but about ending colonial rule. For that fight to be successful he needed to curb the baser instincts of his followers and, perhaps, in his own case he really did not want to be the prime minister. Who needs to be a 'neta' when you can be a 'mahatma'?

When we stop expecting today's politicians to be saints we might succeed in coercing them to do what they should be doing which is govern the country. It is when we expect high morality that politicians respond with the drivel poor Kesri was reduced to: *Hum samman key bhookey hain, satta ke nahin* (we are hungry for respect, not power). Rubbish.

What we should ask Kesri and the Congress party is whether they have any idea of the damage the country's economy has suffered on account of their whims. No budget, no finance bill, crores lost on the stock exchange, many more crores lost forever from foreign investors who may have begun to think of India as a good investment.

We need answers on why Kesri timed his shoddy little coup at the very moment that India and Pakistan were talking to each other for the first time in three years and moments before more than forty foreign ministers were due to arrive in Delhi for the NAM meeting.

There are other questions. Can the Congress party do more for us than Deve Gowda and his gang? Can they give us a better budget? A better foreign policy? Can they finally after nearly fifty years in power give us health and education policies that would provide our people with minimum literacy and healthcare? Do they have schemes that would succeed in making our towns and cities less unsanitary, less polluted?

Those are the things we need from our political leaders. We do not need saintly behaviour or all we can expect is the sort of result that A.K. Antony delivered as chief minister of Kerala. They used to say of him that he was so worried about preserving his saintly image that he avoided decisions altogether. This is not what we want. So go ahead Mr Kesri and have your lust for power but tell us what you can do for us.

REMEMBERING RAJIV GANDHI

26 May 1991

There is so much horror and tragedy in the manner of Rajiv Gandhi's death that it is hard to write about him just yet except in the eulogistic tone obituaries naturally assume for those who die young. In my case an objective assessment is particularly difficult because I knew Rajiv as a friend before I knew him as a politician. But, if I do not try and assess his contribution to Indian politics objectively and unemotionally I feel that I would be no better than the sycophants who destroyed his legacy.

I first met Rajiv during the Emergency. It was at a dinner party a week after his mother locked up the Opposition and declared this necessary for putting 'democracy on the rails'. Among the guests at this dinner was Biju Patnaik's son, Naveen, whose father was among those jailed. The other guests were socialites, young scions of industry and commerce and glitzy creatures from the worlds of advertising and art. They hovered around the Gandhis, kowtowing, flattering, utterly abject in their devotion. The only person who noticed Naveen Patnaik was Sonia Gandhi who said uncomfortably that it could not be nice for him to have his father in jail, or words to that effect. This was the political remark of the evening.

There followed similar parties throughout the Emergency to which I was invited but always urged by everyone not to say anything political. This resulted in my not speaking to Rajiv at all because with Emergency 'excesses' raging outside it seemed ridiculous to be talking to Indira Gandhi's son about whether he liked flying Avros or jets. Finally, when the Janata government came to power I could restrain myself no longer. Catching Rajiv sitting by himself at yet another dinner party I asked him how much he knew about the excesses. He looked me straight in the eye and said quietly, 'Very little. But whatever I did find out I told Mummy.'

As he said this a look of relief crossed his face and I realized that far from not wanting to talk about politics he had longed for someone to mention the unmentionable. We talked at length that evening about what he had felt about the Emergency, what he had known and not known and what he thought about his brother's politics. He never attacked either his mother or brother but tried to explain why they had done certain things. There was so much candour and sincerity in what he said that it was hard not to be completely and utterly charmed by him, as were most other people who met him on a personal level. Many meetings and political conversations were to follow that first encounter and I discovered that although Rajiv's understanding of political things was limited he had the sort of overdeveloped sense of decency and honour that was exactly what national politics needed. Without realizing how prophetic my words would be I often told him that he was the right brother to be in politics.

It was thanks to a lot of persuasion from me that he gave his first interview to *Sunday* magazine and that is how M.J. Akbar first met him. I remember him being really nervous about the interview and insisting that he would give it only on the condition that I sat through it and signalled to him if he was about to say anything wrong. He needn't have worried. Akbar was completely in his thrall by the end of the interview and it was carried on the cover.

Then Sanjay died and he was sucked, much against Sonia's wishes, into the political vacuum his brother left. His immediate reaction was to try and collect around him people with the same sense of values and these tended to be school friends like Arun Singh. In the inner circle around him at that time there were few people against whom aspersions of any kind could be cast. On the fringe, however, lurked the likes of Satish Sharma and loser types from Doon School.

It was Rajiv's misfortune that when he became prime minister it was they who surrounded him. This was particularly true after differences began between him and Arun Singh. This little caboodle of the worst of his friends became the inner circle, they came to be the only ones with the magic key of access to the prime minister's house. They flaunted their access at parties, stomped into government affairs as if they had his permission to do so, and used his name in ways guaranteed to bring discredit and trouble.

Rajiv compounded the problem by using as his spokesmen crass, abrasive persons of the Mani Shankar Aiyar variety who made it easy to forget Rajiv's own charm and who were also unable throughout to project any of the good things his government did. And, good things there were. There was the first serious attempt to liberalize India's shackled, stagnant economy. There were attempts to make people aware of how fast the rest of the world was moving and how we would get completely left behind unless we realized what was happening in the world of computers and new technology. There were, initially, serious attempts to restructure the Congress Party so that the power of corrupt, party bosses and influence-peddlers could be reduced. But, because of the inability of his spokesmen to project anything except their own boorishness, most of these achievements remained in the background as did the excellent work done by people like Sam Pitroda.

Rajiv's own increasing inaccessibility, God only knows under whose stupid advice, made him unpopular with the press. So everyone was waiting to pounce when Bofors happened. This, again, was handled with such monumental ineptitude that Rajiv came across as guilty even before the evidence began to be compiled. Forgotten immediately were his political successes, his charm, his decency and all that remained was the image of an isolated prince surrounded by a corrupt and foolish bunch of courtiers. It is not the sort of image you win elections with. He lost. Would he have won this time? I very much doubt it but I wish so much that he could have had another chance.

DELUSIONS OF DYNASTY

9 June 1991

Myths and legends are the stuff of dynasties. The Nehru-Gandhi dynasty is no exception. But, even for those of us who mourn Rajiv, and I count myself among them, the time has come to examine these myths to understand the damage they have done to India as a country and us as a people.

The dynasty began, as dynasties do, amid troubled, turbulent times. Colonialism had broken the spirit of India and the terrible violence of Partition had broken her heart. It was a tattered, poisoned sort of freedom that came after all those years of struggle and one that became instantly stained with the blood of Gandhiji. It was easy in such a situation for the whole country to cling to the image of Jawaharlal Nehru, larger than life anyway, as a symbol of unity, integrity and hope. It was easy perhaps necessary to forgive him his mistakes. The disastrous policy in Kashmir, the incomprehension of the language issue in Punjab, the blind belief in the Soviet model of development, the China war.

When he died there should have been analysis of the things that had gone wrong, some attempt to rectify mistakes but as a people we like gods so we deified him. Like Gandhiji before him, he entered the political pantheon and criticism of him was looked upon as treason, even blasphemy. As a child I remember reading eulogies to him in textbooks, as a whole generation must have done, so where was the question of looking at him as a mere mortal? Naturally, when his party decided to appoint his daughter as the next prime minister, she came invested with the extraordinary qualities attributed to him, if not in the minds of the cynical party bosses who supported her, certainly in the minds of the people.

She was good at perpetuating myths—like the myth of her being the messiah of the poor (anti-princes, bank nationalization), and though the poor saw no dramatic change in their lives the myth grew. After the Bangladesh war there was the myth of Durga; even Opposition leaders saw her as the goddess. It was easy to overlook the increasingly powerful coterie of stenographers and sycophants around her, easy to ignore her patronage of Sanjay's schemes and her destruction of the Congress party until the Emergency. Then, for two years, and because she really did go too far, the scales fell from people's eyes, but the myth of Indira's political cunning was so great that the Janata government spent its time in office mesmerized by the inevitability of her return.

In retrospect, it is easy to see that she won in 1980 because the Opposition split and she may have won even in 1977 had they remained divided, but at the time her triumphant return became the stuff of a new myth. India could only be ruled by the Congress and the party could only be ruled by the Nehru-Gandhi dynasty. This, we were told, was stability. This was 'the unity and integrity' of India.

In the four years that followed Indira Gandhi became a victim of her own myths. So convinced was she that India's 'unity and integrity' were synonymous with her that she created the problems in Punjab and Kashmir, almost casually, certain that once she had extracted her short-term electoral gains she could put the genies back into their bottles, because she was India's 'unity and integrity'. When we look back at what happened, even her most ardent admirers find it hard not to concede that had she not toppled Farooq Abdullah's government in 1983 and indulged, at least initially, the antics of a certain Punjab priest, we would not have a Punjab and Kashmir problem today. But, the myth of 'stability' survived and got transferred to Rajiv, despite the horrific pogroms against the Sikhs in the first two days of his rule.

So powerful is the mythology surrounding the Nehru-Gandhi name that Rajiv justified the pogroms and could still go into the general elections as a knight in shining armour. Poor Chandra Shekhar, for his part, has never been credited with ensuring that there was no violence after Rajiv's assassination. The foreign press, in particular, spent far more time on the end of the dynasty and on end-of-India scenarios than on trying to find out why there was no violence this time. We, in the Indian press, are equally culpable. Senior newspaper editors gave interviews to the BBC saying only a Nehru or Gandhi can ensure India's unity.

We create new myths. Sonia's dignified restraint is evidence of her leadership qualities. Priyanka (for some reason not Rahul) has the making of a future prime minister. When I hear this from journalists and Congress party sycophants I ask how they have concluded this about a teenager studying home economics and they say that she campaigned for her father and always asked the staff questions. If these are the only qualities required to rule India then we should be able to find a prime minister in every Indian home.

These myths demean us. Dynastic succession may have kept the Congress party together but it has debilitated India. Institutions have been diminished. You see the effects everywhere. Chief ministers are subservient to the stenographers who control access to the court, judges kowtow, bureaucrats align themselves openly and blur the barriers between politics and administration. The fourth estate, that powerful pillar of democracy, is brought to heel by feudal tactics. It is no secret that journalists who speak their mind are treated as enemies.

The essence of democracy is debate and debate is anathema to dynasty. In the Congress party the consequences are evident. There is not a single leader who can be considered as having a political *raison d'etre* that goes beyond loyalty to the Gandhi family. One of the most specious arguments advanced for why we should accept dynastic democracy is that 'the people want it'. How can the people want anything else when for forty years they have been told by their political leaders that the country will fall apart unless it is ruled by a Nehru-Gandhi? If our leaders grow up the people will as well. Dynasties thrive by making everyone else seem like dwarfs. It is time now for the dwarfs to show us how tall they can grow.

KILLERS IN KHAKI

8 December 1991

Raghunath's death was so routine, so inconsequential that it barely made the papers. The two Delhi newspapers that reported the story carried the same photograph of a young man with an Amitabh Bachchan hairstyle and sunglasses, posing with a nonchalance and confidence unusual in young men who come from Bihar looking for jobs in the big city. His friends say it was probably his confidence that caused his death, because it may have irritated the policemen who beat him to death.

They told newspaper reporters that Raghunath was the smartest among them and that he incurred the wrath of the police as he was the only one who had the courage to protest. This is how Raghunath's friends described what the police did. 'They had his hair cut. He was trussed up, tied upside down with his head between two tables and beaten with a baton...The torture went on for three days...'

When Raghunath was released and returned to the cramped one-room servant's quarter he shared with several cousins and a brother his condition rapidly worsened. On the afternoon of 29 November he vomited blood and died. When his killers in the GTB Enclave police station heard of his death they threatened his relatives with dire consequences unless they cremated the body instantly without an autopsy. The terrified relatives obeyed, and the killers are now in the happy position of being able to get away with murder.

Raghunath was killed for nothing. He was not charged with being involved personally in the theft the police were investigating, but he protested about police methods of interrogation so they taught him a lesson. What will happen now? Nothing. If there is enough noise in the newspapers an internal inquiry may be ordered, a couple of lower level policemen may be transferred or suspended and that will be it. That is how the Indian justice system works.

In Delhi alone there is a death in police custody almost every other month. Inevitable, since the police know only one method of interrogating a suspect. In Raghunath's case he was only the friend of the suspected thieves, but this is reason enough to be arrested if your friends are domestic servants and there is a theft in the household. Raghunath's friends were suspected of stealing three lakh rupees from their employers who handed them to the police only after they had beaten them within an inch of their lives but failed to find the money.

Raghunath's death is unlikely to evoke much mention in the political columns of major newspapers. They concern themselves with bigger things. There is the general decline in law and order, the increase in terrorism, the entry of criminals into politics, all sorts of big, serious matters. Yet, Raghunath's death is directly linked to all those big things.

So inextricably linked that unless we start to deal with the 'smaller things' like Raghunath's death there is no hope of containing terrorism, naxalism, separatism or whatever other name we give the inexorable breakdown of law and order.

We are in a peculiar situation. The police are more powerful today than they have ever been before. Some of our most troubled states (Punjab, Kashmir) are being ruled by ex-policemen, which must mean that the home ministry trusts their judgement implicitly and yet there is no doubt in anyone's mind that there is no institution in India more corrupt and dishonest than the police. In Delhi we overcome this dichotomy by convincing ourselves that however bad the police may be they are essential in terrorist-affected areas, because only they can restore normalcy. But we do not yet see the first signs of normalcy in either Punjab or Kashmir.

We are unlikely to either, because the average citizen in both these states sees our so-called guardians of law and order as much bigger criminals than the criminals. If deaths in police custody are routine in Delhi it requires little imagination to see what happens in the police stations of sleepy mofussil towns and villages. Senior police officers, especially in Punjab, start frothing at the mouth when human rights groups talk of 'fake encounters'. But, in the villages few people have any doubts that most encounters are fake.

Those killed in encounters could be the lucky ones, because death is painless compared to being killed in police custody. Torture is the rule when interrogating suspected terrorists and sometimes the victims are barely in their teens. A process of brutalization and revenge begins and when it comes to their turn the terrorist groups kill children if they happen to be the children of policemen.

The cycle of violence becomes endless and we make laws that protect the police and not citizens. I recently visited a maximum security prison in Nabha in which trials of those arrested under TADA (Terrorism and Disruptive Practices Act) are being held. The courtroom was a prison cell in which iron bars divided the lawyer from the accused, who are brought manacled and handcuffed and treated as guilty till proven innocent. Is justice possible in secret courtrooms? Draconian laws like TADA are sometimes necessary, but can we put them in the hands of policemen who kill innocent people for nothing?

CONGRESS WITHOUT AN (I)

2 February 1992

Something strange is happening to the Congress (I). Or have you not noticed? When you pick up your daily *Times* or *Express* or *Hindustan Times* these days do you observe headlines like 'Rao's move to woo party MPs' and 'Singh revolts against Rao'. Do you note that even sidekick Congress leaders, never heard of in the past, are suddenly expressing their views on everything under the sun? Could it be, could it finally be, that the shadow of dynasty is beginning slowly to lift and the ruling party is taking its first trembling steps towards becoming a proper political party?

It is still too early to say. Number 10 Janpath continues to remain so powerful a political force that little Miss Priyanka had barely to get elected (albeit unwillingly) to the Congress party from Uttar Pradesh for everyone to start rethinking their equations. Not just in the party but, alas, even in the press. Leading dailies instantly sent ace reporters off to track her down in college, only to have them return cooing and gushing. 'She's terribly fair isn't she? I saw her eating chhole bhatoore at the canteen with her friend Sonia.' It is not easy to forget forty years of democratic monarchy.

But, change is in the air. The clowns, courtiers and tumblers that once infested the grounds of the AICC(I) have gone. No longer do you see the likes of K.K. Tewary singing paeans to the Gandhi family, no longer do you hear people like Kalpnath Rai warning newsmen not to 'touch the diamond

(Rajiv)' and it is hard to imagine even a Simi Garewal making a film called *India's Narasimha.*

There are other changes. In the old days it was not possible to enter the drawing room of a Congress (I) leader without being zapped by Gandhi family memorabilia. There would be clocks with Rajiv's face smiling out from under the arms and 3-D pictures of Indira Gandhi so real they looked as if she was on the verge of walking out of the frame. Sycophantic mementos can still be seen in the offices of ministers but that they are less evident in drawing rooms must be a sign of changing times.

More significant are the actual political changes. In the old days an atmosphere of paranoia and suspicion surrounded the court, so if you wanted to be considered a loyal Congress (I) *chamcha* then you avoided as far as possible all contact with Opposition leaders. This led to misunderstandings at the top. Opposition leaders were treated as pariahs, untouchables. This unhealthy approach to parliamentary democracy is changing slowly but surely.

Inner party democracy, alien to Congress culture, is also putting down tiny shoots, as is evident from open dissidence on important issues. But the idea is still feeble and uncertain if you remember that there are no complaints when Sonia's friends—like a certain interior designing lady—get national awards that are wholly undeserved. Other leftovers of past traditions persist. The Rajiv Gandhi Foundation represents what remains of dynastic power and nobody objects when letters are sent to government officers, above the rank of joint secretary, asking them to contribute to the foundation. The prime minister needs to ask himself why this is being allowed and why some industrialists still fall over themselves raising money for the foundation. If it is merely out of charity then the economic reforms must have brought about a big change in the heart of Indian industry.

Old habits die hard, especially bad ones, but we have reasons to hope. When Delhi tried to impose its will on the Congress (I) chief minister of Karnataka over the Cauvery waters issue, he resisted and continues to remain in power.

This would have been unheard of in days of yore. Remember Rajiv's problems with Sharad Pawar? Then we have Arjun Singh raring to go on full attack against the Madhya Pradesh government despite the prime minister advising restraint. Even S.B. Chavan, always associated in the past with doormat politics, has not hesitated to make it clear that he does not approve of Rajesh Pilot interfering in Kashmir and Punjab. Pilot considers himself the prime minister's personal troubleshooter and believes he should have carte blanche, like Satish Sharma once had, but he has been shot down by the home minister.

On the economic front there is open dissent. Ministers of socialist bent do not hesitate to oppose the finance minister's attempts to liberalize the economy. This may be only because of vested interests but in a democracy dissent is healthy and a breath of fresh air after years of obeisance to the dynasty that has ruled India for nearly forty years. A dynasty so powerful that when Indira Gandhi declared a state of internal Emergency in 1975 she did not consult her cabinet and nobody complained. Later, we heard that 'stalwarts' like Jagjivan Ram and Y.B. Chavan had protested, but so feeble was their protest that nobody knew of it. And the President of India happily rubber-stamped the suspension of our fundamental rights because if Mrs Gandhi considered it necessary then necessary it must be.

At a more frivolous time there was Rajiv Gandhi's 'Freedom Run'. When he slipped into a tracksuit and raced off to win India her freedom nobody dared point out that India had been free since 1947. Pot-bellied ministers and ageing bureaucrats wore tracksuits and ran alongside. Rajiv was not just prime minister of India but the heir to the Nehru-Gandhi dynasty so he must know best. If Narasimha Rao declared an Emergency and suspended democracy would everyone go along happily? If he slipped out of his dhoti into trackpants would his ministers follow? Inconceivable. Right? Could we be moving towards a time when the Congress party will drop the (I) for Indira?

THE MAHARAJAS OF SOCIALISM

1 March 1992

This is budget week and there will be much ponderous analysis of the economy, ninety per cent of which nobody will understand. There will also be much breast-beating about the demise of socialism (much of it began months ago) and this is something everyone understands. At least we think we do, because years of rhetoric from our 'great leaders' taught us that if you are on the side of socialism you are on the side of the good guys and if you are on the side of capitalism you are evil.

This simple economic philosophy has permeated the Indian psyche. It gets reflected in our newspapers, in our cinema and, of course, Doordarshan goes out of its way to propagate it because it serves the interests of our rulers who are the only category of Indians to have visibly benefited from the 'gains of socialism'. I live in the jurisdiction of the richest, most privileged municipality in the whole of India, the New Delhi Municipal Committee (NDMC). Very few private citizens are lucky enough to find room in the NDMC area because this is Lutyens' Delhi, reserved almost entirely for those who govern us. My reason for being here is a grandfather who worked with Edwin Lutyens when the city was being built. At that time Lutyens' Delhi was inhabited by many private citizens.

Today it is almost a gated city, reserved for VVIPs and the richest Indians. The prime minister, the president, the whole cabinet and the vast majority of MPs and bureaucrats live here. There are benefits. We do not have power cuts or water shortages and remain unaffected by traffic jams and pollution because here the roads are wide and tree-lined. There are public parks and houses are set in vast, sprawling gardens. Fountains play on hot summer nights and when the children of the poor try and use them for their daily bath they are kicked firmly out. The 'maharajas of socialism' are more feudal than the old maharajas were. They have the confidence of being democratically elected.

This confidence allows them to do things that ordinary Indians could go to jail for. Electricity bills can remain unpaid for months and years and nobody will do anything. Ditto, telephone bills. Once you have moved into the NDMC area you need never leave. Taxpayers' money pays for many ex-ministers and ex-MPs to live in princely style for the rest of their lives. Jagannath Pahadia, former Rajasthan chief minister, cannot be evicted from his residence in Bikaner House although he is said to owe the Rajasthan government more than Rs. 25 lakh. He is not entitled to government accommodation.

A letter has been written to the prime minister about this but what can he do when he himself occupies almost an entire street and when so many of his own colleagues are VIP squatters. Raja Dinesh Singh has become something of a legend for having occupied his ministerial bungalow for twenty-five years despite spells in between (and now) when he has not been a minister or an MP. This former prince is in the vanguard of those mourning the demise of 'socialism'.

Never for a moment do 'socialists' like him notice that the money spent on subsidizing the living standards of former politicians alone could pay for roads, electricity and drinking water in several villages. And we are a poor country. In most rich Western countries MPs and ministers are entitled only to humble accommodation. Nowhere do you see them occupying prime residential property, whether in London, Washington or Paris.

In India because we are 'socialist' we have ensured that the easiest route to a privileged lifestyle is either by becoming a civil servant or an MP. Listen to the 'perks' that an ordinary

MP enjoys and you will find it easier to understand why in our country people kill to get a parliamentary ticket and burn themselves alive when it looks like government jobs may become fewer.

An ordinary MP gets Rs. 5500 in hand as salary. This sounds humble and socialist but listen to the rest. From the minute he gets into Parliament he is entitled to accommodation in Lutyens' Delhi where market rents range between Rs. 25,000 a month for a flat to Rs. 2 lakh for a five-acre bungalow. The government (taxpayers' money) supplies him with any number of air conditioners for a very small charge and if he does not pay his electricity bill it does not matter. The central government writes off crores of rupees every year.

Technically he is only allowed 30,000 free telephone calls a year but he can make any number and not bother to pay. Nobody would dare cut his telephone connection. Then there is travel. The railways offer him unlimited first-class trips anywhere in the country and Indian Airlines gives him sixteen free 'intermediate' trips in addition to free travel to and from Parliament sessions. Other perks include the right to provide forty-eight gas connections and fifteen phones a year to deserving constituents. In our socialist economy these things are in short supply, so MPs are tempted to sell their quotas. Houses and even servant quarters are rented out so that a clever MP makes more than Rs. 50,000 a month putting his perks to commercial use.

Ministers and senior bureaucrats are more privileged. Perks include cars, staff and just about anything else they may need. This pattern of subsidizing our elected representatives and officials exists all the way down to the state and district level, so you can see that 'socialism' has become a burden for the taxpayer. But, budgets come and go, and although we hear about cutting other subsidies, we never hear about cutting down the subsidized lifestyle of our politicians and officials. What kind of socialism is it that allows the vast majority of our people to live without schools, drinking water, roads and hospitals forty years after Independence while our politicians and officials live like kings?

SEASON OF SABRE-RATTLING

3 March 1992

Next week we will see another Kashmir yatra. A Pakistani one, led by one of Kashmir's oldest 'freedom fighters', Amanullah Khan. Could he have been inspired by Shri Murli Manohar Joshi's venture? It certainly seems that way because when I, along with a group of Indian journalists, met the JLKF leader in Islamabad six weeks ago he mentioned nothing about marching with 50,000 people to the line of control. Something has happened since to persuade him to be more aggressive.

Or it could just be that time of year again when India and Pakistan rattle their sabres at each other. Hostile noises emanate from both foreign ministries but it's hard to take them seriously since our prime ministers have been having a friendly old time in lovely Davos. Think back over the past few years and you will notice that generally around this time, almost every year, tensions have escalated between India and Pakistan. In 1987 there was the 'eyeball-to-eyeball' confrontation over Brasstacks. In 1990 we had V.P. Singh virtually threatening Pakistan with war. In between there were problems over Siachen, Kashmir, Punjab and even one episode in which Rajiv accused Pakistan of trying to bump him off using a lone terrorist with a homemade gun (Rajghat, 1986).

This time tensions have heightened not just because of the proposed JKLF (Jammu Kashmir Liberation Front) march but because of an interview given by the Pakistani high commissioner in Delhi, a man known to choose his words carefully, in which he accused India of 'bludgeoning Kashmir into submission'. This is not the sort of language you normally hear from diplomats so could it be frustration? Desperate talk?

Things have changed dramatically over the past few months where our Kashmir problem is concerned. With the most obvious change being in the attitude of the West. Suddenly, we hear more about Pakistani-sponsored terrorism than about human rights. In the past two years, all we heard about was human rights violations by Indian security forces. For the West to withdraw moral support is almost more important than Pakistan withdrawing military support in Kashmir. When the movement for 'azadi' took a violent turn in January 1990 it was to a significant extent inspired by the wall coming down in Berlin and borders changing in Europe.

I was in Kashmir at the time and remember being astonished by the number of people I met in little towns and villages who talked knowledgeably about these changes and pointed out that an independent Kashmir (not Pakistani) was an idea whose time had come. Pakistan did not start the uprising but leapt in at this stage to take advantage of a situation created by our own mistaken Kashmir policy.

Things have now changed again and if Pakistan shows its frustration we can afford to be indulgent. If only our foreign ministry spokesmen had ignored Mr Abdul Sattar's remarks or dismissed them as merely an expression of Pakistani frustration we could perhaps have moved a tiny step closer to peace in the subcontinent. Instead they reacted in high dudgeon. As did our political leaders, once again bringing us down to the same level as Pakistan. Why do they always do this?

India is not Pakistan. Despite the best efforts of the RSS we are a long way from becoming a small-minded theocracy controlled by Generals. There is no reason for us to follow a policy of reciprocity in our relations with Pakistan. We are bigger and better in the real sense of those words and our best weapon is India itself. Most Pakistanis have no idea what India is really like because, unfortunately, they have to base their opinion entirely on what our officials and politicians say and usually they sound almost as hawkish as their own lot.

Due to reciprocity being the basis of our foreign policy we do not allow Pakistanis into India, at least not easily, because Pakistan is mean about visas to our citizens. What our policy-makers fail to understand is that Pakistan has things to hide and we do not. Superficially, Pakistan looks more prosperous and developed than India and this often impresses Indians. But they have only to stay for more than a few days to realize that the country has an ugly underside of military and religious repression. You have only to meet a Pakistani mullah or a general to want to flee back across the border as soon as you can. Recently, a group of us hacks from this side of the border had the dubious honour of meeting General Aslam Beg. We returned from this encounter terrified by the thought that till only a few months ago it was his hand on the nuclear button. In India it would be really hard to find generals as hawkish as General Beg. This is something Pakistanis are not aware of.

They think of India as some kind of giant monster waiting to swallow up Pakistan. Other absurd notions prevail which can only be disabused if we make it easier for Pakistanis to come to India. Those who do come are pleasantly surprised by our plurality, our open society and the general disinterest in Pakistan that exists beyond northern India. Hindi cinema has its own special magic for Pakistanis, as does a society that allows simple pleasures like a drink in a discotheque, watching a dance performance or lying on a beach in Goa without a mullah breathing down your neck. It is in India's interest to stop thinking in terms of reciprocity and make it easier for Pakistanis to come across the border. It would strengthen the hands of those people in Pakistan who are tired of these annual seasons of sabre-rattling.

APATHY REIGNS SUPREME

18 October 1992

In the week that General Arun Vaidya's killers, Sukha and Jinda, were taken to the gallows shouting 'Khalistan Zindabad', the *Pioneer* reported what is the first official admission that the killings of the Sikhs in Delhi after Indira Gandhi's assassination were planned and not spontaneous. Justice for the general in six years, a short wait by Indian standards, and not even the beginnings of justice for three thousand widows who have been waiting since 1984. Should we not be asking why?

It is fashionable in political circles to bemoan the decline of democratic institutions but when reasons for the decline stare us in the face we look the other way. After the *Pioneer* report the only political party to demand an explanation from the government was the CPI(M). From the Janata Dal there was not a peep. When I rang Jaipal Reddy and asked for his reaction he said, 'I'm shocked. But not surprised. The government owes a definite explanation to the nation.' There has been silence not just from our political parties but even from the press. Nobody bothered to pick up on the *Pioneer*'s report.

The newspaper reports that a senior police officer, Deputy Commissioner of Police Chandra Prakash, one of the officers charged with failing to do his duty during the 1984 massacres, has told the home ministry that a decision not to impose curfew in Delhi immediately after the assassination was taken in the prime minister's house at a meeting attended by the then home minister, P.V. Narasimha Rao. Chandra Prakash, who was in charge of south Delhi at the time, made this allegation while defending himself in an internal inquiry being conducted by the home ministry.

Prakash said, 'I suggested to Gautam Kaul that the situation had taken a very ugly turn and rioting and arson had spread over a vast area. I recommended to him that curfew should be immediately imposed and army called out to assist the civil administration. Gautam Kaul turned down my recommendation stating that a meeting had already taken place some time earlier in the prime minister's house where the home minister was also present and a decision had been taken not to impose curfew and call out the army at this stage.'

As someone who covered the massacres in those first terrible days after Indira Gandhi was assassinated let me say without hesitation that curfew was the key. More than 3000 Sikhs would still be alive if it had been imposed on time. As soon as it came into force and the army began patrolling the streets of Delhi the violence stopped. Prakash corroborates this. He says, 'If my recommendation for imposing of curfew and calling out of the army had been accepted immediately, possibly most of the tragic events that followed could have been averted.'

When I rang the home ministry to get an official reaction to Prakash's devastating testimony I was told curtly that there was none. Home Secretary Madhav Godbole, who was at least good enough to come on the telephone after six joint secretaries were in a meeting, out of the room, or on tour, said, 'There can be no comment, because there is a departmental inquiry going on at the moment.'

Departmental inquiries may be useful for the home ministry's functioning but they are no use to us because proceedings remain top secret and buried in some dusty archive. If there were public hearings we might find out what prevents policemen from doing the job they are paid to do, which is primarily to protect ordinary citizens from violence.

In 1984 they failed to do this and more than 3000 Sikhs were killed in Delhi in three days. All we have had since then by way of justice is inquiries, inquiries and more inquiries. They are a foolproof method of procrastination. The Supreme Court recently passed severe strictures against the endless delays that have been created by policemen implicated in the violence but other than that there has been general apathy over the deliberately delayed justice.

One of the reasons for this apathy is that people associate sympathy for the victims with sympathy for the Sikh cause. The opposite is true. Sikhs who believe in Khalistan would prefer justice never to be done because their whole case for a separate country is based on the idea that Sikhs are second class citizens in India and can never get justice. If the killers of 1984 are brought to justice it will strengthen moderate Sikh opinion. More than that it will strengthen India as a country.

It will also help our Punjab problem. There has been some improvement in the state, the number of terrorist killings has dropped, cities bustle with activity and in the villages people are daring to hope that after ten years of violence peace may finally be possible. The situation has improved because ordinary people are more eager to help the police with information than they were before, but there are aspects of the problem that go beyond simple law and order. The most important of these is the Sikh sense of alienation not so much because of Operation Bluestar but because of the pogroms that followed Indira Gandhi's assassination. Our judicial system has failed in the past. Victims of police brutality in Meerut and Malliana still wait for justice, as do the victims of countless other communal riots, and this is shameful. But what happened in Delhi in 1984 was our first state-sponsored pogrom. It was not a communal riot and this makes the need for justice to be done even more important.

The victims were ordinary people. Voiceless, unarmed, tragically vulnerable. They were mostly dalits from Rajasthan without any interest in Punjab politics. The state's failure to protect them is criminal and if the justice system fails as well it compounds the horror of what happened.

OUR MONEY'S WORTH

21 March 1993

How many more innocent people will have to die before the government realizes that our intelligence agencies have completely collapsed? Realization should have dawned earlier. Much earlier if you consider the gradual collapse of national security that we have witnessed in the past decade. There was the Khalistan movement which grew and gathered strength and was financed by mysterious financiers abroad despite many a trip abroad by intelligence operatives who supposedly went to bring back vital information. Nobody asked any questions. Not even after Operation Bluestar, when the army lost hundreds of soldiers because civilian intelligence could not even give them an accurate list of entrances to the Golden Temple. I have it from a general involved in Bluestar that had they known of the number of entrances they would not have begun the attack from the main entrance which was heavily fortified.

After Bluestar the country got its first real taste of terrorism. Again, intelligence agencies were provided with vast secret funds. They came up with nothing. It was left to the police to give us details of the Pakistani hand and the evidence they provided was based on interrogation reports of terrorists they had caught and who admitted to being trained next door. Pakistan dismissed the evidence, pointing out that subcontinental policemen used methods of interrogation that could get anyone to say anything in custody. Our intelligence agencies then came up with a list of alleged 'training camps' in Pakistan. It was given to me on a visit to Karachi by one of our diplomats who had full faith in it. Using it as a guide I went looking for the camps and found through my own investigations that although there were no camps there was training. Most of it in Faisalabad jail where Sikh youths who fled after Operation Bluestar were technically incarcerated.

This was later confirmed when terrorists crossed back into our Punjab and got caught. The map of training camps was quietly forgotten but our intelligence agencies carried on as usual, and if heads rolled nobody heard about it. Then Mrs Gandhi was assassinated. Again, heads should have rolled and there should have been some kind of major intelligence overhaul, some effort to rectify things that were clearly going wrong. Nothing happened.

Conditions within our major intelligence agencies deteriorated to such an extent that when V.P. Singh became prime minister, disgruntled elements in the Research and Analysis Wing (RAW) came up with a note on the misdemeanors of their own agency. They demanded that the new government produce a white paper on what RAW had been up to by way of destabilizing activities in Assam and Punjab. As far as anyone knows the allegations were not investigated. Since then Rajiv Gandhi has been assassinated and a major secessionist movement has begun in Kashmir. If our intelligence agencies provided us with warnings, a hint of prior information, these have remained secret.

You may have noticed that they are very good at telling us how much advance information they had after something happens. So, after Bombay's horrific bombings the press carried reports of an intelligence warning that came the day before. If there was a warning why was it not in the press a day earlier? Why were there no warnings to the public on television and radio and, most importantly, can the intelligence agencies tell us what they did about the information they had? Were cars searched for bombs? Were suspects detained?

What happened in Bombay is typical of what always

happens. Immediately after the bombings we were told that intelligence agencies had information that the Inter-Services Intelligence (ISI) was planning a major strike in Bombay. Then, a Sri Lankan suspect who had supposedly been under surveillance for more than a month was produced and detained for questioning. The Bombay police after being clueless on the day of the bombing was suddenly, according to the police commissioner, 'full of clues' with many leads being pursued. Within two days they found an Iranian called Yakub Memon who we are told is the evil genius behind the attack.

It is he, they say, who reserved rooms in the Centaur and Sea Rock hotels in the names of Ramesh Saxena, Sanjeev Rai and Advani. He left leads everywhere. We are to believe he was stupid enough to have left his own car filled with AK-56 rifles and hand grenades parked carelessly in a Bombay street. Is this credible? Are we to believe that someone who could mastermind one of the most sophisticated, meticulously synchronized acts of terrorism in the world would be stupid enough to make such mistakes?

Most people will believe it, though, because our intelligence agencies are treated as sacrosanct. Nobody will ask any questions until the next tragedy and the next and so it will go on until the government realizes that revamping these agencies should be top priority. And that we should be retraining and redeploying our anti-terrorism forces.

The National Security Guard (NSG) and the Special Protection Group (SPG) were formed immediately after Mrs Gandhi's assassination. The bravest and the brightest of men were selected from our police and armed forces and put through months of special commando training. The problem is that the NSG, popularly known as Black Cats because of their black fatigues, and the SPG have mostly been used to defend VIPs against terrorist attack. The SPG guards the prime minister and the NSG guards ministers, MPs and those who can persuade the home ministry that they face an imminent terrorist threat. The list of endangered VIPs is long and unconvincing and it has become fashionable in political circles to acquire your personal Black Cats. In Delhi, VIPs measure their importance by the number of commandos who protect them. Black Cats can be seen waiting outside drawing rooms and the glittering halls of five star hotels when they could be much better employed in Kashmir protecting ordinary citizens.

Not a thought has been given to these things and the official response to a terrorist act remains the same. After the event VIPs, protected by their specially trained commandos, fly down to the scene of the crime in hordes. They make sympathetic noises and distract the police from what they should be doing and then they fly off again and the average Indian citizen remains as vulnerable as ever. What is the point of VIP visits? Why does the home minister never explain what he has done to improve the functioning of our intelligence agencies? Why are they so ineffectual compared with our neighbour's ISI? So many questions. But they remain unasked—until the next terrorist act and then the next.

SYCOPHANTS STILL

28 March 1993

If Sonia Gandhi is genuinely not interested in taking over the Congress party she could perhaps consider lending the All India Congress Committee (AICC) a pair of sandals that could be placed on a velvet cushion in a place of honour at party headquarters. It should then be made obligatory for dissidents and loyalists (and Sharad Pawar's fence-sitters) to file past every morning and kowtow. This might prevent the ruling party from splitting and, who knows, may even lead one day to Ramrajya. We have been ruled before for fourteen long years by a pair of sandals and from all accounts it was a very successful experiment. Would Soniaji do us the honour of dedicating to the nation an attractive pair of Italian sandals so that we can return to dealing with some of our real problems?

There is a long list of things that need to be tackled urgently—international terrorist conspiracies, communal tensions so serious that they could break the country, and a secessionist movement in Kashmir that may do the same. This is before we even get to chronic, but equally grim, problems like uncontrolled population growth, the dearth of primary education and basic health facilities, starvation in Orissa and Bihar and at the top of it all, a bloated, useless bureaucracy that puts paid to all Manmohan Singh's brave new plans for economic reform but that we can do nothing about because of 'vested interests'.

If the Congress party could sort itself out these are the

things that should have been discussed at the All India Congress Committee (AICC) meeting in Surajkund. It was only a year ago, when the AICC last met in Tirupati, that the prime minister made his passionate plea for change. After explaining how the public sector had been devouring resources that should have gone to health and education he said, 'We have the largest illiterate population in the world and it continues to grow. So, if I get Rs. 500 crore from somewhere else (foreign investment) for a power project, please imagine how many schools will be built, how many more teachers there will be. There are certain areas where money is being wasted and we have to cut mercilessly.'

Of course, no merciless cuts have been made and as for the man who made the speech, he has recently returned to his old job of faithful retainer of the Gandhi family. When he realized that he was making a mess of being Congress president he went off to grovel before Sonia Gandhi. Could she not help? Would she be good enough to consider becoming Congress president so that he could at least try and do a decent job of running the government? We do not know what the enigmatic Sonia said, that is something we will never know for sure, but it is whispered that she did not say an outright no.

Meanwhile, despite Mr P.V. Narasimha Rao's protestations that he had only paid a 'routine visit' (what are these routine visits?), his foes in the Congress party got wind of what he was up to and immediately tried to play the same game themselves. If he could grovel before Sonia they could do a much better job. So that master sycophant, K.K. Tewary, was resurrected from oblivion and sent off to 10 Janpath to plead for permission to fast at Rajiv's samadhi in protest against an imagined slight to the dead leader.

The alleged slight having come in a letter by Rao supporters which implied that it was not Rao but Rajiv Gandhi who should be blamed for the rise of the Bharatiya Janata Party. Arjun Singh, a pretty clever groveller himself, immediately saw his chance. He shot off his own letter to the prime minister saying, 'It is possible that for a few Congressmen, loyalty to

Rajivji and fidelity to the cause he espoused ended at his grave. It must be understood, however, that for Congressmen at all levels in the country, Rajivji lives in the hearts and minds as a shining symbol of a life dedicated to the cause of the nation. It is, therefore, very difficult to reconcile ourselves to this kind of denigration of a leader of his stature.'

So there we have it. We have a party in power that cannot rule or stay united without endlessly expressing its devotion to the Gandhi family and the only member of the family who could instantly replace Rajiv is unwilling, so what solution can there be other than for the affairs of the Congress party to be conducted in future in the name of Sonia's sandals? This would put an end to all dissidence, confusion and speculation and we would not have to read hidden meanings into everything.

At the moment Sonia has barely to make an appearance at an Iftar party and we have reams of analysis in the next day's papers about what could possibly be the meaning of it. She has barely to meet an MP or a minister, which she does on a daily basis, and all kinds of rumours result. After Rajiv's assassination, when the Congress Working Committee made her president of the party, she wisely declined. She had never had anything to do with politics in the years she had been a prime minister's wife and daughter-in-law and nothing to do with the party. Her refusal to take her late husband's job helped the party move away from its dependance on the Nehru-Gandhi dynasty and there were signs that it was on its way to becoming a proper political party again. Inner party democracy began to burgeon, dissidence flourished and there were even hints of debate at the Tirupati session last year.

Somewhere along the way Narasimha Rao lost his nerve or was reminded that he had his job only because of Sonia Gandhi having chosen him for it and not because he was a popular leader. The grovelling began. Governance and political issues were put on a backburner and the prime minister concentrated on kowtowing and obeisance to Number 10. So Soniaji let's have a nice pair of sandals, please! It's an old Indian tradition.

MORE HOT AIR ON HUMAN RIGHTS FROM BENAZIR

22 February 1994

If it wasn't so irritating it would be quite funny to be lectured on human rights by Pakistan. And, if it weren't so pathetic there would be entertainment to be derived from the spectacle of Benazir Bhutto strutting around the world waving the Pakistani flag on the human rights front. This is the same white-veiled lady, please remember, who was incarcerated for years in her own humane country for daring to speak of democracy and fundamental rights. The same lady whose father, Pakistan's only democratically elected prime minister, was executed on the flimsiest of charges. And who before he died wrote in praise of the 'noise and chaos' of India's democracy despite his pathological hatred for this country.

Either Ms Bhutto has a short memory or she can no longer see the generals in Islamabad. Generals who execute democratically elected prime ministers, care little for human rights, and cared less for the people of Bangladesh. Three million people killed in nine months, dear Benazir, three million 'freedom fighters' (nearly the entire population of the Kashmir Valley) under the orders of a general who, if I am not mistaken, is a member of your People's Party. When Bangladesh happened you were perhaps too young, too apolitical to notice that darling, adored daddy was partly responsible for what happened. He wanted to be prime minister and could not care less that Mujib had more seats. Remember? So, the generals were sent in.

Passionate as you are about human rights, 'Serbian shells could not deter Prime Minister Bhutto from visiting the suffering people of Sarajevo'—you do appear to have a flawed view of history. It is nice to make comparisons between Bangladesh and Kashmir (as Pakistanis like doing), nice because it makes you feel that you are fighting for a just and noble cause. Alas, there is no comparison. India's soldiers and paramilitaries may not have a blameless record on human rights but have you not noticed that things are different here? Our security forces have the Indian and foreign press on their case twenty-four hours a day. Much of the information that you get about human rights violations in Kashmir comes from Indian newspapers. There were not many Pakistani journalists covering what happened in Bangladesh were there?

There have been human rights violations in Kashmir, and many Indians are deeply ashamed of them, but comparisons with 'the holocaust' can only be dismissed with contempt. And, I am not 'a rented Muslim' out to please my Hindu masters, as your government has called Salman Khurshid. We have a free press so the minister of state for external affairs has been widely attacked for his description of you as a hot-air balloon. Personally, I thought it an accurate description, because when you talk of human rights hot air unfailingly comes to mind. We are not perfect. Our policemen often think they still represent a colonial government when dealing with ordinary Indians. But, since you probably do not see Indian newspapers much, you may not have noticed that they are under constant attack.

They are attacked when they violate any human being's rights. Not just when they violate the rights of Hindus. You appear to be only concerned about Muslims. We have heard a great deal from you on what is happening to Muslims in Bosnia and Muslims in Kashmir but when was the last time you made an impassioned statement about what is happening to Hindus in Sindh? Is it only a coincidence that even your bandits in Sindh seem to prefer attacking Hindu homes?

Our two countries are different in more ways than can be detailed here. We have had 'the noise and chaos' of democracy longer than you can remember. We do not execute our prime ministers. We do not have any experience of military dictatorships and 'guided' democracy. The only serious repression we have had to deal with was for two years when Mrs Gandhi mistakenly believed that if other countries could have dictators then so could India. She had to give up the idea in a hurry and when she had an election you saw what happened. Your country continues to have 'limited' democracy whatever that is. And, as far as anyone has noticed, you have done nothing about changing the president's right to dismiss a legally elected government. For that matter, what have you done to change the Islamic-military law that reduces women to half human beings? So, please, no more lectures on human rights.

THE MAHATMA IS NOT UNTOUCHABLE

27 March 1994

Even gods can have feet of clay but not India's political leaders. This is why there is the current fuss over a comment about Gandhiji by the Bahujan Samaj Party's Mayawati. She is not a fan of Mohandas Karamchand Gandhi and should be entitled to her views. If I were an untouchable in the 1930s, when even animals were treated better than shudras, I would have been on Ambedkar's side in wanting to demolish the caste system. Gandhiji was not. He believed it would cause social tension to tamper with the structure of Indian society. Even giving shudras separate electorates, he thought, might cause too much social tension for Hindu society to handle. So, he came up with the idea of renaming untouchables harijans and making them touchable by living among them, eating with them and even cleaning other people's excrement as they were ordained to do under the laws of the caste system as it worked then. Would flush toilets not have been a more revolutionary idea?

Ambedkar's way was different from that of Gandhi. He believed the caste system was evil and needed to be destroyed if untouchability was to end. Being an untouchable himself he knew what it felt like to go to a classroom where upper caste children objected even to his presence. In those days, please remember, if you were untouchable you would have to in certain parts of India scream before you came out in public so that your shadow did not pollute a brahmin's path. And, there were untouchables whose only sustenance came from the grains that they could pick out of cow dung. The caste system was a sick, degenerate thing and time has shown us that, perhaps, Ambedkar was right in trying to demolish it completely since there is still not a village in India where harijans do not live in segregated quarters.

In the cities municipal water supply, public transport and flush toilets have reduced some of the horror of being born a harijan, but if you look around you there are still very few harijan doctors, lawyers, teachers, industrialists, movie stars. Not even many harijan hacks of my acquaintance. So, Ambedkar could have been right. Gandhi's more gentle approach could have been wrong. Mayawati must have the right to criticize Gandhi if she feels he 'did not do anything for the dalits'. If she feels, as Ambedkar did, that renaming untouchables harijans was a silly idea because all that it did was evade the real issue then she has every right to say so. She has explained, in several interviews, that she did not call Gandhiji the son of a devil but was merely quoting Ambedkar, who asked why only they should be called children of god?

Why did upper caste Hindus, he is reported to have asked, not call themselves harijans as well. Were they sons of the devil? It is hard to see what is wrong with either this question or with what Mayawati is reported to have said. But, observe the fuss. In the Lok Sabha, MPs broke party lines to voice unanimous condemnation. One of them even said that Mayawati had caused India 'global humiliation'. The Uttar Pradesh Congress Committee (UPCC) went a step further and demanded that the UP government be dismissed immediately 'for its anti-Mahatma Gandhi and anti-scheduled caste approach' and for its 'intolerable insults to the nation'.

Gandhiji was a great man. A very great man, but he was not the nation. He was not India. To say that he was is a bigger insult to the country than anything Mayawati said. The minute we allow ourselves to start believing that a political leader is India we leave ourselves open to the kind of rubbish that the Congress has been shovelling down our throats for more than forty years. Once Gandhiji and Nehruji were lost to us we needed some new leader to become India and Congress president Dev Kant Barooah proclaimed that 'Indira is India and India in Indira'. She had just declared a state of internal Emergency and anyone who did not share this opinion went straight to jail.

Deification of politicians is dangerous in a country like ours where reverence comes naturally after centuries of kowtowing to our colonial masters. In Tamil Nadu there is an MGR temple in which the idol, like the late chief minister, wears dark glasses and a woolly cap, and at the rate his friend and heir Jayalalitha is going there will be more than one temple to her in days to come. Jayalalitha is so allergic to criticism that, until she dropped them recently, she had more than a hundred cases against journalists, including one against your humble columnist. Journalists in Tamil Nadu have been stripped in public, beaten up and even killed for daring to oppose the government. This is how politicians invariably end up behaving if they are allowed to believe they are deities.

Congress would like us to believe that all leaders whose surnames are Nehru or Gandhi, are not just mahatmas but gods. Their names are invoked at Congress meetings like mantras, so speeches invariably begin in the name of Nehruji, Indiraji and Rajivji. Even our prime minister (whose name is neither Nehru nor Gandhi) cannot take credit for his government's economic reforms without saying he is only doing the work that Rajivji started. So reluctant are we to criticize our dead leaders that it is impossible to get anyone to admit that Nehru was directly responsible for creating the infamous licence raj and for crushing what Manmohan Singh likes to call the creative genius of the Indian people. Nehru's foreign policy was wise and enlightened for its time. His attitude to democracy and its institutions was healthy and worthy of respect. But, as far as the economy was concerned, he goofed up by thinking that the Soviet Union was a model to emulate. Why is it so hard for us to admit this?

Why are there so few biographies of Nehru or Gandhi that really look at what they believed in and see whether their ideas have stood the test of time? What are we afraid of? Could it be that we are scared of seeing those feet of clay?

A WELFARE STATE THAT KNOCKS ON HELL'S DOOR

3 July 1994

Remember Deepa? Deepa, aged twelve, also known as Parminder Kaur? No? Why should you. She was just an ordinary little girl with an ordinary everyday story of how our 'social welfare state' functions. Deepa was found wandering around some weeks ago wearing only a vest and covered in deep wounds and burn scars. A kindly rickshawallah picked her up and took her to a police station where she told this story. She had been sexually abused by her father and several cousins from the age of five and abandoned when she developed epilepsy. She was put into a nari niketan in Meerut. Here she was subjected to regular physical torture because her epileptic fits were a nuisance for the Raksha Graha's women attendants.

On the night that she was found half-naked and covered in injuries the staff tortured her for 'stealing' a packet of tea. This is how a Delhi newspaper reported what happened. 'Deepa alleged that Sushila summoned Seema and ordered her to cut her hair while Champa branded her with burning wood, hot iron rods and tongs and beat her up with *lathis*. According to Parminder (Deepa) the four women branded her all over her back, her thighs, legs and even on her private parts.' Deepa was then thrown out into the streets. Why are we not more shocked by Deepa's story? Why are our politicians not jumping up and down and making a racket in our legislative assemblies? Why do our national newspapers not even think the story worth following up? Because we know that horrific though it is, Deepa's story is not unusual.

Deepa at least survived to tell her tale. That makes her luckier than the two boys—one deaf and dumb, the other epileptic—who died of negligence in Delhi's observation home. The only people who protested were street children who know the observation home is a hellhole. In its efforts to introduce street children to the joys of the Indian social welfare state the Delhi police regularly picks them up and locks them up in the observation home. Here they are beaten, tortured and forced to work for the staff. Conditions are so intolerable that most try to escape at the first chance. Many claim this special home for vagrant children is worse than being in adult jail. Conditions in state institutions for the mentally sick are even worse. Every now and then some newspaper has a report about how inmates are confined to cells naked, untended and covered in their own filth. The story is quickly forgotten.

We are all to blame for what goes on in India in the name of social welfare. We in the press are to blame for not considering these stories important enough. Other things always seem more important, like whether Mulayam Singh gets on with Kanshi Ram. And, all of you out there are to blame for not reacting more angrily to what you see and read. But in the end blame must lie with the state itself. It controls hundreds of social welfare institutions and most of them are run so badly, they are hidden away from prying reporters and the general public. Permission to visit one of these institutions is almost impossible to get and television cameras are not allowed. Why? Is the government afraid we would find out that it is incapable of running social welfare institutions with even minimum compassion? Is it afraid we would find out these institutions are run more to provide jobs for government employees than to provide welfare?

Why can these institutions not be handed over to NGOs? There are hundreds of NGOs, especially those working with women and children, in our towns and cities who would be more than willing to take over the nari niketans and the children's homes but the state refuses to allow them to even get a foot through the door. One organization that has been trying to take over the observation home in Delhi said that the government would not consider its offer because it would deprive its own staff of jobs. Can we continue to allow this to be the main consideration? If these institutions could be handed over to NGOs flush with foreign funds, the government would have time to concentrate on wider issues of social welfare and human development. The recently released Human Development Report for 1994 is a particularly sad document for India. We are ranked 134 in the Human Development Index (two steps lower than Pakistan) in terms of what our government is able to provide by way of education, healthcare, safe drinking water and essential family planning services. This is a disgrace and things will only improve if we acknowledge how serious the problem is.

Look at the state of government hospitals. Even in cities like Bombay and Delhi, if you want proper care and hygienic conditions you have to go to a private hospital. Government hospitals are filthy and hopelessly inadequate. Conditions in rural hospitals and health centres are horrific beyond description. Yet have you ever heard the health minister speak about this? Has there ever been a debate in Parliament? Instead, the health ministry concentrates on churning out glossy posters and pamphlets telling people to beware of AIDS and malaria and urging everyone to have fewer children. It overlooks the small problem that nearly half our people cannot read. Which brings us to schools. Even in our cities there are so few government schools available that poor people, desperate to give their children opportunities they never had, spend their entire time looking for someone who can help with admissions. In the villages, conditions are even more desperate. If there is a school, there are no books, and if there are books, there are no teachers. All we get from the HRD ministry is advice in colourful printed posters. Teach your children to read, they say, attend adult literacy classes, bring light into someone's life by making one person literate.

The social welfare state has not collapsed suddenly. This is how it has always been. The difference is that with liberalization, the urgency for the social welfare state to start functioning properly is greater then ever before. Otherwise, the benefits of a liberalized economy will be confined to the 200 million Indians who are estimated to constitute the urban middle class. Only the market will matter. Is this the kind of economic reform we need?

THE REAL INDIA, WARTS AND ALL

21 August 1994

A new breed of lower caste politicians is turning the caste system so much on its head that it has become a hot subject of political discourse among us political pundits and even in Delhi's drawing rooms. Since everyone in these circles is from the upper sections of the caste system we are shocked that in Mulayam Singh's Uttar Pradesh and Laloo Yadav's Bihar bureaucrats are transferred just because they are brahmin. We are puzzled by Kanshi Ram's venom. What is it, we ask ourselves, as we sip tea from elegant china in our genteel drawing rooms, that makes the man so angry? Why does he say horrible things like *Tilak, tarazu aur talwar, Inko maaro joote char*? Why should he hate the brahmin, bania and kshatriya so much that he insults their symbols in his political slogans and orders them out of his public meetings?

The answers are hard to find for those of us who are upper caste and bred on Gandhiji's idyllic vision of India as a rural paradise. Gandhiji's fantasy world of happy peasants living in pretty villages surrounded by green fields is something we all bought into. Politicians, journalists, writers, filmmakers, activists, lefties, intellectuals, the lot of us. Our images of village India are of beautiful Rajasthani girls on tourism posters, of cows chewing cud in neat stone courtyards, of simple proud people who are the bricks and mortar of this country. Occasionally, when these simple, proud people hack harijans to death or execute children for marrying into the wrong caste we are shocked but we treat these things as aberrations.

Last week a film arrived in Delhi which rattled the teacups in many a pretty drawing room and let in for a few devastating moments the stench of the real India. What came in were not the gentle scents of Gandhiji's idyllic village republics but the stink of Ambedkar's cesspools of ignorance, superstition and backwardness. It is not often that a film can hold a mirror to an upside down reality and succeed in putting it right side up. Shekhar Kapur's *Bandit Queen* does this, which is why in my view, it is the first serious political film to be made in India. It will not be seen much in rural India and even if it is there will be little effect on people who believe so firmly in their ways, but if it is allowed, relatively uncensored, to be shown in our cities and towns it might succeed in explaining to the middle classes the meaning of being lower caste and a woman, in the real India.

The film is about Phoolan Devi. We are still fascinated by her story but have never tried to see it in a wider context. Kapur's film lifts her story out of its individual reality and merges it with the reality of what happens every day in some Indian village or other to low caste women. We know that little girls are married off to much older men every day. The occasion is celebrated in states like Rajasthan where there are mass marriages of children on the auspicious day of Akkha Teej (Akshaya Tritya). We know that little girls are raped by their aged husbands as a marital right but it's only when you see it happening in Kapur's *Bandit Queen* that the full horror manifests itself.

The Censor Board, armed with a new set of instructions to curb cinematic sex and violence, will find the scissors itching in its fingers, but if it is serious about wanting some of our uglier social realities to change it must resist the temptation to cut. There are moments that would ordinarily face censorship. The scene of Phoolan being gang-raped in Behmai, the scene in which she is made to walk into the village square naked to draw water from the well. We know this happened, we know that it was what made her return to the village with a gang that killed every Thakur man they could find. But we do not like to admit that these are realities that low caste women face every day in our villages. When we are confronted with stories like what happened, not long ago, in Dauna village near Allahabad where a middle-aged harijan woman was paraded naked through the village by upper caste landowners we pretend that these are aberrations. This is why things do not change. Shekhar Kapur's *Bandit Queen* compels us to look, it compels us to pay attention to the horror that is the real India.

THE HEADY DAYS OF MRS GANDHI

6 November 1994

If anyone doubted that as a nation we are a pathetic bunch of snivelling sycophants it should have been put at rest by the eulogies to Indira Gandhi that filled our newspapers last week. From a bureaucrat who worked for her, 'Few persons have left as cataclysmic a mark on the recent history of this subcontinent as Indira Gandhi. She has been the only leader who won a victory for India outside India after Chandragupta Maurya's victory over Selukos Nikator in the third century BC.' From her friend and biographer, Pupul Jayakar, 'When she was at the helm, India held its head up in the comity of nations; today we crawl around on our knees. I remember her telling me that the end of India will be when we allow multinationals to come. She said, "Watch, Pupul, it will be like the East India Company."' From the *Hindustan Times*, which dedicated its Sunday supplement to paeans, 'Perhaps the most remarkable woman to be born to this cathartic century, Indira Gandhi had one illusion—India, and one disillusion—the men around her.' Only one newspaper, this one, dared to print a critical assessment of her reign in which Swapan Dasgupta dispassionately analysed her political and economic contribution to this country and concluded that she presided over 'two wasted decades'. And, how!

Is it merely sycophancy that blinds us to the irreparable damage done to this country on account of Mrs Gandhi's policies or do we seriously believe that she was the best thing that happened to us? One of her praise-singers credited her with being the 'creator of India today'. Yes, and take a look at it. With 'head held high in the comity of nations' we can proudly say that we are among the poorest, most backward countries in the world unable to provide a decent standard of living to nearly half our people. Pupul Jayakar (who should concentrate on culture and hagiography) believes that foreign investment makes countries crawl. What about begging for foreign aid as we used to do during her friend's reign? Perhaps she thinks it is possible to beg with head held high?

Mrs Gandhi had charisma, she was loved by the masses, she was a brilliant politician who was very good at convincing ordinary Indians that she was their champion, their saviour. That her love for them was sufficient to make their poverty vanish. She made a good impression on the world stage. She spoke English and French and wore pretty saris. She was a good mother. A very good mother. And, a good employer. Her flunkeys loved her. History, though, will judge her on what she did for India and it is hard to think of too many things she did which can be considered beneficial ten years on.

When you say this her fans and hagiographers leap up and yell, Bangladesh, Bangladesh, what about Bangladesh? At the time of the Bangladesh war it did seem like a brilliant thing to do. Opposition leaders sang her praises, we rejoiced at this Durga reincarnate, at the licking we gave Pakistan. But, in retrospect, did we not do Pakistan a favour by cutting off its impoverished, ungovernable other half, making it possible for it to become richer, more powerful and a nuclear thorn in our side? All Bangladesh has done for us is send a constant stream of its poorest people illegally across our friendly border.

It was Mrs Gandhi's domestic policies that did the most damage. She understood economics about as much as Mrs Jayakar does and set us on the road to socialism. With head held high she nationalized, controlled, licensed and strangled the economy even as communist China opened its economy to the world. She returned to power (1980) at the time that Deng Xiao Ping began his economic reforms and had she copied him we would today have been ahead of the Asian 'tiger' economies who have developed so fast they now sneer at our socialistic ways. Mr Rao and Dr Manmohan Singh are trying to right some of the wrongs she did but we are way behind.

Now let us examine Mrs Gandhi's political legacy. She gave us the Emergency, press censorship, state-controlled television, diminished democratic institutions, authoritarianism, a Congress party of yes-men, secessionist movements in Punjab and Kashmir, a deeply troubled northeast, a durbar in Delhi and dynastic secession. Which of these things should 'a grateful nation' remember her for? We are told that she cared about India in more ways than political and economic. That she cared about the environment. Will somebody explain why the Himalayas lost most of their forest cover during her tenure, why corrupt forest officials were not punished for this and why our sacred rivers were allowed to become polluted sewers? The 'people' she supposedly loved so much were allowed to remain illiterate, poor and without the basic amenities of the twentieth century—clean water, electricity, healthcare, primary education.

Mrs Gandhi's policies left India a second-rate, backward country whose shoddy goods and mediocre ideas the world was uninterested in and whose foreign policy died with the Cold War. If this means holding one's head high in the comity of nations, then thank you very much, Mrs Jayakar, we would rather crawl.

THE RICH AND THE POOR DIVIDE

8 January 1995

On New Year's Eve in Khan Market, Delhi's fanciest, most fashionable shopping centre, I saw something I have never seen before outside Calcutta. At a garbage dump, near a fast-food restaurant, I saw a gaggle of small, barefoot children foraging desperately among the dead flowers, waste paper and rotting fruit, looking for food. They had plastic bags in their hands and into these they deposited anything edible that they could find. Half-eaten buns went in, along with pieces of meat, and once their bags were full, the children raced off to feast on what they had found. Some started eating, even while they searched, and one little boy made himself a sort of hamburger and bit gleefully into it while his other hand continued to scavenge for more. It was a sad, shaming sight, made sadder by the fact that it was New Year's Eve.

That night, champagne flowed in Delhi's drawing rooms and five star hotels and there was dancing, mirth and merriment on a scale that we would never have seen in the days when we were still pretending to be socialist. In those pre-liberalization days ostentation was almost a criminal offence. Too much wining and dining and you would have the tax raiders on your case in minutes, unless you had important political friends. So, maharajas hid their fabulous jewels or smuggled them quietly out of the country. Industrialists tried to live as humbly as possible and our new khadi-clad maharajas salted away fortunes in Swiss bank accounts but pretended, all the while, to be

Gandhians in their heart and Nehruvian socialists in their mind.

There is no question in my mind that we are well rid of the hypocrisy of those days. We will only become a rich country if we respect economic policies that seek to create wealth and respect those that create wealth. This is, incidentally, very much a part of 'the Indian ethos', since we are probably the only country in the world that worships a goddess of wealth, Lakshmi. Diwali, our most important festival, is dedicated not to a carpenter's child born in a manger but to Lakshmi. If she enters your house, the old Hindu saying goes, break her legs so she can never leave.

Foreign observers often make the mistake of believing that it is Western consumerism that is corrupting Indian spirituality. They are wrong. It was a series of confused economic policies and even more confused political ideas that kept India poor and, if you like, spiritual. Children scavenging in garbage dumps is a gift not of liberalization but of socialism. Calcutta, the capital of our only communist state, is where you see this happen most commonly.

What liberalization has done is make the sight of starving children unacceptable. In the old days, when even the richest Indians were pretending to be poor, it was easy to accept poverty, bonded labour, child slavery and all those other fearful things that we got so used to living with. It no longer is. Narasimha Rao's biggest failure is not that he has been unable to contain Arjun Singh and N.D. Tiwari but that he has not understood that he has to change the old ways of 'alleviating poverty'.

He must accept that the vast governmental machinery that was set up in the name of socialism to alleviate poverty was not alleviating anyone's poverty other than that of the officials who manned the machinery. Rajiv Gandhi once admitted publicly that only fifteen paise of every rupee that the government spent on anti-poverty programmes actually reached the poor. Much newsprint went into gasps of dismay at this admission, many editorials expressed shock and horror. Then the fuss died down, as it always does, and the matter was forgotten.

So, most of the money that the government pours into alleviating poverty continues to end up in the pockets of officials. Not just because of their personal corruption but because the system ensures that it stays that way.

Look, for instance, at the fact that there are more than 700 million ration cards in India, which allow people to buy food and other essentials at subsidized rates. Are there 700 million Indians whose children need to forage for food in garbage dumps? No. But, because the government chooses to spread its largesse thin those people who really need subsidized food never get it. Can this not be changed? Can ration cards not be distributed on the basis of family incomes instead of to all and sundry? The truth is that nobody has given it serious thought and what we get, instead, from the prime minister are apologetic statements. 'I agree we have to go into the issue of deployment of resources in a systematic manner,' he said in an interview to the *Hindustan Times* last week '... We are discussing some reorientation of programmes and strategies. I recognize that there has been only partial impact of our economic policies. More impact has to be generated.'

This is simply not good enough, Mr Rao, nor are things going to change dramatically if we finally get a bunch of new faces in the cabinet. The only way there can be real change is if the government throws out all its old anti-poverty programmes and starts thinking anew. Why, for instance, are we sitting on huge stocks of food grain? We are believed to have three times more food grain in stock than we would need if there was a dire emergency like a war. Why are we sitting on it when we know that most of it, thanks to our brilliant methods of storage, will end up in the bellies of rats or rot with damp. And we sit on it when children eat out of garbage dumps in the streets of Delhi.

Our attitude to food is the same as it is to health and education. University education, as has been pointed out before in this column, is virtually free for all Indians, whether you are a Birla or the son of a bonded labourer from Bihar.

Not only does this make no sense but it doesn't help anyone either. Our universities are crumbling before our eyes because they are starved of funds, so the rich send their children abroad and the poor suffer. Similarly with healthcare. It should be the government's primary concern to provide free medical facilities and healthcare to those who cannot afford to pay and let the rich look after their own needs. But, no, we must have an All India Institute of Medical Sciences, which is now such an exclusive place that you have to be a politician or a bureaucrat to avail of its free facilities. Is it not better to have an Escorts heart hospital, which charges everyone equally and keeps no special rooms reserved for political VIPs? Things have gone very, very wrong with our so-called welfare state. When is the government going to wake up to this?

SO LONG FOR WHINING

21 May 1995

The one thing that leaders cannot afford to do is whine. It demoralizes the people they claim to lead and makes the leaders themselves look less like leaders and more like a pathetic bunch of snivelling schoolboys. Yet ours get away with whining constantly, even in our moments of gravest crisis. The 'Pakistan hand', they wail, whenever something terrible happens, as if by saying it often enough they can absolve themselves of both guilt and responsibility. The pattern has been repeated during the Charar-e-Sharif disaster with a small variation from Rajesh Pilot, whose blood-and-thunder speech on the BBC about unfinished agendas in Kashmir was almost as pointless as the collective whining of his colleagues.

Yet, when the 'Pakistan hand' actually spoke from Islamabad in a menacing, threatening voice our government inexplicably did nothing. A day after the Charar-e-Sharif shrine was burned down, a Pakistani gentleman by the name of Maulana Mohammed Farooq, leader of the Harkat-ul-Ansar militant group, warned us from Islamabad that 'India should remember that the fire of Charar-e-Sharif will not be confined to Kashmir alone. Now this fire will burn Delhi and Bombay.' Had we had proper leaders in Delhi instead of a bunch of whiners this was their chance to point out (in calm, unwhining tones) to the international community that here was clear evidence of Pakistan supporting terrorist activity from its territory.

The Pakistan government continues to maintain that it is only providing 'moral support to freedom fighters' in Kashmir but, surely, if India is threatened with terrorist violence by a group operating out of Islamabad it constitutes more than moral support? Have we demanded that this Maulana fellow be arrested? Have we asked for an explanation?

No, of course not. We have grown accustomed to merely whining and beating our breast like some bereaved widow. Are we going to wait till bombs go off in Bombay and Delhi before we do anything else?

The 'Pakistan hand' is really no longer sufficient explanation for our political troubles. We did not vote for the government in Islamabad so it owes us nothing. We vote for the one that rules from Delhi and we need to know why it has been able to do nothing all these years to either stop or cut off the 'Pakistan hand'. If Pakistan is nurturing terrorists who are responsible for subversive activities in our country we want to know what Narasimha Rao's government is doing about this. What have our intelligence agencies been doing? What is the home ministry doing? And what are our security forces doing?

The absence of answers to these vital questions has seriously undermined the credibility of the government in Delhi. So seriously that even when we know that they would not have any interest in burning down the Charar-e-Sharif shrine the explanations have a hollow ring. They tell us, for instance, that they intercepted conversations between Mast Gul and his masters in Pakistan but the story would have been more convincing if we had heard tape-recordings of the conversations. They tell us that they did all they could to prevent the militants from burning the shrine down but if this was true why did they prevent journalists from being at the spot? Have they forgotten the propaganda victory that K.P.S. Gill won by allowing us ringside seats at the Golden Temple for Operation Black Thunder? Why does the government continue to behave as if it had something to hide if it does not?

If we in the rest of India are finding the government's explanations hard to swallow please remember that they are even more unconvincing to the average Kashmiri. And until some measure of credibility is regained in the valley we can forget about a political solution or even a political process in Kashmir.

It will not be easy for the government to regain credibility with the Kashmiris but transparency would be a good start. We have now been pursuing a military solution in the valley for more than five years. Should we not be told exactly how successful this has been? All that we get from the government are statements of 'the elections will be held', 'the militants are on the run' variety; we never get any details of what strategy is being followed. The same is true of our alleged attempts to start up a political process in the valley. All that we know is that the government is keen for this to happen and that it was with this in mind that leaders like Shabir Shah and Yasin Malik were released. Should we not have a right to know what else the government plans to do? What else it has done? Who are the people that it is working through to start this so-called political process?

Since there are never any answers from either the home ministry or the prime minister's office, which is now in charge of Kashmir, the impression continues to grow and spread that not only does Delhi not have any defined policy for our most politically troubled state but that it also does not quite know what to do about it.

So we go back every time to the 'Pakistani hand'. Pakistan is ruining us. Pakistan does not want a political process. Pakistan wants to spread terrorism throughout India. Let us assume that it does. It is, after all, a rather sad irrelevant little country whose only international importance comes from the trouble it can make in Kashmir. With the Cold War over and the Russians long gone from Afghanistan its significance to the rest of the world has diminished to approximately that of one of our lesser provinces. So, it will make trouble for us if only to stay on the map.

What we need to know is why our government can do nothing about it other than weep and wail. Where is the Indian hand? Does it exist? And if it doesn't, will somebody explain why we are spending such vast, secret funds on our intelligence agencies and even vaster resources on our security forces? Is the 'Pakistan hand' responsible for their failure as well? The whining has gone on too long. The government must now give us some answers or hand power over to someone who can.

WHAT DOES SONIA WANT?

28 May 1995

What does Sonia Gandhi want? I ask the question with some trepidation because every time this column dares to mention the name of the Congress party's reigning 'rajmata' I find myself under attack from one or other of her many supporters in Delhi's political and social circles. Why do you have to write about her, they say, she is not in politics and she is never going to be. That, alas, is where the differences begin. I believe, despite the denials of her friends, that she is playing a definite role in Indian politics even if it is like Sanjay Gandhi during the Emergency an extra-constitutional one. If the sordid shenanigans that the Congress party treated us to in recent days achieved anything at all it was to establish that there is little point now in Sonia continuing to deny that she is in politics.

People who are not in politics do not spend their entire time meeting politicians. They do not involve themselves personally in the affairs of a political party and they do not inspire statements of the following kind from 'veteran Congressmen'. 'Only Soniaji can save the Congress and us. Let her take charge of the party.' 'Being the seniormost representative of the Nehru-Gandhi family, partymen look upon her with respect and affection. Mr Rao became the prime minister because at that critical juncture after Rajiv Gandhi's assassination, she wrote only one letter and that was addressed to Mr Rao. Other contenders like Arjun Singh and Sharad Pawar were automatically marginalized because of her signal that she supported Mr Rao. If she were to give an indication of who would be the leader after Rao, partymen will flock to him.'

Her friends like to contend that it is not her fault that politicians want to say things like this, that they want to meet her. How can she refuse to meet her husband's colleagues?

Please remember that in the days when it was her husband who was in politics she found it very easy to avoid meeting politicians altogether. She made it clear that she despised politics and politicians.

If she now spends her whole time amidst politics and politicians, albeit as the innocent, unspeaking lotus in a smelly cesspool, it has to mean that she has changed her earlier views. So, we come back to who is she, or what her role is, and what does she want? We know she likes foreign dignitaries calling on her and paying their respects. We know she likes these visitations to be televised and reported in the press. We know she likes people to see her as someone who is working night and day for the public good, for the 'poor and downtrodden'. We know she likes playing Mrs Robin Hood by achieving their betterment through the enormous funds that the Rajiv Gandhi Foundation collects from rich industrialists who would not have been so generous to an organization with lesser political credentials. What we do not know is what all this high profile good work and seemingly selfless political activity is leading to.

In many ways Sonia already has a unique and enviable position in Indian politics. As reigning deity of our ruling party she is the most powerful woman in India without having to fulfil any responsibilities. Why should she want to swap this for becoming merely another political leader? Yet, there is an ambivalence. On the one hand she seems quite happy backseat driving and on the other she reaches out every now and then and bops the driver—poor weak old Narasimha Rao—on the head. This approach, whether she likes to admit it or not, has been directly responsible for the collapse of the Congress party.

Had she not gone out of her way to encourage dissidence in these past months by always lending an ear to anyone who had a complaint against Mr Rao, and by coming up with her own list of complaints, it is unlikely that has-beens like N.D. Tewari and Arjun Singh would ever have gone to the extent of splitting the party. She made a last-minute appeal for unity but at the dissidents' rally it was she who was the real leader. The party workers who came in thousands from as far away as Tamil Nadu carried placards of her smiling at Rajiv's side. When the dissidents spoke of the prime minister's flaws one of their biggest grievances was that nothing had been done to punish Rajiv Gandhi's assassins. This, as we know, is Sonia's main complaint against the government. If you asked any of the rallyists what they thought of Sonia Gandhi, they said immediately that she was the only one who could save the party. It was Sonia's show all the way even if she wasn't seated, begarlanded and bedecked, on the stage. So, if Congress unity is really what she wants she achieved the opposite.

Her role will continue to be destructive as long as she remains ambivalent. If the Congress were not in power this ambivalence would affect only the party. As things are, she has succeeded in crippling the government. Poor Mr Rao's efforts to put the economy at the top of the political agenda have failed as we return to the Gandhi dynasty's old list—socialism, secularism and democracy. Meaningless but politically powerful words that have long persuaded people to vote for vague rather than concrete reasons.

Mr Rao is not blameless. It is his fault that ordinary Indians have not yet understood why he decided to reform the economy or what he hoped to achieve. He has been an outstandingly ineffective Congress president. But, in fairness to him, it must be said that he would have been able to be more forthright if Sonia's long shadow had not hovered, and lengthened, constantly in the background. She must decide what she wants. You cannot be in politics and not be in it at the same time and what you definitely cannot do is backseat drive.

A BALANCE SHEET ON RAO

26 June 1995

One day when Narasimha Rao's rule is examined from the perspective of history instead of the instant analysis of journalism it will probably be acknowledged that he was the best prime minister this country has ever had. If you say this today people think you have gone a bit mad. How can you say this, they gasp, when he has virtually destroyed the Congress party, when he allowed the Babri Masjid to fall, when he has allowed corruption to achieve new heights, when he has shown himself to be such a ditherer on Kashmir. The trouble with Mr Rao is he is not a popular leader. He is charmless and uncharismatic and when he tries to reach out to that section of the voting public that we call 'the masses' he generally ends up boring them to tears. His idea of a public speech is to launch forth into lengthy philosophical monologues that nobody has the patience to sit through.

Congress advertisements that attempt to project his thoughts and achievements make him look like a caricature from one of Laxman's cartoons. His rare appearances on television have done little to improve his image, again because of his weakness for mistaking philosophical soliloquies for public speaking. But, in this week of the fourth anniversary of his becoming prime minister, we need to look beyond his obvious failings. It is then you notice that he has done more for this country than he is given credit for.

Much as his opponents (and some of his colleagues) would

have us believe that he ruined the economy and sold the country's 'sovereignty' to foreign investors, the opposite is true. He inherited a bankrupt, stagnant economy that had run out of ideas and steam but spluttered along on the fuel of a confused, dying version of 'socialist' ideology. Mr Rao had the courage to recognize that the only real achievement of this ideology had been to concentrate economic power in the hands of politicians and bureaucrats. He decontrolled and delicensed. The system fought back as it did when Rajiv Gandhi tried to bring political change but Mr Rao persevered. He was charged with being a lackey of the International Monetary Fund, of allowing his Budget to be dictated in Washington. He had the courage to continue along the path he had taken and today, despite yowls from the flag bearers of swadeshi, India is attracting more foreign investment than ever before and is being taken seriously as an emerging economic power.

There are still enormous problems of poverty and rural backwardness but those who try to blame these on Mr Rao need to explain when things were better. Besides, surely there is more chance of being able to eliminate poverty when the economy is growing than when it is stagnating, as it has done for most of the years of our glorious Independence.

Mr Rao's detractors accuse him of not having the sort of foreign policy that will make India a world player. They forget that our foreign policy died with the Cold War, which ended shortly after Mr Rao became prime minister. In the new world what makes countries world players is their economic strength not leftover rhetoric from 'non-alignment' days. If India succeeds in becoming a major economic power, as many of our far eastern neighbours have, we will matter in the world. If the flag bearers of swadeshi have their way and we close the Indian economy again, we have had it. Mr Rao is one of the few political leaders in the country who understands this.

There are other things that can be counted among Narasimha Rao's achievements. Peace returned to Punjab and Kashmir. Things may not have got much better, but they are not much worse either. Inner party democracy has been allowed to put small roots down in the Congress party. In the Delhi Durbar there is more dissent than ever before, which is healthy. Would Arjun Singh or N.D. Tewari have dared open their mouths in Rajiv's time? Would they have dared challenge Indira Gandhi?

Television, although it remains state-controlled, has been freed enough for it to at least try and compete with the satellite channels that invaded our skies soon after Mr Rao took over. Having praised Mr Rao we need to look at what he has not done. In the opinion of this column his biggest failures have been in the social sector—education, healthcare, population control. Nothing has happened at all. Nothing much happened before either, so we face the shameful situation in which South African blacks, under apartheid, managed to achieve a higher literacy rate than we in independent India, but Mr Rao must be blamed for doing nothing about this. He must also accept responsibility for having been unable to come up with anything new in the areas of family planning and healthcare.

Perhaps the fault lies in Mr Rao's choice of ministers, and this is another of his failures. He appears to choose ministers for caste, communal and political reasons rather than competence. This system may have worked well enough in the old days, when politics was more important than governance, it cannot work any more. The results are there for anyone to see. Ministries headed by competent ministers like Manmohan Singh and P. Chidambaram have done extraordinarily well, those headed by ministers chosen for credentials other than competence have barely functioned at all.

Another of Mr Rao's failures has been his inability to cut down the size of the government. Not only do we have sixty union ministers but we continue to have thousands of extra officials and thousands of unnecessary departments. There are other failures. Mr Rao has not been able to do anything about the way the police functions, nothing to improve the appalling conditions of our courts and so much needs to be done. But he has managed to make India look a little less shoddy, a little less second rate. Is it not time that he was given credit for this?

THE CENTRE CANNOT HOLD

26 May 1996

Old governments are as forgettable as yesterday's kisses so there are no tears today for Narasimha Rao or his colleagues. Not even for Dr Manmohan Singh. But let me make a small prediction: it will be only a matter of months before we begin to look back on his regime with nostalgia and respect. This may not have happened if Atal Bihari Vajpayee's government survived a couple of years but there is unanimity in the corridors of political punditry that it is not going to and that soon India will have a new prime minister in the form of Karnataka's Deve Gowda. Optimists say this will be a good thing, India will be saved from communalism (long live casteism though) and since Gowda's strength comes from regional parties there will be much needed decentralization of economic and political power.

Even if only decentralization happens we should be looking forward to the reign of Gowda. But, I have a few personal doubts because none of the chief ministers in his circle have ever articulated the need for it. In fact, we have Chandrababu Naidu demanding central government money to bail him out. Genuine decentralization should mean that Andhra Pradesh pay for its own populism. It wasn't Delhi that encouraged 'two-rupee rice' or prohibition which lost the state more than Rs. 3000 crore, so why should the centre pay? Then, there is Mulayam Singh Yadav, who has never been heard saying that Uttar Pradesh should pay for its own poverty and bad governance. Nor has Laloo Yadav. None of this collection of chief ministers or former chief ministers have been heard admitting that they should themselves pay for the appalling mess their state electricity boards are in. On the contrary, they spend their time avoiding payment of their dues to the centre. Decentralization has to mean taking responsibility not just for decisions but also for their consequences so, as I said, I have my doubts.

If we cancel this one possible benefit we are left with the prospect of a government which will be able to do almost nothing for India. Lip service will be paid to the economic reforms, because Congress support is vital, but will there be any actual changes? No. There cannot be because it is simply not possible to satisfy the concerns of all the parties in the group. There is the additional problem that neither Deve Gowda nor his colleagues have even minimum comprehension of economic reforms or international realities. In the one interview I have had with Gowda he railed against GATT and Dunkel as if they were personally responsible for India's poverty. He then showed up in Davos for the World Economic Forum's annual meeting and checked into the most expensive hotel in Klosters with a vast retinue of family and flunkeys. He seems to have treated the expedition as a holiday rather than work. Some of his flunkeys spent their time ringing Indian businessmen to come and meet Deve Gowda but neither they nor their boss were seen wooing foreign investors or listening to the debates on global issues.

Then we have Mulayam Singh, who seriously believes that America was involved in a conspiracy to topple his government and that the American ambassador personally came to Uttar Pradesh during the recent election campaign to help the BJP win. When I tried pointing out that there could be few people in the US state department who had an inkling of Uttar Pradesh, leave alone him, he said that the Indian economy had been deliberately destroyed by the World Bank and the IMF. 'Look how the dollar has gone up and the rupee gone down.'

Unsurprisingly, Mulayam appears to have made little

difference to Uttar Pradesh in his tenure as chief minister but again he blames it all on 'imperialism'. In Laloo's case we can see from the 'gawala' scandal that he and his ministers knew their arithmetic but in terms of how much good this has done Bihar we come up with a zero. Think, what an incredible service these two Yadav gentlemen could have done India if they had managed to bring even the first ray of prosperity to the two poorest, most illiterate states in India?

So, forgive me if I do not share the widespread optimism in Delhi's Left-dominated political pundit circles about the advent of a United Front government. To be honest the BJP government has not inspired much euphoria in its brief moments either, what with Ram Jethmalani shooting his mouth off, Sikander Bakht sulking, Sushma Swaraj trying to censor advertisements and the prime minister finding time to kowtow at Rajiv Gandhi's samadhi. But it would have at least been a reasonably credible, cohesive government capable of making a few decisions. This is more than we can say for Deve Gowda, but then, this is exactly what the Congress wants. Perhaps, Narasimha Rao really is as Machiavellian as they say he is. Good for him. But what about the country?

A COALITION OF CASTE CHIEFTAINS

2 June 1996

The BJP government has been thrown out. Communalism has been defeated. India has been saved. What more can we want? We now have a shiny, new, secular (key word) government which we are assured will keep the country together as it consists of regional parties and is so keen to please 'minorities' that Mulayam Singh Yadav would like to bring Pakistan and Bangladesh back into the fold. Poor simple mofussil Mulayam is unaware that his statement in the Lok Sabha would have sent a chill down our neighbours' spines. He meant no harm, no revival of Akhand Bharat, only to please the millions of Muslims back home in Uttar Pradesh who think of him as the messiah of secularism.

What puzzles me about the triumph of secularism is that nobody in Delhi seems jubilant. In the Lok Sabha and in public they may appear to be but spend a few moments alone with our political leaders, talking 'off-the-record', and what you get is gloom. This is not just because a fourteen-party government totally dependent on slippery Congress support is unlikely to function but also because this uncertain arrangement replaces a government that could have worked well. The same leaders who revile the BJP publicly tell you privately that they believe Mr Vajpayee's government would have done a good job and that they do not think Deve Gowda's will. Many also admit that they do not think the BJP would have dared do anything in power that could be seen as 'communal'. The only real members of the fear-and-loathe-BJP club are our Marxist comrades and caste chieftains. Even they concede that the BJP would govern well but quickly explain that this is not important when weighed against the communalism drawback.

Secularism takes precedence over governance. This could be dangerous. Let me give you a glimpse of the scenario that I see develop in the next few months. Our new government is here only because of its secular credentials so secularism is likely to be its main contribution. I fear that this is not going to be enough. If you had spent as much time travelling in the boondocks as I did during the election campaign you would have discovered that what the average voter wants is governance. Wherever I went, people told me that they wanted their lives to improve. They wanted electricity not in occasional flashes but twenty-four hours a day. They wanted drinking water not at the end of a kilometre-long walk but at their doorstep. They wanted schools for their children, public transport, roads and even telephones.

The only political party that has talked about governance during the political soap opera of the past few weeks has been the BJP. In the presidential address, in which Atal Behari Vajapyee's thirteen-day government laid out its agenda before it was voted out, we heard of drinking water schemes and the need to improve power, telecommunications, ports and roads. We heard of the need to identity five crore of the poorest families in the country to give them special assistance. When Mr Vajpayee sought support for his government in the Lok Sabha he went further, pointing out that it should concern every political party that India continued to be counted amongst the poorest countries in the world.

Not a single speaker from the other side mentioned governance. They made passionate speeches about the fears of Muslims, about the evils of the RSS, about the right of Northeastern people to eat beef and about the BJP's non-comprehension of the pluralism of India's culture, but nobody mentioned one word about governance. What I fear is that if they are unable to govern then secularism could end up being associated with bad governance. And what happens then? Next time round there will be fewer and fewer people who will pay any attention to those who talk of secularism. This will be interpreted by the BJP's lunatic fringe as a vote for Hindutva, especially if the party manages to win a full majority. Then it will not be Vajpayee's emphasis on governance that we will get but exactly the saffron-flavoured pilav that our secular leaders feared the BJP would dish out this time.

We can only hope that in the secular pilav that we have got instead there will be a flavour of governance. Our new leaders need to stop talking about common minimum programmes and start talking instead about the maximum they can provide. How can they do this when all their energy is likely to be spent on trying to stay put?

SUKH RAM'S SMALL CHANGE

25 August 1996

For such a very poor country isn't it fascinating how very rich our ministers and ex-ministers have become? And isn't it wonderful that the CBI has finally decided to stop harassing poor businessmen and go for the really big guns instead. I have always believed that the richest people in our poverty-stricken land are not your Rahul Bajajs and Ratan Tatas but your Sukh Rams and your...wait for the next raid. Never in all those years of raiding businessmen has the CBI come upon three crore rupees casually lying around the house in bedsheets and bags, and please do not imagine for a minute that this is all the money that our former telecommunications minister has to his name. Far from it. According to one of Sukh Ram's former ministerial colleagues, the reason why the money was left lying around so casually was because it was only the 'small change'.

Socialism was really good for our politicians. Yes, yes, I am aware that the view from the Left is that this kind of corruption is the direct consequence of liberalization but, as usual, they are talking garbage. In truly liberalized economies there are clear rules about investment and transparent methods of attracting it. In our own fair land we have had for the past fifty years a police state where our economic rights are concerned and the policemen have been politicians. It has been in their hands to decide who invests where and in their hands to change the rules, the games and even the goalposts as and when they liked.

Why old Narasimha Rao did nothing to change this is because he must have realized that transparency would result in a lack of what our political leaders like to call 'party funds'. He must have realized that the competition that his semi-liberalization brought would result in competition on the party funds front, so he put his key men (like Sukh Ram) in ministries like telecom and petroleum.

The nation owes Sukh Ram a debt of gratitude for leaving so much 'small change' lying about his house. Because, finally, ordinary Indians will be able to get a glimpse of the kind of money we are talking about when we say that our politicians and bureaucrats have made huge fortunes out of public service. Those of us whose jobs compel us to wander about the government bungalows of Lutyens' Delhi have known for some time that we are talking about really big bucks.

We have gauged this from the jewels that mantriji's wife wears, from the fleets of cars that his children travel around in, from the number of times he seems able to travel abroad (first class) with family, from the kind of hotels he is suddenly able to afford, from the foreign education he can give his children, from the foreign medical treatment that his family rushes off for and from his expensive tastes in general. I mean, take someone even as humble as our prime minister. The first time I ran into him on foreign soil was in Davos, where I discovered, to my humble surprise, that he and his family were staying in several expensive suites in the most expensive hotel in Klosters. It is famous for being Prince Charles' favourite hotel. How can we hold it against him when everyone else including our oh-so-humble BJP leaders do the same sort of thing. When exactly did public life become such a lucrative business? If we have to pinpoint it we would have to say that it has always been part of our socialist culture, but that it became more evident in Rajiv Gandhi's heyday, when we noticed for the first time that the money was being stashed away in foreign bank accounts. We also noticed how, in slavish imitation of their Leader, such an extraordinarily large number of Congressmen were suddenly able to wear gold Rolex watches, Mont Blanc pens and Gucci shoes. They were a stylish bunch—those Gucci Gandhians—but we have to remember that the trends they imitated from Rajiv would have had to be paid for in foreign exchange at a time when the rest of us were allowed no more than a couple of hundred dollars on our travels abroad.

In any case, they set a trend that continues to be followed to this day even by people who wear their humbleness and honesty on their khadi sleeves. Even our mighty honest-man-of-the-year, Shri T.N. Seshan, wears a gold Rolex and Mulayam Singh a Mont Blanc pen. I happen to think it's quite stylish to do so but isn't it about time that our rulers were made to explain how they afford their lifestyles?

GOVERNANCE, NOT POLITICS

20 October 1996

Let me begin by speaking plainly. I don't approve of humble farmers as prime ministers. I believe they do not qualify for the job. When you rule a country the size of a continent you need, at the very least, to be educated, sophisticated, economically literate, aware of international realities and capable of making policies that would provide direction to the country. I do not believe that native intelligence and peasant cunning are adequate or suitable substitutes for the qualifications above listed. Having said this let me add that despite my conviction that Haradanahalli Deve Gowda was unqualified to rule India I was prepared to give him a fair chance. If only because, despite his predecessors having been eminently more qualified, he did inherit a country that was a mess despite five years of economic reform.

It may seem as scam after scam is unearthed that the reforms were nothing but an excuse for ministers to make even more money and some leftist leaders have said as much. But they are wrong. The economic reforms were the best thing that happened to us and the government that does not continue with them and speed up the process could be putting us back on the old road to 'socialism' and ruin. I fear that the humble farmer is doing exactly this if we are to go by the populist nonsense that he has lately taken to spouting.

Listen to this comment from his interpreter and chief spokesman C.N. Ibrahim in an address to farmers during the recent election campaign in Uttar Pradesh. 'In cities, the government ensured water for bathing pet dogs, 56,000 UP villages do not have drinking water. In cities, the electricity boards ensure power for air conditioning houses, farmers do not get power for four hours to run pump sets. When my prime minister announced ten rupees subsidy on power for farmers Vajpayeeji objected saying it would cause losses to electricity board.'

Assuming that this was a reflection of the prime minister's convictions and not just campaign rhetoric, let us examine what was said. All right, water for bathing pet dogs. There is not a single city in India where there is an adequate supply of water, not even Delhi. If UP still has 56,000 villages without drinking water it is because it has always had too much politics and too little governance. Next, power for air conditioning. In most cities electricity is in such short supply that hospitals and other vital services rely on generators. Besides, Humble Farmerji, have you noticed that in the cities people pay huge electricity bills which enables politicians like you to give free power to farmers. It is a bad policy that has bankrupted our state electricity boards.

What is more disturbing than the prime minister's shameless populism is his inability to understand the issues he is addressing. While discussing the housing problem at a seminar in Delhi last week this was his explanation for why millions of Indians continue to be shelterless. 'There is a nexus between the politicians and the bureaucrats, and this has to be broken to provide shelter to the poor. The politicians and the bureaucrats live in big houses by paying nominal lease fees. All these need to be exposed to have a proper housing policy.'

Since Mr Gowda grew up in a village in the styx of Karnataka he is probably unaware that housing in urban India is in short supply because of bad policies. Private developers were banned from entering the real estate market in the sixties because the state took upon itself the task of building affordable housing for the poor and the low of income. Then to keep rents low because we were 'socialist' it passed laws that restricted how much urban land individual citizens could own and how much rent could be charged by landlords. The real estate market collapsed and slumlords and mafiosi took charge of low cost housing in cities like Bombay.

As for the nexus between bureaucrats and politicians that entitles them to big houses at nominal rents, this is indeed true and the prime minister would be setting a fine example if he moved his ministers and himself into humbler private houses. If this example was followed by state governments there would be vast tracts of land available in the finest localities in our cities where houses could be built for the poor and the rich. Will the prime minister put his money where his mouth is?

LET'S TALK TO, NOT AT EACH OTHER

23 March 1997

So we are taking to Pakistan again. Should we consider this good news? A major foreign policy achievement? An indication of the success of what we call the Gujral doctrine? It depends on whether we are really talking or simply going through the motions of an exercise we have gone through many times before. Generally what happens is that our officials tell Pakistan to stop promoting terrorism and lay off Kashmir. It is an internal affair of India, they say, and Pakistan's officials respond for the nth time that if we do not talk about Kashmir there is no point in talking about anything else.

Then these worthy gentlemen gather for dinner in one of Delhi's better hotels and our officials try to impress the visitors with our multi-culturalism by reciting bad Urdu poetry badly and by serving greasy, red-meaty, Punjabi food to prove how much we know about their culture. Then everyone goes home and we forget about the peace process till their thugs kill a few more innocent people in Kashmir or one of their leaders makes another silly statement.

We have had variations of this depressing pattern for fifty years and got no closer to peace in the subcontinent. We cannot get any closer until we break with the patterns of the past and start talking to each other rather than *at* each other. If we were talking to each other we would make our position clear. We think of the LoC (the Line of Control) as the border and we will not consider changes to our borders. It is not going to happen and if either side is serious about finding a solution in Kashmir then it's time to start calling the LoC the border and get on with the rest of our lives. It would be terrific, actually, if we could forget about Kashmir and get on with the rest of our lives but it cannot happen. For the simple reason that it is because of Kashmir that governments on both sides of the border spend more money on guns and soldiers than on doctors and teachers, making us two of the most wretchedly poor countries in the world.

In my view India is more to blame for relations being stuck in a rut than Pakistan and the reason why we are to blame is because we have honoured that sad little country across the LoC by insisting on a doctrine of reciprocity. The dusty corridors of Indian babudom limit even the brightest minds, so the best secretaries and foreign secretaries in the MEA (ministry of external affairs) appear to have never noticed that India is not Pakistan and, Allah be praised, will never be. How can we be reciprocal with a country whose very *raison d'etre* limits it? As V.S. Naipaul said in a recent interview, 'Pakistan was created on this very bad premise of dividing people. The Bosnia of 1947... And the dream is being pushed and pushed, the ethnic cleansing dream. It's a mess. It's a lost generation.'

In the same interview he points out that even if a few rational Pakistanis have come to the fore, behind them always lurks the ugly shadow of the mullahs. Not to mention the generals. Can we be reciprocal in our approach? Do we not shame India by even attempting reciprocity, which on the ground translates into *you give me one visa I give you one, you beat up one of my diplomats, I beat up one of yours*.

Reciprocity can work among equals. Despite the strenuous efforts of the BJP's lunatic fringe we are never going to be a Hindu Pakistan. So we need to behave like the bigger, older country. Which is why Inder Gujral needs to be praised for what he is trying to do to liberalize the visa process. He should go further. Pakistanis should be given tourist visas without any difficulty and there should be no police reporting. It is a ludicrous practice which gives the wrong impression about

India and makes extra work for our policemen. We need to remember that the thugs Pakistan trains to kill innocent people in Kashmir and Punjab manage to come across the border without visas.

It is to our advantage that ordinary Pakistanis come to India because what most discover is that the lunatics who tore down the Babri Masjid are not representative of India. They also discover what their own country could be if they could rid themselves of their meddlesome mullahs. It is when ordinary people on both sides of the border start demanding peace that peace will come.

UPHAAR'S VILLAINS

21 July 1997

Raman Siddhu came to see me. He told me a story that has in it the whole horror of India. His wife, two daughters, sister, two nieces and a nephew died because they went to see *Border* on the day it opened at Uphaar cinema in Delhi. In almost no other country in the world would they or the fifty-two other victims have needed to die in such tragic, needless fashion. That is why it is important for you to hear and really listen to Raman's story, again and again and again.

His entire family did not die, you see, because there was a fire in the basement of the cinema. They died because of the insensitivity, callousness and criminal apathy of the Indian state. It is this that we are inclined to forget in the plethora of commissions, committees and whitewashes that will go into the incident. When smoke started filling the hall, Raman's wife, Sonika, had the presence of mind to call him on her mobile phone and tell him exactly what had happened. For several minutes she spoke to him describing the pitch blackness, the smoke, the milling, terrified crowds, the fact that they were holding on to each other's hands to make sure that none of the children got lost. Then she began to tell him of those who were dying. Before she died herself she said, 'They're all dead.'

The conversation would have lasted long enough for everyone in the hall to have been saved. But people will continue to die like Raman's family did. They will die over and over, in incident after incident, until we recognize that the Indian state is now so venal, so apathetic, so inhuman that it could not care less. We need to realize that until all of us—you, me, everybody—gets up and says enough is enough, nothing is going to change. Raman has made it the mission of his broken, tormented life to see that the guilty do not go unpunished. It should be as much our mission if we want things to change.

'Nothing worked,' Raman says, 'nothing at all. This is what I would like you to understand. The ambulances arrived without oxygen. The firemen without the right equipment, without water. The hospital had not even the minimum facilities to handle an emergency of this kind. And as for the police, all they did was try to prevent me from taking the bodies of my family away on the ground that they needed to do autopsies.'

Raman then gave me a copy of the Naresh Kumar Inquiry Committee's report and I tried to plough through its eighty-six pages of officialese. Despite the verbiage that officials usually use to hide their sins it comes through loud and clear that the cinema's management and the Delhi authorities are guilty enough for us to actually be able to demand the arrest of the lieutenant governor himself. In fact, this is perhaps the only way that things will change. Until Delhi's top officials and the Ansal family who own Uphaar are held personally culpable justice will not have been fully done.

The Ansals are fine upstanding members of Delhi's haute society and yet they gave us a cinema which was a death trap. Is this not already a criminal act? Delhi's authorities, who were supposed to at least ensure that their safety specifications and building rules were met did not bother to do even this. Can they be absolved of the ultimate responsibility for the tragedy?

The Naresh Kumar report is no more than a namby-pamby effort at telling the horrible truth of what happened. Nevertheless, it allows it to slip through that if the cinema management had not wasted time nobody would have died: 'When Mr Malhotra (the manager), I along with other staff members realized that the fire could not be brought under control, they came out of the cinema hall leaving everybody behind esp. (sic) the viewers to their fate. Had the management not wasted these precious ten minutes; the lives of the innocent viewers would have been saved.'

The report adds that when the manager realized the fire was out of control he first saved his cash box and his car. When he finally found time to call the police and the fire brigade they did less to save people than ordinary citizens did. Who is to blame for this? Is it not the lieutenant governor? Then, there is the horror of our hospitals. Their outdated equipment, their hopelessly outdated procedures, their shameful inability to deal with emergencies. Is the Delhi government not to blame for allowing these conditions to exist year after year, tragedy after tragedy?

We need to admit that the Indian state gets away with these things because of our own apathy. If Delhi's citizens had reacted to the Uphaar tragedy by boycotting cinemas, the lieutenant governor would have been forced to close them until they met basic safety standards. But *Border* continued to run to full houses. The army chief proceeded to organize a glittering, star-studded screening thirteen days after the tragedy and people paid vast sums to attend.

What kind of people are we? How many more tragedies is it going to take for us to wake up to the truth that Raman's fight has to be our fight? It is a month since the Uphaar fire and all that has happened is the usual procedural delays. In another month we will have begun to forget and in a year we will probably have forgotten altogether. When are we going to realize that we cannot afford to forget any more?

(Published in *India Today*)

ABOLISH VIP HEALTHCARE

28 July 1997

One of our worse legacies from the Nehruvian socialist era is the abject acceptance of government servants and politicians as having a position in society more equal than our own. As in China, the Soviet Union and other former Marxist countries, our peculiar brand of socialism took for granted that those who worked for the government or the ruling party were entitled to more exalted status than your average common or garden comrade. It was not an idea that went down well anywhere. One of the reasons why the once mighty communist empire now lies in ruins behind what used to be the Iron Curtain is that people got sick of the inequities of this kind of socialism.

We who leapt straight from colonialism to socialism are more confused and therefore more accepting of this idea. We have Indianized the concept to such an extent that we cannot identify it anywhere else. It has become the building block of what I think of as the 'sahibji syndrome', which manifests itself in our villages in the debasing spectacle of the average villager—in his shabby clothes and cheap shoes—falling at the feet of some suited and booted pomposity of an IAS officer and begging for a favour that is his right: 'Sahibji, water, please give us water, one little hand pump. Sahibji please, a road and we will be eternally grateful. Just one small road.' Of course, we educated types do not usually fall at the feet of IAS officers. Yet, we have our own ways of showing that we too are afflicted by the sahibji syndrome. And one of the ways that has been much on my mind since Delhi's Uphaar cinema fire tragedy is the manner in which we politely accept that while our hospitals lack even such fundamental necessities as oxygen masks and the ability to deal with emergencies our leaders think nothing of flying to the most expensive hospitals in the world for their own healthcare.

While women and children were dying in Delhi's best government hospitals because there were no oxygen masks V.P. Singh was being tended to in London at taxpayers' expense. Not only were we paying for his treatment we were paying for him to stay in considerable luxury for many many weeks at the St James Court Hotel. For a man who made his name in Indian politics by talking endlessly about the Mandal route to 'equity' it makes you wonder whether he ever thinks of the inequity of his own situation. How many thousand oxygen masks could his medical treatment pay for? Our new health minister, Renuka Chowdhury, went down considerably in my estimation when she had a fit because she was handed what she appeared to consider the lowly portfolio of health. But she improved her standing marginally when she led a group of concerned citizens to Delhi's lieutenant governor last week to urge him to take action against those responsible for the Uphaar tragedy. Not many other ministers were ready to take up such a cause. For doing so Chowdhury deserves public acknowledgement. She will get much more if she publicly admits that had the hospitals under her charge been functioning with minimum efficiency half the victims would have lived.

Jagdeep Mann, who lost his wife and three children in the Uphaar disaster, says: 'My wife was alive when they brought her to the All India Institute of Medical Sciences. She would have lived if oxygen had been available. They didn't even have a torch and spent several minutes finding one. Nor did they have the equipment to revive the heart. Others who went to Moolchand (a private hospital) survived.'

How many thousands of others must have over the past fifty years died for similar reasons. Our healthcare is not just a mess it is a myth—virtual reality. You can see this is no exaggeration when you remember that most Indian children who die before they are five years old die of diseases that are completely preventable.

Diarrhoea is the biggest killer and has been since independence. This means that almost nothing has been done to improve our healthcare in fifty years. If you need further proof of this consider the fact that China's infant mortality, which was 150 per 1000 live births in 1960, came down to 31 by 1990. Ours, which was 165 in 1960 came down to 80 in the same period. Even Sri Lanka reduced its rate from 71 to 26. Add to this the fact that our best government hospitals are worse than the worst hospitals in most other countries and you begin to understand why Indian healthcare is nothing more than virtual reality. Chowdhury is health minister in a government that is on daily wages. There are limits to what she can do to improve the appalling legacy she has inherited. But there is one thing she can do: abolish VIP healthcare.

Only when V.P. Singh, Sitaram Kesri, P.V. Narasimha Rao and the many other leaders who have had their hearts, kidneys and lungs fixed in western hospitals at taxpayers' expense have to rely on what Indian government hospitals have to offer will things improve. Chowdhury has a reputation for being courageous, for daring to step where others fear to tread. Will she have the guts to admit that her ministry can no longer afford VIP healthcare because the money is needed for ordinary people? That would be real socialism, would it not?

(Published in *India Today*)

LIES TO THE LETTER

15 December 1997

Did it occur to you, as you followed the political farce in Delhi over the past few weeks, that it was all happening in the interest of 'strengthening national integration and upholding the cause of the Indian nation?' This is what the Congress claims it was doing when it decided to destabilize I.K. Gujral's government. Sitaram Kesri, the Congress president, said as much when he wrote his letter to the president, withdrawing support to Gujral.

Kesri reminded the president, in case it had escaped his notice, that the Congress always did what was in the interest of the people: 'Since its inception, the Congress has given ample proof that secularism, national interests (sic) and interests of the people are overriding priorities in its agenda. Perhaps you will agree that it is this commitment that brought this up since our government came into existence in June 1996 and the party has continued to sustain it so far in spite of so many detracting factors.'

In the extraordinary attention we have been forced to pay to the slow and not always certain murder of Gujral's government, most of us have failed to take sufficient notice of Kesri's farewell letter. This is unfortunate because a careful reading of it reveals exactly what is wrong with today's politics. What is wrong is that our politicians continue to believe the average Indian voter is a semi-literate dimwit who will swallow any old lie they choose to tell. To make sure this continues to happen we routinely hear them tell us, as V.N. Gadgil did on a television show this past week, that the Indian voter may be illiterate but he never makes mistakes. Ha ha.

To come back to Kesri's missive. He tells us it was the Congress' concern for secularism, national interest and the people's interest that made it support the United Front government. Lies. It was the Congress' inability to form its own government and its terror of the BJP that forced it to do so. Besides, will Kesri explain how it was in the 'people's interest' to have eighteen months of constant political instability? Caused not by the government's internal problems but by the Congress' incapacity to let any prime minister function unless he behaved like a domestic servant. Poor humble H.D. Deve Gowda. Do you remember how many times a week he went and rubbed his nose at the doorsteps of P.V. Narasimha Rao and Kesri?

Gujral was more dignified but as aware of the need not just to be a Congress stooge but to be seen as one. So he graced every Gandhi-Nehru family birth and death anniversary, smiling obsequiously at Sonia Gandhi who rarely acknowledged his presence. Was it in the 'national interest' for the prime minister of India to behave like some flunkey?

As for secularism, it is amazing that Congress politicians dare mention this word after what happened to the Sikhs in 1984. What did happen to the Ranganath Mishra Commission's report? Did it not recommend prosecution of Congress MPs and workers for their direct involvement in the pogrom that followed Indira Gandhi's assassination? Has the Congress forgotten that Rajiv Gandhi justified the killings?

There are other reasons why the Congress should be ashamed to mention secularism. Recall the 1987 riots in Meerut and Malliana? Remember that more than seventy Muslim males, aged between thirteen and sixty-five, were taken to the banks of a river and shot by a police force serving a Congress government in Uttar Pradesh. Their bodies were then dumped into the river. It was only because of a couple of survivors that the story came out. As far as I know, no action was ever taken against the killer policemen.

Kesri's letter tells more lies when he speaks of his party's role in Sri Lanka. He says Congress governments under Indira Gandhi and Rajiv Gandhi provided Tamil refugees with only 'necessary shelter and relief'. What about the training camps, Mr Kesri? Was it some foreign government which ran these in Tamil Nadu during beloved leader Indiraji and beloved leader Rajivji's time?

It is Kesri's sanctimonious tone when he talks about national integration that is most irritating. Has he forgotten it is to the Congress' unusual concept of national integration that we owe secessionist movements in Punjab, Kashmir and the Northeast? It is now widely accepted that these regions would not have erupted in the manner they did if Congress policies had been wiser and more sincere.

Due to the Congress' approach to 'national integration', we wasted the 1970s and '80s on political problems when we should have been addressing our economic failures. Now, when it was finally beginning to seem as if it were the economy that would take priority, we have the Congress forcing politics back into the forefront. Is this in the national interest Mr Kesri? Is it in the national interest for us to have had virtually no government in Delhi for weeks now?

Personally, I have never expected politicians to be paragons of virtue. The mahatma type of political leader died with Gandhiji and, really, is not required any more. We want politicians with an ability to govern, not necessarily saints. But I wish people like Sitaram Kesri would stop insulting our intelligence by expecting us to believe their shameless lies.

(Published in *India Today*)

SECOND DECADE
(1998–2007)

MY FAMILY AND ITS FLUNKEYS

2 February 1998

Is it just me or are there a few of you who are as shamed as I am at the thought of India having an Italian prime minister? Nine hundred million people, a civilization as old as time, a country the size of a continent. Yet we appear so utterly bankrupt politically, intellectually and in our sense of identity as a nation that we turn to someone who has only been an Indian citizen for thirteen years as our 'saviour'. There should be something shaming about this. But wandering lately along the campaign trail, let me tell you I have met a disturbing number of people—both uneducated rural and educated urban—who say they are not at all worried about the fact that Sonia Gandhi is Italian by birth.

In Sriperumbudur, after the new Mrs Gandhi made her first election speech, there was unanimity among the people I interviewed that here was our next prime minister. In Chennai, I asked a Tamil intellectual whether he did not think it would demoralize us as a people to have a foreigner as prime minister. He said if the Constitution did not recognize her as a foreigner, she was Indian enough for him.

Wait a minute. What if she comes to power and decides she wants a few more Italians in her cabinet? Would she be able to do so simply by making them Indian citizens? The intellectual replied it would be no worse than if Phoolan Devi became prime minister and appointed a cabinet of bandits and no worse than Bihar being handed over to a semi-literate chief minister's even less literate wife.

A few days later I caught up with Atal Bihari Vajpayee's campaign in Chhindwara, Madhya Pradesh. I asked him whether it bothered him that his main opponent in this election was Italian. He said it did not and it would not be made an election issue. This, from a party whose economic policy makes it clear it will favour Indian companies over foreign ones.

Vajpayee is, at least, restrained about applauding Sonia's advent. Our two Yadav giants, Mulayam and Laloo, have actually welcomed her as someone who can stop 'communal forces'. Only one politician, N. Chandrababu Naidu, has pointed out that what the Congress is doing is mortgaging India's self-respect by begging at an Italian lady's door.

I could not have put it better myself. Even if I represent only a small minority, I have to say that the prospect of a foreign prime minister definitely bothers me. But there are other equally important reasons why Sonia's rise as the biggest star of this election bothers me. Now that she has, at long last, spoken and we know what she thinks, her political and economic views bother me almost as much as her being a foreigner.

Her basic message is that she is here to restore her family's glory and fulfil Rajiv Gandhi's dream: 'The family to which I belong has made several sacrifices for the country. There are many who would belittle its great contribution to the nation and sully its image. I have come before you to uphold the great tradition of the family.' What is this 'great tradition'?

Jawaharlal Nehru, who is revered as the builder of modern India, is synonymous with the socialism we put our faith in for fifty years. This socialism amounted to a virtual economic dictatorship in which the state decided what would be produced, by whom and in what quantities. The state arrogated to itself the role of being our only big industrialist. It produced everything from bread and milk to missiles and tanks. This involved so much business activity that the state had little time to ensure such things as literacy and healthcare. When Nehru died we were about as poor a country as we had been when he took over.

His daughter continued the economic dictatorship and added, even after the Emergency, a political one as well. Democratic institutions were emasculated and instead of a government in Delhi we saw the creation of a durbar. Courtiers, court jesters and sycophants were promoted to the highest offices in the land while dissenters, thinkers and men of honour and conviction were quickly shown the door.

It is from her mother-in-law that Sonia appears to have learnt her politics. Within two weeks of her entry we have seen the return of sycophancy as a political ideology. In Sriperumbudur, Tamil leaders compared her to Mother Teresa and, believe it or not, God. You are our God, they sang, we worship you. A more nauseating display of sycophancy is hard to remember even from Indira Gandhi's days. So much for the glorious tradition Sonia wants to restore.

Let us now come to Rajiv and his alleged dream. In Sonia's view, he was a paragon of secularism and would have stood in front of the Babri Masjid rather than let it be demolished. Would she like to tell us where he was in 1984 when 3000 Sikhs were killed on the streets of Delhi at his party's behest? Would she like to tell us why he opened the Babri Masjid to Hindus for worship when he could have prevented this despite what happened in the courts? Was it a secular gesture for him to begin his election campaign in 1989 from Ayodhya by facilitating the laying of the foundation stone of a Ram temple and promising Ramrajya?

As for Rajiv's dream, what was it? As far as we know, he was an airline pilot who reluctantly entered politics at all leave alone entered it with a dream. No wonder what Sonia is offering us, politically and economically (socialism), is almost as worrying as her being a foreigner.

(Published in *India Today*)

LAND THE WORLD FORGOT

16 February 1998

For the past four years or so, on the last Thursday of January, I have found myself in the little Swiss town of Davos. Its name has become a synonym for what is probably the most impressive gathering of political leaders, businessmen, scientists and thinkers on the planet. This is the World Economic Forum's annual meeting. For me, it has become a chance to look at India with the objectivity of distance and also, over the years, examine whether we have come any closer to speaking a language the world understands. I may as well begin by telling you the answer: no.

Four kinds of Indians come to Davos regularly: political leaders, bureaucrats, businessmen and journalists. They react in different ways to this gathering of the world's elite. Most of our political leaders, with the exception of P. Chidambaram, react with abject puzzlement. Even the supposedly sophisticated ones, who pride themselves on their Oxbridge accents, find they have little to say and almost no answers to the questions they are asked.

Our bureaucrats react, as they usually do when confused, with sneering arrogance. This year we had the cabinet secretary and the finance secretary as the main representatives of the Government of India. One of them was heard saying, 'We don't need Davos, we have people queuing up to invest in India.' Mercifully, our businessmen make up for this chippy arrogance by listening, observing and trying to learn; and we hacks try hard to hide the fact that we are either bedazzled or befuddled or both. I long for the year when I will be able to come here and report that like other Asians (Chinese, Malaysians, Indonesians, Thais) we have also learnt to react normally.

Let me explain. The only political leader at Davos this year from South Asia was Nawaz Sharif, Pakistan's prime minister. He addressed a session called 'Emerging powerhouses: Managing the volatility of globalization'. Poor old Nawaz was completely out of his depth. His speech had clearly been written by some bureaucrat accustomed to reading lectures to semi-literate audiences to whom the word globalization had to be actually explained. When it came to answering questions, Nawaz was so completely befuddled that he referred to the motorway built between Lahore and Islamabad as an example of regional cooperation.

Don't laugh. Our own political leaders are not much better and our bureaucrats are as bad. In contrast, the Chinese—who do not have the advantage we have of familiarity with the English language—now speak with the confidence of real members of the global community. After poor old Nawaz, as if to show him up completely, came a session called 'What terms for China's integration into the global political and economic systems?'

China was represented by Li Lanquing, its vice-premier. He spoke in halting English but made the point that China should no longer be kept out of the World Trade Organization. In the clearest language, he proceeded to outline why and to give details of exactly where China would be going in the next ten years. How much infrastructure it would require, what its growth rate could be expected to be and which areas of economic growth would get top priority.

Sitting in the audience, I wondered which of our own political leaders would be able to come to Davos after the next election and speak with equal intelligence about India's economic problems. Only two, I am afraid: Manmohan Singh and P. Chidambaram. The reason for this is that for too long we have allowed our political leaders to get away with concentrating on the sort of subjects that allow endless hours of meaningless waffling—secularism, communalism, nationalism. From the Laloos and Mulayams come a whole bunch of silly local issues that have no relevance to whether India will become a confident, prosperous country in the twenty-first century or not. Surely this has to be our main goal, item number one on our political agenda?

So inconsequential have we become because of our insularity and our isolation, that India quite simply disappears from the newspapers and news bulletins of the world while you are travelling. For the amount of attention it receives in the international press, the Lok Sabha election may as well not be happening. In the week I have been away from India, I have seen only one story—it was about Sonia Gandhi launching her campaign in Amethi. In Davos, during a week of sessions that begin at 8 a.m. and end after dinner, there has not been a single one dealing with India. South Asia has barely been mentioned, despite Sharif's presence.

We could react as our chippy bureaucrats do by simply shrugging our shoulders and saying we couldn't care less. This would be stupid. Globalization may only be a buzzword in India but it is a reality everywhere else. If we want to be part of it, we must start demanding that our political leaders and high and mighty officials speak in a language the world understands. For a start, they have to become economically literate.

It is no longer good enough for us to be told, ad nauseam, that India is a poor country with vast problems. We need to know why it is still a poor country and what our political parties are going to do about it. When they learn to answer our questions, they will learn to answer the questions of the world.

(Published in *India Today*)

BEWARE THE NUCLEAR YOGIS

1 June 1998

The trouble with the BJP is that for every sane man it can count among its ranks, there are at least ten loonies. The party has been careful since it finally got its chance to rule India to keep its lunatic elements locked up. But the nuclear tests appear to have freed them.

Hence the absurd idea (later junked) to carry Pokhran dust—'sacred soil'—in sanctified vessels across the country in yet another set of yatras, this time in the name of gaurav or pride. Hence the even more ludicrous idea of building a temple to the bomb: a shaktipeeth. This latter idea emanates, unsurprisingly, from the Vishwa Hindu Parishad (VHP), and is unlikely to be abandoned since Ashok Singhal, its president, has shown himself in the past to be ever capable of the worst kind of dementia, especially when he thinks it has religious sanction.

This time his excuse is that religious leaders have favoured India going nuclear since 1974. Think of it, a temple to a weapon of mass destruction in a country where we still sacrifice children to satisfy some god's imagined bloodlust and where we still worship girls who dare to commit sati.

It is an invitation, in our wondrously illiterate land, to the most terrifying kind of superstition and stupidity. Those who still believe in human sacrifice and in burning inconvenient widows on their husbands' funeral pyres will undoubtedly soon think of radioactivity and related nuclear horrors as new objects of reverence. If the government wants to be taken seriously in its new role as custodian of a nuclear India, then it needs to put down its loonies fast or at least direct them in a more constructive direction.

For instance, why can't our religious leaders get together and clean the Ganga and the Yamuna before the next Kumbh Mela? They can do it more easily than any government or any conglomerate of environmental groups. All the shankaracharyas need to do is issue a collective appeal against the dumping of human and other waste into these sacred rivers. God-fearing Hindus across the land will almost certainly obey.

There are other worthy causes that they would do well to pay attention to. The Sangh Parivar fancies itself the guardian of Indian culture but so far its contribution in this area has been largely limited to burning M.F. Husain's paintings, attacking his home and so on. It was frightening to see Kushabhau Thakre, the BJP's new president, rise to the defence of the looters who targeted the artist's Mumbai home recently.

Thakre went on national television to announce that the attack was justified as Hindu sentiment had been hurt by Husain's depiction of Sita. Well, my sentiments as an Indian are deeply hurt by Thakre's justification of thuggery. So would he consider it all right if I stormed into his home with my own gang of thugs?

Again, however, even hurt religious sentiment can be put to good use. Maybe the BJP government's more lunatic supporters could be employed by the department of culture (DOC), of which Murli Manohar Joshi is the new boss. They could be asked to take care of some of our ancient temples and monuments that are falling to pieces on account of bureaucratic neglect.

The bureaucracy has dealt with preservation with the same benign neglect it has reserved for everything else over fifty years. Thus, many of our finest monuments are being destroyed. Konarak, Hampi, Nalanda and ancient temples may disappear altogether in the twenty-first century unless we adopt a radical new approach.

There are museums across the country where priceless artefacts are falling to pieces due to the same benign neglect. Some of the best museums in BJP-ruled states like Uttar Pradesh don't even have proper buildings to house their treasures. This tragedy is largely on account of a culture policy that sneers at commercialization. So museums are not allowed to make money out of shops or restaurants. If they did, they would be able to pay for their needs. But for this to happen we need a new culture policy, some action from Joshi.

Modern Indian culture is in no better shape. Fifty years after we got rid of the British it is still Indian writing in English that the world knows most about. Writers writing in Indian languages resent the fuss made about Arundhati Roy or Salman Rushdie. But the truth is had these writers written in Malayalam or Urdu, their audience would have been so limited as to be inconsequential in today's global village.

The Culture Department should have been responsible for facilitating decent translations of modern Indian literature. But like every other government department, it seems to spend most of its resources paying salaries to armies of officials. With so much work to be done in the area of promoting Hindu 'gaurav', the BJP needs to persuade its more lunatic sister organizations to lay off such things as nuclear bomb temples and nuclear dust pilgrimages. Their fallout could be harder to control than the international anger the tests generated.

(Published in *India Today*)

GET BACK TO BASICS

8 June 1998

All right, the government has had its moment of nuclear glory. Now it's time for work. In this past week, I have spent much time wandering about Delhi's corridors of power, meeting ministers, chatting with bureaucrats, looking for signs of change. Alas, all that anyone has talked about are the Pokhran tests.

What did I think of the fact that ninety per cent of Indians have supported the government? Wasn't I proud as an Indian? How did I react to the news that important American politicians like Jimmy Carter and Newt Gingrich attacked Bill Clinton's sanctions? Wasn't I delighted to see Pakistan squirm and splutter? Whether I talked to lowly officials or to ministers, this was the mood. If I tried to change the subject to something like literacy, healthcare or the economy, I failed.

The time has come to start talking about these other things. Otherwise, the government could find its support vanishing as suddenly as it appeared. Already the mutterings have started. Sonia Gandhi and her many spokesmen—does she have so many because she finds it so hard to speak herself?—have started making their disapproval clear. Madam herself, at a recent event where she did in fact speak, informed us in her charming Italian-accented Hindi that from her vast understanding of political issues she had concluded sanyam (restraint) was better than an open display of shakti (power).

The left parties made their position clear within hours of

the explosions. They objected to India trying to go nuclear because it might annoy China. It is only a matter of time before the ninety per cent of ordinary Indians who allegedly favour the bomb get less euphoric—unless Atal Bihari Vajpayee's government can show us it is capable of the kind of governance India desperately needs if it is ever to become a real superpower.

A country that has nearly half its population living in absolute poverty, that has an illiterate population more than 2.5 times that of sub-Saharan Africa, that has more than half its children over the age of four living in malnourishment can never be a superpower.

As the above figures indicate, our biggest failures have been in the human development area. We rank a shameful 135th out of 174 countries in the human development index, a point that Lal Krishna Advani eloquently made during his Swaran Jayanti Yatra in 1997. 'When I looked at the report,' he said, 'I knew India couldn't be in the first 20. So I started looking in the first 50. But we weren't even there. Then I started looking in the last 50 and was shamed to discover we were 135, behind even Sri Lanka.'

Of course, at that time it was easy to blame everything on Congress misgovernance. It no longer is. The government now needs to tell us what it can do. If it really means business, it may find that it will need to begin by abolishing the ministries that deal with things like literacy, healthcare, population control and sanitation—and start again from scratch. Otherwise, it could find—as it must have done in the states it has ruled, such as Rajasthan, Maharashtra and Uttar Pradesh—that the armies of officials who run these ministries will strangle even the best schemes with red tape.

Vajpayee needs to seriously consider putting these ministries under people like Mahbub-ul-Haq, who brings out the annual Human Development Report. He is a Pakistani and I am not suggesting we employ him. But there are people like him in India who will be able to make a serious contribution. Haq believes our worst mistake in the past fifty years was the failure to invest in health and education. He also believes we can rectify this mistake by investing liberally in basic education in the next five to ten years.

Writing about South Asia in a recent article, Haq says, 'If all children are to be put in primary schools in the next five years, this means creating school facilities for sixty-five million children and training about two million additional teachers, preferably three-fourths of them female. The recurrent cost is modest: only $1 billion a year in the next five years, or a mere one-third of one per cent of the combined income of the region. Even if capital expenditure is included, the total additional cost will be less than one per cent of the combined GNP of South Asia.'

If we can afford nuclear weapons, then we can afford this investment. But first we have got to change the mindset of the ministries given the job of providing India healthcare and literacy. Unless this is done, Vajpayee could find himself immobilized by officials who have perfected, over the years, the art of appearing to be very busy while doing nothing.

During my wanderings in the corridors of power this past week I ran into many ministers—formerly bursting with dynamism and new ideas—who had already been felled by the bureaucracy. When I reminded them of changes they had earlier talked about, they unfailingly answered, 'We suggested it but they tell us that it can't be done that way for a variety of reasons.'

Actually, it can be done, it has been done elsewhere. But most of our bureaucrats react badly to change. This is why most of them will be happy as larks if the Congress comes back to power. It will too unless Vajpayee realizes euphoria is ephemeral. Real work is not.

(Published in *India Today*)

ABC OF INDIA'S FUTURE

15 March 1999

As someone who believes fundamentally that India will be a developed country only if we manage to make every Indian literate I seize any chance to bring up the subject. This time it is the finance minister's budget and its criminal neglect of primary education that gives me my chance. Yashwant Sinha is not unusual in this. He has behaved as every Indian finance minister has done since independence: treated primary education with the peculiar mix of contempt and tokenism that has made us one of the most illiterate countries in the world.

Let me first give you some statistics. There are thirteen districts in India in which more than eighty-five per cent of the women are illiterate and they are all in Bihar, Madhya Pradesh, Rajasthan, Orissa and Uttar Pradesh. The two with the most abysmal record, Barmer and Jalore (more than ninety-two per cent), are in Rajasthan. The point I seek to make is that we know everything we already need to know about the scale of our literacy problem. We also know exactly which districts need special attention. So why are successive governments in Delhi so completely incapable of formulating policies that will deal specifically with these problem districts?

Surely when we know from the United Nations Development Programme's latest report on India that it is likely to take ninety-two years to achieve universal literacy in Uttar Pradesh and a hundred and twenty one years in Bihar—while Kerala has already got there—then should we not expect emergency measures in states where the problem is acute?

If you ask these questions in Delhi's corridors of power you are likely to be told that the reason why no union government has been able to do much is because education is a state subject. It is a silly excuse because, as the most recent exercise in Bihar proves, Delhi rarely hesitates to intervene when it thinks a state government is incapable of handling things on its own.

The states in which these thirteen districts lie have proved themselves incapable of dealing with what is already an educational emergency. The centre must intervene and it does not even need to dismiss the state governments to do so. What it does need is a proper education minister at the head of an education ministry that is not also dealing with sports, women's welfare, culture, archaeology and god only knows what else. The human resources development ministry (instead of education ministry) was one of Rajiv Gandhi's most illiterate ideas. Why are we continuing with it?

It is because we continue to not have an education ministry at the centre that primary education remains an area of scandalous neglect. Sinha's budget allots it Rs. 3,034.95 crore, Rs. 254 crore more than the previous year, while giving secondary and university education Rs. 1,136.69 crore, an increase of an almost similar amount at Rs. 213 crore. This despite everyone in the government, including the prime minister, telling us they recognize the vital importance of primary education.

If we had a proper education minister (and if we had the good fortune not to have Murli Manohar Joshi) he would already have come up with a policy that sought to privatize university education so that government could concentrate on primary schools. Perhaps he might have managed to give us some idea of how the country's thirteen most illiterate districts had to be helped.

It has been said before but it needs to be repeated ad nauseam that literacy is the key to development, healthcare and jobs. It is the key to population control. It has been proved over and over that literate women have fewer babies. To drive through states like Uttar Pradesh and Bihar is to understand in all its horror the extent of our population problem. In village after village you see that it is the poorest, most illiterate women who have the most children.

The conditions in which these women and children live are often worse than those in which the village's animals live. This in a country in which many are still basking in the radioactive glow of our nuclear tests. There is something sickening about India going into the twenty-first century as a nuclear power but with the largest number of illiterate people. Isn't it possible to shame our political leaders into doing something?

All those other ideas about mid-day meal programmes and education guarantee schemes can be implemented in double measure. Wherever it seems the state governments cannot cope the centre must step in. If Rabri Devi's government could be dismissed because it failed to protect the lives of the poor then why shouldn't it be possible to intervene when a state government fails to empower the poorest of the poor? There can be no empowerment—such a fashionable word these days—without literacy.

Once there is a scheme in place for our thirteen most illiterate districts it could be extended to other districts with similar problems. These are almost entirely in the Hindi heartland.

First we need an education ministry in Delhi. The prime minister needs to put his best man in charge of this ministry and should personally monitor his performance. Unless something drastic is done immediately we should reconcile ourselves to entering the next millennium as a country that despite its proud nuclear status will really be quite irrelevant to the world.

(Published in *India Today*)

MOURNING IN BANARAS

5 April 1999

When Atal Bihari Vajpayee quoted—at the governor's reception in Lahore a month ago—Ali Sardar Jafri's beautiful line about the morning light of Banaras it had special meaning for me, gone as I had almost directly from Banaras to Lahore. The verse is about friendship between India and Pakistan: *Tum aao gulshan-e-Lahore se chaman bardosh, hum aayen subh-e-Banaras ki roshni leykar, phir uske baad yeh poochein ke kaun dushman hai*. Loosely translated it means: You bring with you the scents of the gardens of Lahore and we will bring the morning light of Banaras, and then let someone ask who the enemy is.

The prime minister could not have chosen a more beautifully appropriate bit of poetry to express the mood on that first day after his Wagah crossing. But it made me wonder, reluctant though I am to be a spoilsport, when it was that he had last seen the sun rise over the Ganga in that oldest and most sacred of India's cities.

The morning light is still as beautiful as ever but have any of our political or religious leaders noticed what we have done to Banaras? To the Ganga? The last time I was in Banaras was to cover a riot so I had little time for aesthetics. This time I went with a friend who has the keys to secret India—keys that open the doors to the magic and beauty that make this land special. So it was my aesthetic rather than political senses that were at work.

I watched, mesmerized, the ceremonies at the Vishwanath temple on Shivratri, wandered through narrow streets into tiny rooms filled with fabulous brocades, silks and satins, listened in awe to professors at Banaras Hindu University and breathed deeply in the peace that still pervades Sarnath. But try as I did to not notice the filth, pollution and terrifying congestion of the streets of Banaras I failed.

Those who live in the filth every day say that the secret of enjoying Banaras is to rise above it. You have to exist at a spiritual plane, they say, and ignore the dead rats, the open drains, the swarms of flies, the human excrement at every corner and the fact that the Ganga is terrifyingly polluted. I mentioned to senior officials and policemen that traffic in the city was fast reaching a stage where it would not only become impossible to move but even to breathe because of the automobile exhaust that fills the air.

The senior police officer in charge of traffic smiled complacently and told me that in India things only start to improve when they hit rock bottom. 'It will have to get much worse,' he said, 'before people start demanding that it get better.' The same answer applies to cleanliness. It is only when the city decays completely and the Ganga becomes a sewer that those who celebrate the 'morning light of Banaras' will wake up to the reality that the city, and perhaps even the river, is in its death throes.

Banaras is believed to be not just the oldest city in India but the oldest city in the world. In another country it would be cherished as a national treasure and everyone would join the effort to save it. But here, despite Hindutva governments ruling Uttar Pradesh and India, nothing at all is being done. True, there was the Ganga Action Plan, but the end result appears to have been that crores and crores of rupees have disappeared into unseen pockets.

The river remains as polluted as it was before the plan got started in 1985. Mainly because you cannot clean the Ganga unless municipalities in towns and cities along its banks are forced to stop dumping raw sewage into it.

Once the government does its bit, it is time for others to do theirs. Instead of worrying about conversions, why are organizations like the RSS and the VHP not using their vast armies of Hindutva supporters to help clean Hinduism's most sacred city? Where are the shankaracharyas? Why is not one of them able to stand up and announce that any good Hindu guilty of using the banks of the Ganga as a toilet is making seriously bad karma for himself?

And where pray are those noisy environmentalists? Instead of making doomsday prophecies from the relatively safe environs of Delhi and Mumbai, instead of worrying about some building in Mumbai breaking a few building bye-laws that are usually unreasonable in the first place, why are they not sitting in Banaras and setting up a Save Banaras Society? Vast funds have been collected for Venice in this way. They have been spent on preventing the city from sinking and on preserving its unique beauty. Why not Banaras?

Where are our Hindu businessmen who spend fortunes on building ugly modern temples? Why are they not concerned about spending some money on cleaning the Ganga? The first business group to show some initiative in this area is, ironically, Parsi. Godrej is re-launching its Ganga soap next month with an advertising campaign that promises not only that the soap is made from Ganga jal 'collected from the pure and pollution-free heights of the Himalayas' but that part of the profits will go towards cleaning the Ganga. All we need is a few more big business groups to join the effort and not just the Ganga but even Banaras may be saved.

Nothing will happen, though, until the prime minister personally takes an initiative and starts the Save Banaras, Save the Ganga campaign. Not a single political party will object. More important, future generations of Indians may also have a chance to celebrate the special light that illuminates their most sacred city at dawn.

(Published in *India Today*)

DR JJ THROWS A TANTRUM

19 April 1999

If it wasn't obscene, it would be quite funny to hear Jayalalitha give 'national interest' as her reason for subjecting the country to yet another period of political uncertainty. It makes you wonder whether provincial political leaders understand such things as national interest at all. And whether the real lesson of the past few years isn't that provincial politicians should be kept firmly where they belong: in the provinces.

Jayalalitha Jayaram wreaked havoc on Tamil Nadu during her reign but, because she ruled only one Indian state, her depredations were limited. Ever since she has had the chance to treat all of India as her stage, she has spent most of her time ensuring that nobody misses her presence for even a moment. It was clear from day one to even the politically illiterate that national interest was the last thing on her mind. But so deceived does she appear to be by illusions of her own grandeur that she hasn't noticed everyone has her figured out. And that she currently epitomizes the ugly Indian politician. Even more than Laloo Yadav does.

She wins first prize because of her inability to understand that national interest is not the same as self-interest. It could be in her interest to keep the government quaking and quivering every time she rolls into Delhi. In her interest to have her tea parties splashed across the front pages while more important news gets buried inside. Very much in her interest to be the hottest political story in the country. But, it is not in the national interest.

What is in the national interest is for Atal Bihari Vajpayee's government to be allowed to get on with the business of governance. This it had just begun to do when Jayalalitha decided it was time for her 'political earthquake'. An earthquake created ostensibly by the prime minister's refusal to concede Jayalalitha's 'reasonable' demands. These included the setting up of a joint parliamentary committee to investigate the dismissal of former navy chief Vishnu Bhagwat and the transfer of George Fernandes to a ministry 'less sensitive' than defence. Why, you may well ask, is Dr JJ so interested in the defence ministry?

And if you did ask you would be in good company since many people in Delhi's political circles are asking the same question. What we also need to ask is whether Jayalalitha has the right to interfere in decisions that should be taken only by the prime minister, especially since Jayalalitha has such a peculiar understanding of national interest.

If she really understood or cared about the nation Jayalalitha would have realized that there could not have been a worse moment to create political turmoil. She timed it to coincide with the exact moment when things were beginning to look up for the country. Vajpayee's government has taken a long time getting into governance mode. It has spent a year bogged down in largely irrelevant issues. Initially, there was the Jayalalitha problem, then there were the nuclear tests, then there were settling-down problems, then there was the problem of the BJP's lunatic fringe trying to push its agenda. Conversions became more important than governance and swadeshi nearly succeeded in reversing the process of economic liberalization. So it has only been since the beginning of this year that the prime minister has shown any signs of being in control.

As a result we have seen the beginnings of a sensible, new foreign policy and a budget that sent the stock markets on an upward spiral unseen since the heady days of 1991—when P.V. Narasimha Rao began the process of economic reform.

Economists and businessmen are in agreement that the economy was definitely on the road to recovery. Then, along comes Jayalalitha with her tea parties and her glib one-liners about political earthquakes and we are back to square one. Moving backwards is the last thing the country can afford because there is so much that needs to be done.

It is clear, for instance, that the economy is not going to recover in any major sense unless the government starts to invest in infrastructure instead of simply talking about it. The grandiose highway network that the prime minister announced in 1998 has remained a paper highway.

If someone sensible is put in charge of surface transport he is likely to point out that we need to choose a road that has the highest traffic density—Delhi to Mumbai, for example—and convert it into a modern expressway before going any further. Government investment on one road and a couple of other big projects could help boost the economy.

Next the government must seriously consider cutting costs. We can no longer afford a central government that employs four million people and costs taxpayers Rs. 32,000 crore. We can no longer afford ministries that should have been closed down long ago. Steel, food processing, hotels, airlines, television, telecommunications—why is the government still involved in these areas, especially since most of them lose vast amounts of taxpayers' money?

If Jayalalitha were not so provincial in her comprehension of national interest, these are the things she would be making a noise about. But then perhaps she is not really her own woman. Perhaps she is only being used by the Congress to do its dirty work and once it is done she will be allowed to fall—with an earthquakely thud—between two stools.

(Published in *India Today*)

THAT THIRST FOR POWER

10 May 1999

You know the old line 'it isn't over till the fat lady sings'? Well, in our case the variation is: it isn't over till the Fat Lady goes back to Chennai. And she has. Forty-eight suitcases, flunkeys and all. Meanwhile, the Thin Lady—she who emerged briefly out of purdah into the glare of television cameras to inform us that she had 272 MPs and many more coming—has had her prime ministerial ambitions dashed and, for the moment, also gone back behind the veil. But between them, with some invaluable help from Rashtrapati Bhavan, they have departed only after pushing the country into a general election that we could well have done without.

The only source of good cheer in an otherwise dismal scenario is that both ladies have done severe damage to themselves in the process of bringing down Atal Bihari Vajpayee's government. In Jayalalitha's case, there was little at stake to start with. Most polls indicate that few Indians think highly of her, despite her recent attempts to improve her image by singing romantic Hindi songs on television and talking about the absence of 'unconditional love' in her life.

In the case of Indira Gandhi's daughter-in-law, there was more at stake. In the past couple of years Sonia Gandhi has carefully cultivated the image of a reluctant politician. She really only wanted to live a quiet life, her spin doctors let it be known, and she would have been perfectly happy doing this had the Congress not needed her help so desperately. Then, when she came out to 'save the party', the impression was carefully spread around that her campaigning, her many good works were not to promote her own career in any way but for the good of the country (read: Congress). She would never be prime minister herself. She would choose someone like the good Dr Manmohan Singh for this job, while she went about with her altruistic deeds unsung and unheard in the background.

It came then as a shock to many Indians when she emerged late last month not just as the Congress candidate for prime minister but also as just another politician. Not a very good one either when you consider the mess she landed herself in. Her first mistake was that display of arrogant overconfidence at her first press conference outside Rashtrapati Bhavan. 'How much do they say they have: 270?' she asked with a snigger. 'Well, we have 272 and we hope to get many more.'

When she was asked whether this meant the BJP's charge that the Congress was resorting to horse-trading was true she had a fit. She accused the BJP of charging others with what it did itself. And the press with not remembering the events of 1998 when the BJP government was formed: 'You are media people... Don't you remember what you wrote then?' As far as anyone can remember, there were no charges of horse-trading at that time because there was a pre-poll alliance. The only recalcitrant ally was Jayalalitha and nobody tried to buy her MPs.

At her next press conference two days later our new Mrs Gandhi's arrogance was in a visibly deflated condition. She appeared from Rashtrapati Bhavan and admitted that the numbers didn't add up. Oh oh, but by that evening the spin doctors were in full swing and Delhi's hyperactive political grapevine buzzed with stories of how she had been misled by her inner circle. How men like Arjun Singh were now in the doghouse. Perhaps. But in politics it really carries no weight at all when political leaders try to blame their domestic staff for the broth being ruined.

Another interesting fallout of Mrs Gandhi's first foray into real politics is that suddenly a surprisingly large number of

Indians are no longer amused by the possibility of having an Italian prime minister. The punditocracy is still divided on this issue, with those of leftist 'secular' persuasion determined to create the impression that Indians are not bothered by her foreign origins. But wander through the bazaars of any Indian city these days and stop to ask a few questions and you meet many people who say they are deeply ashamed that a country of a billion people cannot find a single Indian to lead it.

Cries of *Videshi neta, videshi paisa nahin chalega* were heard even in the Lok Sabha. By revealing her cards before she was actually in the running for prime minister, Sonia could have made her biggest mistake to date. Till a few months ago, senior Congress leaders were busy boasting about how they would get at least 300 seats in the next election. There is no boasting any more and nobody can quite figure out why Sonia was so desperate to be prime minister just yet. As things stand the election is likely to give us pretty much the same sort of result as we got last time. This is why it is vital our political parties realize the urgent need to put some safeguards into our present political system.

One suggestion is that we learn from the Germans and frame a rule that a vote of confidence can only be moved if the Opposition can guarantee an alternative government. A change like this is necessary if we are ever to have governments that can survive long enough to tackle our real problems. We can no longer afford the luxury of some future Fat Lady toppling a government because of some sudden whim, some imagined insult or because the lifts did not work properly in some government hotel.

(Published in *India Today*)

LET'S STOP LYING

26 July 1999

The war is over or should be soon. But if last week's speeches by Pakistan's prime minister and foreign minister are any indication, then it's back to the proxy war we have been fighting in Kashmir for ten years. The Pakistani prime minister talked of peace when he addressed his countrymen but warned, 'Today we have calmed down the volcano of Kargil but tomorrow the volcano can erupt somewhere else, as the lava is boiling. Nobody can suppress the Kashmiris' struggle for freedom.'

His foreign minister was no less restrained when he told the BBC there would be 'ten more Kargils' if the Kashmir problem was not dealt with. What he did not say, but what he seemed to mean, was until it was solved to the satisfaction of the Pakistani government not the people of Kashmir. For Pakistan the only solution is a plebiscite, which, if Allah is in his heaven, is expected to result in an overwhelming vote in Kashmir for absorption into Pakistan. Since there is no way any Indian government in the near future will be able to further divide the country for Islam's sake many Indians ask whether there is any point in talking to Pakistan at all.

Yes, there is. But only if we can begin on the premise that the Line of Control (LoC) is the border. Will this premise be acceptable to Pakistan? No, and we know that it isn't even acceptable to most of our own political parties, who continue to pretend that one day all of Kashmir will become part of the great Hindu motherland. This is not going to happen. So while we should make every effort to convince Pakistan to accept that talking about a plebiscite is a waste of time our own political leaders need to stop lying to the people.

These lies have got us nowhere in fifty years. They must stop if we want to move forward, as Nawaz Sharif suggested, instead of backward. Once the lies on both sides of the border are replaced by recognition, however grudging, of ground realities we can have a proper dialogue instead of the usual Urdu poetry spattered pretence at conversation.

If the lies on our side of the border have served mainly to obfuscate the Kashmir issue, the lies told in Pakistan have been infinitely more dangerous, as we can see from what happened in Kargil. It is outrageous that Pakistani leaders should continue to expect us, and the world, to believe that the men whom our troops so valiantly fought in Kargil were not regular soldiers but mujahideen and 'freedom fighters'.

Everyone, even the Islamic fundamentalist groups in Pakistan from whose ranks these mujahideen are believed to have been recruited, must know by now that without the Pakistani army there would have been no fighting in Kargil, leave alone fighting that lasted nearly two months. If Pakistani leaders continue to pretend to believe their own lies then we are a long way from real dialogue on the Kashmir issue.

There is, meanwhile, much we need to do domestically if we are to win the proxy war that now stares us in the face. At the highest levels of government in Delhi it is now accepted that under the cover of the fighting in Kargil Pakistan has succeeded in infiltrating a small army of terrorists into the Kashmir valley. To fight them we will need a properly trained counter-insurgency force.

Unfortunately, the men we have supposedly trained in this area are all sitting in Delhi protecting our so-called VIP politicians. And as has been pointed out often by many commentators, most of these supposed VIPs face so little real threat that if they walked down a street they would not be recognized. Yet, they set up a howl of protest if anyone tries reducing their armed guards. Because in the exalted circles in which they move Black Cats are as much a sign of social status as Rolex watches and Mont Blanc pens.

The home minister must have the courage to withdraw security from those who no longer need it. He must also spend some time thinking about the absurdity of having a counter-insurgency force (like the Black Cat commandos) that mostly spends its time attending dinner parties in Delhi with sundry supposedly endangered VIPs. Would they not be more useful in Kashmir manning police stations in districts that are known to be infested with terrorists?

The home minister needs to look carefully at what our intelligence agencies have been up to. Given how much money has been poured into these outfits—most of it unaccounted for—they appear to be a sadly ill-informed lot when you consider that shepherds in Kargil first noticed the intruders. They are also disparate and fragmented and often used by our political leaders to spy on each other instead of for the country.

These agencies need not just reorganization but a thorough overhaul. If L.K. Advani is really the 'iron man' his supporters claim, then he should set the process in motion now. There is no point in using the coming general election as an excuse for inactivity. Because if we could fight a war in its shadow then we can surely get on with doing other things as well.

They say that public memory is short. In our country it seems to be particularly so and no sooner is a crisis over than we move on to some new excitement, some new problem. If we do this with Kargil it will be unforgivable since so many young men have died cleaning up the mess created by the incompetence of our political leaders. So stocktaking in the defence and home ministries should be considered a continuing part of the war effort—if the memory of those who died in Kargil is not to be betrayed.

(Published in *India Today*)

BYPASSING THE BABUS

10 January 2000

There is an awesome quality about writing a column that will appear in the first week of a new century. Something that forces you to move away from the events of the moment—even this terrible hijacking—and look at life with a deeper perspective. Indians are an ahistorical people. This is evident from the fact that most Indians voted Indira Gandhi the woman of the millennium in a recent BBC poll. Considering that it was an Indian director who made the most recent film on the life of Elizabeth I, she at least should have been in the running. But no, 'we are like that only'. For us it is always only the recent past that counts or, when we want to justify our civilization, ancient history. It comforts us that we were once a great country.

We have not been for a long long time and we should shed no tears for the passing of the twentieth century because it has not been an Indian century. The next one will be, they say, Asia's. Again we could miss out because when people talk of Asia they usually mean East Asia and China. Those countries have successfully dealt with poverty, illiteracy and disease. Whatever their other problems, they no longer have hordes of beggars in their cities or armies of children working in their factories.

The only progress we have made in these crucial areas is that the beggars in our cities now use empty ice-cream cups, dumped in the streets by the handful of Indians who can afford Baskin Robbins, for begging. If with all the potential in the world we go into the twenty-first century as one of the poorest countries it is the fault of our policymakers. They appear to have got it almost entirely wrong. Jawaharlal Nehru gave us democracy, people point out, at a time when countries were falling into the hands of despots. True, but when his daughter tried despotism during the Emergency she failed miserably. It is not a system of governance that works easily in a country the size of a continent. Democracy with all its flaws is the only way India could have been governed.

Nehru virtually abolished private enterprise and profit and established the idea of the *maibaap sarkar*, leading the average Indian to believe that instead of working hard he could rely on the government to provide him with everything. Even a job for life. So there is still a huge section of Indians hankering after a government job because they know that once they get it they can keep it whether they work or not. It was a bad idea and we are paying a heavy price for it today when the Indian state is not only not benign but malignant and corrupt. Every Indian knows that officialdom often stands in the way of good policies.

If Nehru's legacy has dubious merits that of his daughter is a tale of wasted decades. There was so much she could have done had she, for even a few moments, thought economically and not politically. Instead of creating political problems in Punjab and Kashmir, she could have looked at what was happening in the rest of Asia and asked why. Had she done this we would have been living today in another India.

Then came Rajiv Gandhi with—in political terms—the opportunity almost to order the sun to rise. No political leader in recent memory had a chance quite like this. And what did he do? He threw it away. He became embroiled in some mistaken idea of India becoming a regional military power and domestically did little more than window-dressing. Corruption became respectable and our khadi-clad politicians began to understand perfectly how profitable a career in politics can be.

At the turn of the millennium can we hope that things will

change? With an entirely different party in power in Delhi we should have been able to. But so far A.B. Vajpayee has shown us that the only way he knows how to govern is the way his predecessors did. So, our most important ministries—education, health, roads—continue to be treated as punishment postings. Only the most insignificant politicians are given these portfolios, so how can we expect dramatic change? How can we expect any change at all when we still do not have a ministry of education at the centre?

Do we then go into the twenty-first century shrouded in gloom? No, there is hope and it comes from you and me. The scale of change in areas not controlled by government has been phenomenal even in the past ten years. It comes from the enterprise and energy of ordinary Indians and will continue to come from them. The solution lies in making government irrelevant. We aren't cursed, we've just been unlucky in our leaders. If this does become India's century it will be thanks to you and me.

(Published in *India Today*)

CLUELESS IN KASHMIR

10 July 2000

If only we would sometimes think of Kashmir when it is not in crisis we might find a permanent solution. But, like some secret, unmentionable disease we like to forget about Kashmir until there is trouble on the border, some terrible massacre or some new political drama. So our attention is currently totally focused on Srinagar because Farooq Abdullah's demand for greater autonomy for the state received, last week, the fullest support of the Jammu and Kashmir legislative assembly: only sixteen of eighty-seven legislators voted against the resolution. How did this happen, we gasp, what could have gone so wrong that our favourite Kashmiri leader should suddenly be talking in a language that sounds suspiciously like secession?

In the fifty years we have spent trying to hang on to Kashmir we have learnt to mistrust all talk of autonomy. It's one of those words that, when used in a Kashmiri context, makes us forget the terrible mistakes made by our leaders in Delhi and blame only the Kashmiris for their inability to assimilate themselves more fully into the 'Indian mainstream'. Mention autonomy and we forget that Delhi's paranoid policymakers denied Kashmir fair elections for nearly thirty years, that they viewed any popular Kashmiri leader with misgiving. And that we would probably have had no Kashmir problem at all today if the wrongful dismissal of Farooq's government in 1984 had not led to a series of other irreparable mistakes.

What is more important than the past is the future. Where do we begin the discussion, though, when the A.B. Vajpayee government seems to have no Kashmir policy at all? As the most serious political problem the government inherited Kashmir deserved more attention and at the very least a new beginning. Instead the government inexplicably chose to adopt the mistakes of the past as if they were its own and proceeded to deal with Kashmir in the same befuddled, haphazard manner that created the problem. Politically, there has been a complete absence of coherence and militarily an absence of strategy. This cannot be called a policy.

Farooq's demand for greater autonomy, if viewed without paranoia, offers us a chance of a new beginning. In the cacophony of condemnation that has greeted the autonomy demand there has been one sane voice: that of the union home minister. L.K. Advani has wisely said that autonomy can be discussed and he is right. Some attempt should be made to understand why Farooq chose to put the autonomy report before the assembly at this particular point. There are those who say the timing is all wrong because the country has, by and large, lost sympathy for the Kashmiri cause as a result of Kargil. But try and see it for a moment through Farooq's eyes: if Delhi can discuss azadi with the Hurriyat, why not autonomy with a legally elected state government?

Nobody in Delhi has paid attention to the fact that Farooq's government has been almost completely broke for more than a year. The Fifth Pay Commission added to its problems an annual burden of Rs. 550 crore and this, as in most other states, literally broke the government's back. Says a bureaucrat in Srinagar, 'No matter how much we try to improve the administration, where will we find the money to build schools or provide drinking water and power?'

Delhi could have and should have helped but did not. Even when Farooq received political support he found it insufficient to overcome the usual bureaucratic delays. Then, when it became increasingly evident that Kashmir was in trouble, Vajpayee's government decided to talk to politicians whom it had earlier locked up as militants. Does it make sense? No, and it cannot until the prime minister recognizes the need to evolve a clear policy.

If Vajpayee decides to do this he needs also to look at the international dimensions of the problem. There is no point any longer in insisting that we will not talk to Pakistan or anyone else about Kashmir because, whether we like it or not, it is an international problem. We internationalized it by going to the UN in the first place. So why should we not now consider going back to the UN to have its earlier resolutions abrogated? In Delhi, when I put this question to a senior bureaucrat he dismissed it out of hand on the grounds that we would not get enough support. Should we not also consider international mediation since it is clear we are unable even to speak the same language as Pakistan?

At the highest levels in Delhi you meet policymakers, intelligent important men who continue to believe that good governance is the solution in Kashmir. In which case why are there no secessionist movements in Bihar and Uttar Pradesh? When are we going to admit that we have serious political problems in Kashmir, problems that will not go away unless we find a serious political solution?

(Published in *India Today*)

GIVE NO QUARTER

17 July 2000

The Bharatiya Janata Party faces a clear choice. It can either survive, and grow, as a political party by severing its ties with the RSS or it can die defending the organization it considers the alma mater of the Sangh Parivar. There is no third alternative. Because what the RSS and its uglier spawns, Vishwa Hindu Parishad (VHP) and Bajrang Dal, are doing to Christians, Muslims and lower castes is certain to destroy India. Had these organizations been Muslim or Christian they would not only have been stopped but anti-India labels would have hung around their necks and their leaders charged with treason. It is only because the RSS and its repulsive copycat bodies are Hindu that they have been allowed to get away with spreading hatred and subversion. When will the prime minister, and more significantly his home minister, realize that the RSS is anti-India?

If it were not would its leaders have watched silently as members of the VHP and the Bajrang Dal gave interviews to the national media justifying the targeting of Christians? What can they say, though, when the RSS itself believes that the killing of priests and the burning of churches are not things the government needs to apologize for? Even as the prime minister was assuring the Pope that Christians would be protected in India the RSS national working committee, at its meeting in Gujarat, was passing a resolution condemning his government for being apologetic. I quote from the *Times of India*—'A resolution passed at the end of RSS' national working committee meeting here said, "One fails to understand why the government authorities become apologetic about such reported atrocities." It criticized a major section of church leaders for seeking to internationalize the issue unmindful of the "adverse effect" on the image of our nation.'

Are we to take it then that the RSS believes burning churches, killing priests and raping nuns is unlikely to have an 'adverse effect' unless Christians talk about it?

I have come across some of the pamphlets that are being distributed in remote districts of Madhya Pradesh and Uttar Pradesh and in small towns in Gujarat. Let me give you samples of their content. 'The Hindu samaj needs to resort to social opposition and if necessary by violence attacks (sic) to find a solution to this (Muslim boys marrying Hindu girls). In the case of Halvad village a Muslim boy abducted a brahmin girl. On the day of the court verdict, the Miyo (Muslim) was bold enough to move around the village with the brahmin girl... More than a thousand people pounced on them with pipes and iron rods...and the Muslim and the Hindu girl were beaten to death by the people and their dead bodies were left in the courtroom... The incident is etched in golden letters in the proud history of Hindu samaj. Revenge of this type is necessary against such abduction of our girls.'

The government's response to the attacks on Christians has only been to blame it all on the ISI. Perhaps the ISI is involved but can anyone who has had any connection at all with the RSS deny that the pamphlets in circulation across India reflect their views and that they see Indians converting to other religions as a threat to India?

The prime minister himself, ill-advisedly, once called for a debate on conversion. Why? What is there to debate? Every Indian has a right to choose any religion he wants and why should lower castes not convert if they are treated as untouchable and are not allowed within the precincts of many Hindu temples?

If the RSS were capable of bringing about some kind of

Hindu renaissance there could be some justification for its existence. But I found it hard not to agree with that old maverick Subramanian Swamy when he told me in a recent interview that as a Hindu he believed in a Hindu renaissance but left the Jan Sangh when he realized that all that the RSS wanted was to create hatred against Muslims and Christians in the mistaken belief that this would unite the Hindus.

A renaissance is brought about by scholars, thinkers and philosophers. Not by the sort of semi-literate thugs who fill the ranks of organizations like the Bajrang Dal and the VHP. It is outrageous that Christianity and conversion should become a national issue when we are unable to deal with illiteracy, healthcare and poverty. The UN Human Development Report reminds us that thirty-five per cent of Indians live on less than a dollar a day, seventy-one per cent have no access to sanitation, twenty-five per cent no access to healthcare and nineteen per cent no access to safe water. Why does the vaunted patriotism of the RSS not persuade it to take up issues like these?

The prime minister knows better than anyone that it was his personal image that won the BJP so many seats in the last election. So why is he so afraid of taking action against organizations that, under the shield of his government, are causing serious harm to India?

(Published in *India Today*)

TRUTH OMISSIONS

28 August 2000

When will we get a prime minister who will use his speech from the ramparts of the Red Fort to tell us why India's 'tryst with destiny' has been a disappointment? This was not something we could have hoped for in the forty years when our prime ministers came not just from the same party but usually from the same family. But in the past few years, when so much has changed and so many governments have come and gone, I have waited eagerly every year for a prime minister who would have the courage to tell us the truth. Something along the lines of—brothers, sisters, countrymen, we should be a rich, powerful country and if we are not it is because you have been let down by your leaders.

To make a new beginning you need acknowledgement of past mistakes, and A.B. Vajpayee is in a better position to do this than anyone else. He is a popular prime minister—the most popular in years—and he belongs to a party that has nothing to do with the mistakes of the past. He is also arguably the best orator Indian politics has ever seen. So when he stepped into his bullet-proof glass cubicle to make the first Independence Day address of the twenty-first century I expected him to seize the moment.

And when after the routine sabre-rattling over Kashmir he turned to the economy, I really thought he would. He began by pointing out that seventy per cent of India's population was under the age of thirty-five and that the twenty-first century belonged to them. He explained that economic reform was necessary and that nobody should be afraid of being hurt by it. Now was the moment, I thought, to explain why so much had gone wrong. How we had spent our resources on running airlines, phone companies and hotels when we should have spent this money on schools, hospitals and roads.

With Vajpayee's communication skills, it would have been so easy for him to explain that the wastage had reached a point where governments were spending more on administration and paying interest on loans than on meeting people's basic needs. He could have admitted that it was because of bad housekeeping and a skewed idea of development that India—with its enormous resources—continued to be one of the poorest countries in the world. Why did he not say any of these things? Well, it could be because he has lousy speech writers but more likely it's because we have so far not had a leader who fully understands the importance of telling the truth about the things that have gone wrong.

This is a problem not just in Delhi but in our states as well. So governments come and go, and the average Indian continues to puzzle over why so little changes. Why all that changes visibly is that a new set of faces stares out from the white Ambassador cars with their red lights and their sirens and a new caboodle moves into the high offices and fine homes reserved for our leaders.

On Independence Day several states paid for full-page advertisements in the national newspapers to boast about their achievements in exactly the way governments did when the Soviet Union was our role model. The advertisements assume that the average Indian is an idiot. So they list achievements that would not be considered achievements by anyone with minimum powers of discernment.

From Rabri Devi we hear that the Government of Bihar 'is working round the clock to fight the challenges coming in way (sic) of ensuring social justice to one and all, especially the dalits, backwards, minorities and women'.

Terrific, but will someone explain why Bihar has more

massacres of the poor and the underprivileged than any other Indian state? Or why there seem to be so many more under Rabri's 'committed to social justice' regime.

What can we expect from the chief minister of Bihar, though, when we have so far not had a prime minister who has dared to be different? Not even in the small things has anyone dared make changes. Why, for instance, do we need to annually enact the Red Fort routine when all it does is bring Delhi to a complete halt and when nobody who can be loosely described as 'people' can attend? Security arrangements are a nightmare and even the high officials and politicians who get invited face so many checks en route that it is better to stay home and watch it on TV. Is it not time the prime minister spoke from the safety of his own home?

For me the most poignant image of Independence Day 2000 was the sight of barefoot children selling the national flag at street corners in Mumbai. They were mostly small children but many carried smaller children in their arms as they worked from dawn to dusk on our most important national holiday. One day, if we are lucky, we will get a prime minister who will dare to explain why, more than fifty Independence Days on, this is still the face of the Indian child.

(Published in *India Today*)

LESSON IN EDUCATION

23 April 2001

Bill Clinton came to India to do good work but judging from the national obsession that developed around his culinary tastes you could have been forgiven for thinking he was here to write a Good Food Guide to Indian Cuisine. Before he arrived, chefs of five star hotels supplied newspapers with details of the menus they were preparing and after he came, front pages of major newspapers were filled with accounts of the meals he ate and did not eat—he left Sharad Pawar's breakfast untouched but feasted on vegetarian delicacies at the Ambani lunch. Pawar's chefs then gave interviews expressing their sadness that the former president had not touched their fare. We thought he liked kebabs, they said, and all he did was drink a glass of papaya juice. Some newspapers disputed this, their investigative journalists reported that he did not even drink the juice.

In the process of following Clinton's culinary journey, what got ignored was the single most important comment he made on Indian soil. 'No nation in the world,' said Clinton in the small Uttar Pradesh town of Rampur-Maniharan, 'has so much potential as India as long as education reaches every boy and every girl.'

He was gracious enough not to add that if we did not succeed in doing this, then we are looking at another wasted Indian century. God knows we have had enough wasted centuries already and yet we continue to treat education as if it were one of our less important concerns. How else does one explain the complete absence of the drastic changes that are not just required but necessary? How else does one explain the continuing absence of an education minister at the centre? In his place we have a minister for human resource development whose main obsession is to instil what he thinks are Indian cultural values when what he should be doing is giving us a policy that would make primary education compulsory. Ask them about it in Delhi and they will tell you that nothing more can be done because primary education is a state subject. If the centre is so powerless, why is Dr Murli Manohar Joshi attempting to make any changes at all?

The truth is that A.B. Vajpayee's government is treating education with the same disdain as its predecessors. In the old days, there were explanations for this attitude. We were an illiterate nation led by mainly upper-caste leaders who seemed to believe that it was not such a bad idea for lower castes and Muslims (who constitute the majority of illiterate Indians) to remain in ignorance and poverty because they constituted important vote banks, and vote banks cease to exist when people get a little education. Also, the electorate was so steeped in illiteracy that building schools did not necessarily bring in the votes.

Since then things have changed. It is hard to find a village that does not list schools—along with roads, electricity and drinking water—as the most important items on their election wishlist. So, building schools brings votes and yet the attitude of our political leaders remains unchanged. They continue to fiddle around with silly schemes and 'cultural' changes when what we need is a new policy backed by enough money to implement it.

Nobody is suggesting centralization of primary education, but once a policy—a clear road map—is in place, those state governments that need help can be given it. By now it should be clear that states like Bihar, Uttar Pradesh and Rajasthan have failed completely on the education front and desperately need help and money. If Joshi was serious about bringing changes he would at least have done something to change a system that spends more on the salaries of officials than it does on building schools. On paper we appear to have made progress but anyone who visits a village school will confirm that usually it is a school in name only. When it comes to literacy rates it is pretty much the same story. Anyone who can sign his name is considered literate so our literacy rate is now in the sixties but everyone knows that the reality is quite different.

When it comes to higher education there is as much need for change. Joshi has supposedly been in the process of encouraging private investment in higher education but try setting up a college and you will find it is not encouragement you get from the government but obstacles. Meanwhile, our once fine universities are in a state of decay because nobody dares raise fees that have remained virtually unchanged for fifty years. Joshi, unbothered, concerns himself with introducing astrology as a subject at the university level and making Sanskrit compulsory in schools. Can we please just begin by getting every Indian to read and write? What a shame that a political leader from a distant land can see so clearly what our own netas remain blind to.

(Published in *India Today*)

DEVELOPMENT DUD

7 May 2001

Some time during the course of this Tehelka-troubled session of Parliament, a report was tabled that could wipe the smile off the face of every MP in the land. And perhaps that of every MLA as well. It was the report of the comptroller and auditor-general of India (CAG) for the year ended March 2000, on the Member of Parliament Local Area Development scheme (MPLAD). Concealed in the turgid prose that typifies Indian government reports is a tale of corruption and misuse of taxpayers' money that makes Bangaru Laxman's pathetic little Rs. 1 lakh 'gift' seem like a tip to a peon.

The MPLAD scheme allowing MPs Rs. 2 crore to spend on development works in their constituencies was a gift to members of Parliament from P.V. Narasimha Rao when he was prime minister. He headed a minority government and needed the support of MPs so badly that he wanted to do something that would win their gratitude. So in December 1993, he ordained that MPs would be allowed to spend Rs. 1 crore in their constituencies on creating 'durable assets'. He still needed to buy votes to keep himself in power but that is another story.

The scheme was such a hit with MPs that in 1998 their constituency development allowance was doubled to Rs. 2 crore. They now want more. They want this allowance to go up to Rs. 7 crore per constituency and—unlike real development—this scheme has a trickle-down effect so most state governments have extended similar allowances to MLAs as well. Even wretchedly poor and underdeveloped Bihar sets aside a small fortune for its MLAs to spend. And what does the CAG's audit tell us? 'In its present form, the scheme, in operation since December 1993, has hardly served its main objectives...besides the fact that a significant part of released money was not utilized, the works carried out in a large number of cases did not qualify for the definition of durable assets. A large number remain incomplete. Several others were either inadmissible or were not recommended by the members of Parliament.'

Since 1993, Rs. 5,017.80 crore has been released for the scheme of which only Rs. 3,221.21 crore has actually been spent. Of the 41,955 development works that have been sanctioned, 20,874—nearly half—remain incomplete. The more closely you read the report the worse the story gets. The ministry of statistics and programme implementation, which administers the scheme, admits that it still doesn't have the proper means to monitor the monies it dishes out but continues to dish out more and more money. Under the scheme, the centre transfers money directly to district collectors who then spend it according to the wishes of the local MP.

Technically, an MP should use the money only to build 'durable assets' for the public good. Drinking water schemes, sanitation, schools, tube wells, roads—things that rural India desperately lacks—are the sort of durable assets they should be spending their allowance on. In a country as poor as ours, in which starvation deaths are still reported, in which access to healthcare is still a dream, you would imagine that there would be no shortage of real development works on which the MPs could spend their Rs. 2 crore. But in constituency after constituency, the CAG found the money being spent on 'inadmissible works'. It comes as no surprise that much of the development works that our MPs sanction benefit local officials and the police. Police stadiums have been built, district commissioners' offices have been beautified, and government houses have been constructed. In seven constituencies in Uttar Pradesh Rs. 102.04 lakh was spent on 'boundary wall to DM residence, library and computer room in collectorate', and so on.

It is the usual story of our netas and babus colluding to spend our money on improving their own living conditions and those of their families and friends. Worse still, the CAG has produced a long list of constituencies in which MP development funds have been spent on building private clubs, ashrams and memorials. And, when the money remains unspent it seems to disappear since it doesn't come back to the central government.

When it comes to duplicity and chicanery, the Indian politician is hard to rival. So post-Tehelka we have been subjected to endless sanctimonious speeches about the evils of corruption. For obvious reasons, our Opposition MPs have been particularly vocal and particularly sanctimonious. They began with a demand that the government resign, reduced it to a demand that a joint parliamentary committee investigate Tehelka and shouted so much that it was impossible for Parliament to function for most of the budget session. Well, here is a wonderful opportunity for them to put their money where their mouth is: what about a joint parliamentary committee on the MPLAD? It is, in its way, a bigger scandal than the one unearthed by tehelka.com.

(Published in *India Today*)

STEP THREE FIRST

30 July 2001

It might seem an odd thing to say with the air still thick with debris from Agra's failed summit but, personally, I think we could have in General Pervez Musharraf our first honest interlocutor from the other side. Let me explain. In recent years, we have tried talking peace with Zia-ul-Haq, Benazir Bhutto and Nawaz Sharif in that order and in each case we have faced duplicity, dishonesty and deceit. Zia-ul-Haq wanted to come and watch cricket in India even as he was busy arming secessionist movements in Punjab and Jammu and Kashmir. Benazir, whom we liked best, because her daddy and our Rajiv's mummy signed the Simla Agreement, did nothing to stop the cross-border export of terrorism and Nawaz Sharif 's betrayal in Kargil is too fresh in public memory to need repeating.

If General Musharraf comes as a refreshing if ostensibly nasty change it's only because duplicity—or even diplomacy—is not a thing he has time for even when a bit of either could have saved the Agra summit. The general prefers to spit out exactly what he wants to say. So he tells us that he will not talk about friendship or anything else until we agree to tell him what we plan to do about Kashmir. Call it an issue or whatever you please, he says, but please admit that it is the root cause of our enmity and that it has to be the only subject up for discussion. What is the point of talking about commerce or cultural ties if we do not admit that we will be enemies until there is a solution in Kashmir? He was careful in Agra not to spell out exactly what he meant by a solution but anyone who has passing familiarity with public sentiment in Pakistan knows that the only acceptable solution in their eyes is for us to break India once more in the name of Islam.

Former ISI chief Hamid Gul, who incidentally served under the beauteous Benazir, spelled it out in a Pakistani newspaper recently. 'I believe,' he wrote, 'India cannot live as a political entity as it is today. It has to be fragmented.' He is far from being the only Pakistani who dreams of India's fragmentation. His words reflect a widespread view that this fragmentation hinges on Kashmir. Musharraf was careful not to go quite so far in Agra but did not hesitate to bring Bangladesh into his diatribe. Revenge is one of the things that inspires Pakistan's Islamic warriors.

Well, since the general likes plain-speaking, let us stop pussyfooting and spell out exactly what we want to say. Let us go to what he calls step three of finding a Kashmir solution: negating ideas that are unacceptable. Let us spell out in the plainest language that there will be no more redrawing of India's borders in the name of Islam. Since Pakistanis are so obsessed with Kashmir what can be considered at some point, when the violence lessens, is a softer border. That is all. We could go on then to negate all possibilities—and all talk—of plebiscite and self-determination for the Kashmiri people. This is not going to happen and if the general does not know this already it is time he was told. Once these two possibilities are negated—to use his word—the general could find that there is little else to be discussed on Kashmir except the terrorists he likes to call freedom fighters. More than eighty per cent of them these days are not Kashmiri so it is not azadi they are fighting for but some wider Islamic war whose heroes are Osama bin Laden and the Taliban. We should tell the general that we do not want them around and if he continues to send them into our territory we shall continue to kill them.

Unfortunately what has inhibited such plain-speaking is our domestic problem in Kashmir, which the Vajpayee government has been singularly inept at handling.

It is a problem inherited from the Congress and the first thing that a BJP prime minister should have done was dissociate his government from the mistakes of the past and look at Kashmir anew. He should have admitted to the Kashmiri people that he was aware that they had faced terrible injustice on account of fifty years of rigged elections. It was this denial of basic democracy that caused the armed struggle and now the unending bloodshed. Vajpayee should have attempted a new beginning but did not and if he wants Pakistan's plain-speaking general off his back he better make a new beginning now.

We need a serious effort, not some committee headed by K.C. Pant. If we can solve our internal Kashmir problem, we would have no reason left to discuss it with anyone else at all. Please remember that nobody was haranguing us about Kashmir in the 1970s and 1980s and memories of plebiscite and Partition had all but died. They were revived on account of mistakes made by Indira Gandhi and Rajiv, mistakes that Vajpayee has not distanced his government from.

(Published in *India Today*)

STRIKING TERROR

24 September 2001

When measured against the horror of what happened in New York and Washington last week, our own terrorist problems seem small but in their own way are as significant. Coincidentally, on the very day that hijacked planes crashed into the World Trade Center and the Pentagon, Kashmiri women were forced into purdah by a faceless terrorist group.

Nobody knows who or what the Lashkar-e-Jabbar is but its terror tactics were so impressive that as the veiling deadline (September 10) approached, Kashmiri tailors could not produce burqas fast enough, shopkeepers threw veils over mannequins and the women-in-veils movement spread even to Mumbai, not a well-known Muslim city but a victim in the past of terrorist attacks. Mighty Hindutva charioteers like Sardar Advani remained strangely silent as terrorism won again. They say the silence was because elections in Uttar Pradesh loom dangerously close and nobody wants to put Muslim voters off by speaking out against Islamic dress codes. A sign that our political leaders continue to make compromises on terrorism.

The political leadership deserves most of the blame for these compromises but there is a hidden culprit and it is liberal public opinion. Our liberals and leftists are strident when it comes to attacking what they perceive as the 'saffronization' of India. No sooner do they get a whiff of Hindutva creeping into school textbooks or university courses than they are out on every public platform protesting their heads off. They are vigilant when it comes to seeing saffron but somehow become colour blind when it comes to Islamic green. So there has not been so much as a whisper of protest out of them against the terrorist group that has imposed purdah in Kashmir.

There have been other whispers, though, and they come from liberal journalists who hint that since nobody had heard of the Lashkar-e-Jabbar till it came out with the veiling order it could be a group created by Indian intelligence agencies to malign the genuine mujahideen. That really is a laugh when you consider that our intelligence agencies have to date not shown even enough intelligence to prevent the massacres of innocent people in Kashmir.

It is worth remembering that there has been, ever since militancy began in Kashmir twelve years ago, a calculated attempt to inject Islamic terror in the valley. In the movement's earliest stages we saw Islamic militants forcing hotels to close their bars, smashing bottles of liquor on the streets of Srinagar, closing down beauty salons, all in the name of Islam. There was also an edict on women's dress codes and some women obeyed. So the Lashkar-e-Jabbar is not saying something new, particularly not when you consider that Islamic countries like Saudi Arabia (where funds for violence come from) and Afghanistan (supplier of manpower and training) force similar dress codes on their own women.

But Indian liberals are a truly liberal breed so they manage to weave a Hindu plot around the appalling Lashkar-e-Jabbar. The danger of this kind of warped liberalism is that it is invariably taken advantage of by terrorist groups. So our security forces face a constant barrage of criticism on rights abuses but massacres in Jammu go relatively unnoticed. Since liberal opinion almost never speaks out against Islamic fundamentalism, we find blatantly sectarian organizations like the Students Islamic Movement of India speaking out loudly against the 'communalism' of the RSS and its various clones without noticing the irony of their words.

On account of the weakness of our political leaders and the partisan tinge of liberal public opinion we find ourselves in the dangerous situation of taking orders from terrorists. Militant organizations who kill innocent villagers simply because they happen to be Hindus should not be in any position to enforce dress or moral codes. But this is exactly what the shadowy Lashkar-e-Jabbar has succeeded in doing while our leaders continue to gibber on about terrorists in Kashmir being 'on the run' and our liberals watch from the stands.

Let us hope the full horror of what happened in the US has some effect here. Terrorism is no longer a form of protest by a handful of semi-trained militant groups; it is a war fought without any rules of war. Now that America faces the same war, we can only hope that President George Bush understands that we also would like to 'make no distinction between the terrorists who committed these acts and those who harbour them'. Pakistan and Afghanistan both harbour terrorists and their jehad is as much a threat to us as it is to America. If one terrorist strike can destroy the World Trade Center and the Pentagon the thought of what could happen in India is too horrifying to contemplate. There can be no more compromises on terrorism.

(Published in *India Today*)

DOUBLE-EDGED SWORD

1 October 2001

America's war against terrorism has acquired a surreal quality. On the one hand, we have George W. Bush telling us on a daily basis that states harbouring terrorists will be held as responsible as the evildoers themselves, and on the other, we have America turning to Pakistan for support in fighting its new war. Does America know what it's doing? Is it aware that Pakistan's foreign policy in recent times has been based entirely on supporting militant Islam? The jehad in Kashmir, the rise of the Taliban in Afghanistan and the countless acts of terrorism on Indian soil are part of this foreign policy. Is it possible to take America's war against terrorism seriously when it seeks Pakistan's help to wage it? Is it not a bit like employing Osama bin Laden to catch Osama bin Laden?

Pakistan is delighted with this turn of events. Its military dictator and his foreign minister have lost no chance to appear on CNN and BBC and hold forth on how Pakistan has always supported the global war against terrorism while we in India rub our eyes in amazement. Was it not just the other day in Agra that General Musharraf justified terrorism on the grounds that innocent people sometimes get killed when freedom movements take place? Was it not just the other day that he refused to discuss cross-border terrorism on the grounds that what was happening in Kashmir was a freedom movement? From Pakistan's point of view, the routine massacres of innocent Hindu villagers in Jammu, the barbaric beheading of Hindu priests and brutal killings of Sikhs in the Kashmir valley are all part of a 'freedom movement'. It would be interesting to know if Bush and General Colin Powell share this perception.

It would be interesting to know how they view the fact that the men who hijacked IC-814 two years ago sought refuge in Pakistan. The terrorists released in exchange for the passengers on that unfortunate flight have also taken refuge in Pakistan, not to mention Dawood Ibrahim and the Memon brothers. Does this or doesn't it qualify Pakistan as a state that harbours terrorists?

There is no question that what happened in New York and Washington on September 11 was the worst act of terrorism ever. The whole world—with the exception of a handful of Islamic fundamentalists—felt America's pain and understood its horror and rage. We in India were so eager to be in the vanguard of the new global war against terrorism that we were among the first to offer unconditional support. The prime minister, who has shied away from addressing the nation in most moments of domestic crisis, felt compelled by the events of September 11 to make one of his rare nation-wide addresses on television. The minister of external affairs talked in grandiose language of 'a concert of democracies' against terrorism. It must, then, have come as something of a shock when America ignored our effusive gestures of support and turned instead to Pakistan for help.

To some extent, this is understandable. If Afghanistan is to be the main theatre of this new war—at least in its initial stages—then Pakistan becomes an important frontline state. But America needs to keep in mind that there may not have been a Taliban government in Kabul if Pakistan had not just helped it seize power but provided for most of its financial, defence and other needs thereafter. Pakistan's jehadi foreign policy has brought it to the verge of bankruptcy, so it needs America more than America needs it. The Americans should be in a position then to warn Pakistan that it will need to alter its own sponsorship of terrorism if it is to be considered a serious ally in this new war which, at the best of times, is extremely hard to fight.

Even if Osama bin Laden is killed or brought to justice, it will only be the beginning. Militant Islam is an ideology that has spread its tentacles right into the heart of western democracies, as we can see from the fact that the plot to destroy the World Trade Center and the Pentagon was hatched in Miami and Hamburg.

Many of the Islamic militants we seek take refuge in western capitals like London and are financed by countries whom America counts as its friends, like Saudi Arabia. We can only hope that President Bush has some ideas on how to deal with this. So far all we have heard is a lot of bluster and bombast of the 'wanted dead or alive' kind. This kind of talk might satisfy his domestic constituency but sounds foolish on an international scale.

If America is serious about this 'new war', then it needs to keep on its side those countries that have been fighting terrorism a lot longer than America has. There can be no duplicity. If terrorism on American soil is a barbaric act against America then terrorism in Kashmir or Mumbai must also be viewed as a barbaric act against India. These are some of the things the American president needs to discuss with his current favourite ally Pakistan.

(Published in *India Today*)

GOVERNANCE IN LIMBO

22 October 2001

Cruise missiles pound a country in our neighbourhood. Our old foe Pakistan changes overnight in the eyes of the world from a pariah to a frontline state while we get relegated to bystander status. The roots of Islamic fundamentalism in our country run so deep that students in Srinagar shout *Osama se rishta kya, la ilaha illallah*. Our economy is slowing down before our very eyes. It should be clear that we will not escape the consequences of the first war of the twenty-first century. But in Delhi, it is business as usual for Atal Bihari Vajpayee's government. True, there have been, since the attack on Afghanistan, a couple of emergency meetings of the cabinet at which the nation's security was supposedly pondered over. But there is no indication that either Vajpayee or any member of his government has understood the seriousness of the problems we are likely to face.

The most serious of these relates to the economy. With a global recession looming, there is no chance of India escaping its effects, but nobody in Delhi seems concerned, least of all our finance minister. His thugs, who pass for inspectors, continue to run extortion rackets in the name of income-tax inspection and because nobody can stop them, legitimate businessmen look constantly over their shoulders and hesitate to invest. The finance minister must know what is happening, that his wondrous plans for the economy remain largely unimplemented. But he does nothing.

The other economic ministries are equally somnolent about things that need to be done and equally wideawake about things that do not. So for reasons nobody can understand, the commerce ministry has banned the import of meat and dairy products and raised the duties on wines so high that they may as well be banned. This hardly affects the average Indian, so the reasons are hard to fathom. But it seriously affects the hotel industry, which is currently reeling under a severe downturn.

On account of the war in our neighbourhood, most hotels report that there will be no foreign tourists this winter. Resorts that usually need to be booked a year in advance for the Christmas–New Year period report that all their bookings have been cancelled. Did the government need to impose these ludicrous bans at this point?

No, but we are a Third World country and one of the characteristics of Third World governance is that we concern ourselves with the meaningless and do nothing about things that are important. National security is important, but here again we take a Third World approach. So after our external affairs minister politely escorted those terrorists to Kandahar in exchange for the passengers of IC-814 our security agencies forgot about them. Result? Masood Azhar went on to form the Jaish-e-Mohammed which proudly claimed responsibility for killing thirty-eight innocent people in the bombing of the Jammu and Kashmir assembly two weeks ago. And it turns out that one of the other terrorists we released was responsible for sending large sums of money to Mohammad Atta who led the bombing of the World Trade Center. Would the home ministry like to explain what efforts it made to track the movements of the terrorists it so kindly released?

We are eager to join the global coalition against terrorism and are disappointed that so little attention is being paid to our offers of help. Perhaps we were ignored because we have done such a hopeless job of bringing our own terrorists to justice. With the Taliban regime on the verge of extinction there is likely to be an even larger number of Islamic fundamentalists on the loose in the region with serious consequences for us in Kashmir. Are we prepared?

We have a right to know but nobody is likely to give us any answers because another characteristic of Third World governance is that it takes place—if at all—in total secrecy.

In more advanced democracies, presidents and prime ministers feel the need to keep the people informed about what they are doing. Since the September 11 attacks, President George W. Bush and senior members of his administration have become familiar figures on our TV screens where they explain every important decision they take.

The difference between them and us was so obvious that it briefly inspired our prime minister to address the nation—something he has rarely done in our own moments of crisis. We have also seen a bit more of Jaswant Singh than we did in the past, but so unused are our political leaders to the importance of TV in modern politics that they usually end up sounding like bad actors in a bad play. Their performance never rises above the amateur (perhaps because they are amateurs) and is rarely reassuring. As the country heads into troubled times what we need is reassurance. And some signs of real governance.

(Published in *India Today*)

HOT PURSUIT, COLD FEET

31 December 2001

Everyone except Colin Powell knows that the terrorist attack on the Indian Parliament has Pakistan's fingerprints all over it. Everyone also knows that Kashmir's movement for azadi melted a few years ago into the larger Islamic jehad that destroyed the World Trade Center and the Pentagon and everyone, even Powell, should know that if Afghanistan was the headquarters of Allah's warriors, Pakistan was the war's hinterland. If by the time you read this Osama bin Laden and Mullah Omar remain uncaptured, you can almost be certain that it is to this hinterland that they have fled for shelter and succour. If this happens, the American state department may wake up to the fact that Pervez Musharraf is not General Goody-two-Shoes but we, in India, have more important things to worry about than America's fork-tongued foreign policy.

We don't need the FBI's help to find out if Pakistan's generals back the terrorists that perpetrate vile crimes on our soil. We know that without the support of the Pakistani army, groups like the Lashkar-e-Tayyaba and Jaish-e-Mohammed would collapse just like the Taliban did. The problem is, what can we do about it? Since December 13, the demands that the government 'do something' have reached a crescendo. Barring a handful of leaders in the Congress party and on the lunatic fringe of the Left, there is a consensus that the attack on

Parliament was a defining moment for India and that if the government fails yet again to take convincing steps, there will be a dangerous loss of faith in its ability to act.

What most people mean by decisive action is a strike against Pakistan. They want to see India take revenge just like America does. There is some hesitation about using the word 'war', but much talk of limited war and hot pursuit. This has been heightened by statements of the prime minister and union home minister that indicate that this time they do not plan to just sit back and condemn cross-border terrorism, as they did after IC-814 was hijacked, after the Red Fort was attacked and after the legislative assembly in Srinagar was nearly blown up.

But would an attack on terrorist camps in Pakistan be a solution? Personally, I fear not. Having pursued the terrorist camp trail in the 1980s, I can report that the information given by 'authoritative' sources in the government was wrong. I was given a list of camps that turned out to be inaccurate, and discovered through an accidental meeting with a Sikh priest in Lahore that 'the boys' who came across from Punjab after Operation Bluestar were taken to Faisalabad jail where they were trained in the use of arms and explosives. This information proved accurate when some of these boys returned to India and got arrested by the Punjab police. Nothing that our intelligence agencies have done in the years since indicates that they have improved their information gathering systems. So the question is do they really know where the terrorist camps are now? From all accounts many of Kashmir's terrorists were being trained in camps in Afghanistan that have already been destroyed.

The absence of full comprehension of the nature of the problem we currently face was evident in union home minister L.K. Advani's statement in the Lok Sabha last week. He talked about 'twenty years' of Pakistani terrorism apparently without noticing that the present phase is different. In the 1980s and early '90s, we had political problems in Punjab and Kashmir that bred violence. Currently, we are dealing with jehadi terrorism of an altogether different and more dangerous kind.

It weakens our case to argue that there is any kind of continuity.

The other frightening aspect of the government's understanding of the problem is that almost nothing has been done to train our police force in dealing with terrorism. Those who prevented the suicide squad from entering Parliament House showed remarkable bravery but, by and large, police work in India remains shoddy and amateur. Interrogation methods continue to be primitive and usually when a terrorist act occurs policemen can be seen trampling flat-footedly over evidence instead of sifting through it with the necessary care. The result is that the police is much better at catching innocent citizens than terrorists and it is nearly always after the event that we hear about accomplices being caught. The home ministry needs to concentrate on improved police training instead of worrying about 'hot pursuit'.

The prime minister needs to start asking questions on why the criminal justice system moves so slowly that men like Masood Azhar and Omar Sheikh managed to remain in our jails for five years without facing trial. It would also be interesting to know what steps we took to track down the hijackers of IC-814. The terrorism we now face requires that the criminal justice system be made to function more efficiently. POTO (Prevention of Terrorism Ordinance) is no solution. Nor is war, limited or not.

(Published in *India Today*)

SUFFRAGE CIRCUS

25 February 2002

The only claim to fame of a candidate contesting from an assembly segment of the prime minister's parliamentary constituency was that he had been to jail 242 times. More times than anyone else in the world, he boasted during his election campaign, supplying copies of the *Guinness Book of Records* to anyone who sought proof. In another Uttar Pradesh constituency, a candidate with a criminal record said this should not bother anyone as long as people were ready to vote for him. Elsewhere we had eunuchs contesting on the valid grounds that as men and women had failed so abysmally they who thought of themselves as neither might do a better job.

Proud though we are of our democracy, could it not be said that these elections came as worrying proof that the 'noise and chaos'—which Zulfiqar Ali Bhutto famously praised us for—have become more important than anything else? If eunuchs, criminals and an Italian-born national leader were not ludicrous enough, we had the descent of stars from Bollywood. Govinda dancing at Congress election meetings because of his love for Sonia Gandhi; Amitabh Bachchan singing at Samajwadi Party rallies for his love of Mulayam; and Hema Malini, in her new role as 'Punjab's daughter-in-law', speaking up for the prime minister. Not one of these stars had anything political to say and Govinda was good enough to admit this. 'I am an entertainer,' he said in an interview to Aaj Tak, 'and it is as an entertainer that I am here.' Had he been more political, he could have added that since elections have become entertainment why should there not be real entertainers instead of clowns masquerading as politicians? Indian democracy is going through a bizarre, disheartening phase and this found reflection in the assembly elections. There were, for a start, no issues to speak of although there should have been thousands.

We need to ask why. Is it because our political leaders are raising the wrong issues? Or because the electorate knows it makes little difference who comes to power as nothing changes anyway? That nothing changes has become depressingly evident. For years large sections of the electorate—from extreme left to right—deluded themselves that the BJP would provide change. Those of leftist inclination predicted this fearfully. Fascist parties usually brought a degree of good governance, they would mutter. Had the Nazi party not made the trains run on time? And voters of rightist bent believed the BJP slogan that it was a party with a difference. They were willing to overlook the party's inclination towards militant communal nationalism as long as it could change the way India was governed.

Three years of Shri Atal Bihari have put an end to both leftist fears and rightist hopes. It is not so much that A.B. Vajpayee has been a bad prime minister but that he has been so much a Congress-type prime minister it is sometimes hard to believe he is not. The Congress bequeathed him a corrupt, inefficient, obsolete system of governance and he has done absolutely nothing to change this. So the average Indian continues to fight his way through a jungle of evil officials and evil rules and regulations to obtain the basic necessities. He knows the officials are corrupt and have too much power and that the rules are convoluted and unnecessary. But he is now resigned to the reality that nobody is going to do much to change things.

If things are bad in Delhi, they are infinitely worse in a state like Uttar Pradesh that has over the years degenerated into lawlessness, casteism, religiosity and despair. The foundations of this decline were ably laid by Congress chief ministers, but in recent years it has been BJP chief ministers who have cemented the collapse. So, much as governance should have been a big issue in the recent election, it was not because the voter seems to have given up hope.

Politicians and Delhi's political pundits like to blame the voter for this. It is because voters vote on the basis of caste and creed, they say, that there has been this decline. What nobody appears to notice is that voters would not vote this way if they were given a choice between caste and creed on the one hand and progress and development on the other. Which voter provided with a road, a school, clean drinking water, healthcare and electricity would choose temples or caste instead?

It is when the choice is only between temples and mosques, upper and lower caste leaders that caste and creed become important and, unfortunately, that is usually the choice that the Indian voter has. Is it any wonder that he would rather watch Govinda dance or listen to Amitabh sing than hear some third-rate politician make yet another set of third-rate promises that he is going to break anyway. If that sounds cynical, think of the cynicism of thirty per cent of our people living on less than a dollar a day after fifty years of regular elections.

(Published in *India Today*)

PLUG THE DRAINAGE

4 March 2002

As someone relatively uninterested in who ends up ruling Uttar Pradesh or Punjab while other political pundits puzzled last week over the permutations and configurations of future governments, I found myself wandering through the dreary corridors of the Planning Commission. This crumbling edifice of Indian socialism is for me the symbol of all that is wrong with the way India is governed, so wandering through its corridors is not something I usually like to do. What took me there were rumours that something significant and surprisingly unobserved was going on within.

In a discreetly elegant room in Yojana Bhavan's otherwise decaying atmosphere, Arun Shourie is quietly working at bringing about what could be the most important change India has seen in decades. If he succeeds it will, in my view, make the difference between whether we are a rich country in twenty years or one still impoverished by the profligacy of our governments. The change he is charged with bringing about goes by the name of disinvestment. A word the Indian government had to invent because mere mention of privatization causes socialist hackles to rise. Since socialism is still the abiding faith of most of our political class, even privatization in the guise of disinvestment has hardly been possible, and for a long time all that the government managed to sell was one decrepit bakery. This despite the fact that the government is too poor to build the schools, hospitals and roads the country desperately needs because it spends seventy per cent of the money we pay in taxes on interest on its borrowings. It borrows mainly to waste more money on running and reviving industries that it would have been forced to close down or sell had it been a businessman in the private sector.

When Shourie became minister for disinvestment he tried speeding things up by pushing through the sale of BALCO, and was not only accused of bribery and corruption by the Congress but also taken to court. Luckily for us, the Supreme Court took a stern view of a case that it said should never have been brought before it: there was nothing wrong at all with the sale of BALCO, the judges said, and they would be grateful if people did not misuse the instrument of the PIL (public-interest litigation) on needless litigation.

Since this judgement, there has been less public hysteria when the government tries to sell off what our socialist pals still delude themselves into thinking of as the family silver.

There are now twenty-two transactions under way and in the foreseeable future mighty public sector icons like Maruti and Air-India could also be in private hands. But there is still huge opposition from vested interests ranging from cabinet ministers and senior political figures to ordinary workers and newspaper editors. So, when Paradeep Phosphates was privatized recently, Oriya journalists bemoaned the loss of what they claimed was a fine, profitable company. The truth is that this company, in which Rs. 400 crore of taxpayers' money has been invested, is now worth Rs. 1.2 crore with debts of Rs. 1,140 crore. Should we waste any more money on it?

Should we, for that matter, waste money running the Ashok Hotel when it spends Rs. 52 crore for every Rs. 41 crore that it earns? Of the thirty-one hotels that the India Tourism Development Corporation runs, only one makes a small profit, but every time the disinvestment ministry has tried to rid us of these hotels there is huge resistance from within the government itself. Do you know why? Because if these hotels are privatized, it would make it impossible for ministers and other officials to live in the style to which they have become accustomed: free meals, free accommodation and, according to some estimates, a vital source of income since money is made on virtually every purchase.

Quite simply we cannot afford this any more. Nor can we afford to try and have any more revival packages as they have already cost taxpayers Rs. 40,000 crore without one public sector company showing signs of revival. Besides, is there not something bizarre in sheer business terms of an investment of Rs. 200,000 crore being made for the benefit of 2 million public sector workers?

Think of the schools this money could build. Think of how many more villages could get clean drinking water and decent roads, how many cities could be provided proper sewage systems and decent housing. These are the things we should expect from our elected representatives, not whether they can run steel factories or luxury hotels. If the disinvestment ministry succeeds in what it is doing it could be the most significant contribution of the Vajpayee government. The Opposition even from within the government continues, though, to be strenuous, and rumour has it that if a sale goes through it is generally because it has the prime minister's personal backing. If this is true, and it appears to be, then as someone who has often attacked A.B. Vajpayee's somnolent approach to governance, may I this week salute him.

(Published in *India Today*)

POGROM POLITICS

18 March 2002

The saddest message that comes to us from Gujarat's sickening shaming violence is that we have learned nothing from the terrible pogroms of 1984 that caused more than 3000 innocent Sikhs to be killed on the streets of Delhi in less than three days. We have not even learnt to distinguish between a communal riot and a pogrom. In 1984 what we saw were organized pogroms against Sikhs and in Gujarat what we have just seen are organized pogroms against Muslims. Riots are a different thing altogether and it is important that we make a distinction. In 1984, not a single Hindu lost his life, the dead were all Sikhs, and when we get down to counting the dead in Gujarat, we will probably find that the list has only Muslim names. This makes it a pogrom, not a riot, and as in 1984, a pogrom that appears to have had the tacit approval of the state.

The anti-Sikh pogroms inspired inquiry commissions, internal inquiries by departments of the police and the administration, judicial proceedings and more inquiry commissions, and what a lot of time and taxpayers' money we have wasted since clearly no lessons were learnt.

Had we learnt only Lesson One, the administration of the pathetically incompetent Narendra Modi would have anticipated violence on the day that Hindutva activists were burnt alive by a Muslim mob in Godhra. Had even the simplest preventive measures like curfew in major cities and towns and a ban on public gatherings been taken, there would have been no pogroms. Assuming that the violence was sudden, spontaneous and widespread—as the chief minister would have us believe—it could still have been controlled if the administration wanted it controlled. In 1984, when Indira Gandhi's assassination inspired violence in Delhi on a larger scale than in Gujarat, it was checked as soon as police officers were ordered to shoot at mobs. Mobs are made up not of valiant warriors but of the worst, most contemptible cowards and a gun needs only be pointed in the right direction for the mob to melt away as if it never was.

If this did not happen in Gujarat, it can only mean that either the chief minister, or his patrons in Delhi, did not want the mobs to be reined in too quickly. It must also mean that they wanted revenge and blood-letting instead of justice. Had they wanted justice, the arrests that were made later in Godhra would have been made on day one and they would have been made in the full glare of the media so that ordinary Hindus could have been assured that justice would be done. We are told that those who instigated the violence in Godhra were members of the Congress. If this is so, it would have helped contain public anger if these details were made known instantly. Instead, we had various ministers in the Vajpayee government hinting darkly at an ISI plot without providing an iota of evidence. Why should we believe them now when they tell us that it was not the ISI but the Congress?

Gujarat's chief minister now tells us that his policemen were possibly biased in their reaction to the communal violence because they are members of the community and would be as affected by public sentiment as the next man. Well, had we learnt any lessons from the past we would by now have a police force trained to treat rioters as rioters and not as Hindus, Muslims or Sikhs.

There are other unlearnt lessons from the past, like the need to punish policemen and officials who fail to protect ordinary citizens from violent mobs. Not only have they never been punished, but even the killers themselves usually melt—unidentified and unpunished—into ordinary lives as soon as the violence abates. If in the past fifty years we had been able to punish even a handful of negligent officials, convict just two or three rioters, there would be less likelihood of us having to suffer the shame of what we have just seen in Gujarat.

We like to think of ourselves as a civilized country. We like to sneer at Pakistan for being unable to match our high standards of civilization and yet beneath the veneer of our 'democracy and tolerance' lies a dark barbarous side that politicians find easy to bring to the surface. We need to ask ourselves why. We need to ask ourselves how it can be controlled. We need to ask ourselves how America's leaders managed to keep their people from taking the law into their own hands despite the terrible provocation of 9/11.

We need for a start to ask the prime minister why he finds it so hard to control the Hindutva fanatics his own party has bred and nurtured. Why can they not be ordered instantly to stop their temple-building activities in Ayodhya? If they need work to do, let them go to Gujarat and rebuild the mosques and Muslim shrines that the mobs destroyed. Let them do penance by helping the victims rebuild their ravaged lives. It might go some way in easing the shame of Gujarat.

(Published in *India Today*)

WAY OUT: LET US FOCUS ON VALLEY; LET US HANDLE GEN

2 June 2002

Say something in your first piece about this column returning to the *Express*, the editor of this newspaper said to me, so for the longest time I sat and stared at a blank computer screen trying to find the appropriate words. They did not come but what did were thoughts from 1987 when I first started writing this column in this newspaper.

What a different India we lived in then. Socialism was sacrosanct, the Ambassador car—that shoddy symbol of our socialist workmanship—dominated the roads, the media consisted of badly printed newspapers and dreary old Doordarshan. So many things we now take for granted like private airlines, satellite TV, computers, mobile phones and e-mail were completely unheard of.

When seen from an economic and technological point of view much has changed for the better. Sadly, the same cannot be said of our politics or politicians. Here, it has been downhill at such a rapid pace that at our next general election we face the grim choice between an Italian prime minister on the one hand and a Hindu fascist one on the other.

The deterioration that is more important this week is in our relations with Pakistan. We were not on particularly good terms in 1987 either and there was all that fuss about a military exercise by the Indian Army called Operation Brass Tacks which caused an eyeball-to-eyeball confrontation along our borders but it is hard to think of a time when things were as bad between us as they are today. Whatever else we can blame Atal Bihari Vajpayee for we cannot blame him for this.

If the proxy war turns into open war General Pervez Musharraf will have himself to blame. No Indian prime minister in recent times has done more to try and bring peace to the subcontinent than Vajpayee and if there could have been the smallest reciprocation from the other side we would today have been on the brink of lasting peace and not war.

Why does General Musharraf not see this? Because, judging from his interview to the *Washington Post* and last week's television address, the general appears to be suffering from a serious attack of megalomania.

How else to explain his comment, to Steve Coll of the *Washington Post*, that the present crisis has been created by India in order to destabilize his government? If the general's speech was 'disappointing and dangerous', to use Jaswant Singh's words, the interview is being seen in Delhi's corridors of power as the rantings of a psychopath. There is agreement that all chances of peace with Pakistan will have to be postponed until that country can find itself another ruler.

So, if peace is not possible will there be war? Not if India can help it and not if the Americans can put enough pressure on their current favourite military ruler to get him to desist from exporting terrorism.

But this is where the situation gets tricky. Although the public stand taken by the Vajpayee government is that all acts of terrorism in India are personally ordered by the general, privately senior ministers admit that there is growing evidence that groups like the Lashkar-e-Tayyaba and Jaish-e-Mohammed are now functioning on their own. The jehad is out of control and one of its objectives is to cause a war between India and Pakistan, preferably a nuclear war.

In this terrifying scenario what are India's options? Well if there is nothing we can do about the external aspects of the problem there is much that can and must be done to bring peace inside Kashmir. The Vajpayee government's biggest political failure has been its complete inability to formulate a policy for Kashmir.

In the absence of a policy it has stumbled from one feeble, half-hearted effort to the next so we had that ceasefire two years ago and then when nothing happened there were those almost farcical attempts to hold talks with Kashmiri militant groups with K.C. Pant as the Indian government's interlocutor. And now that all else has failed the government pins its hopes on holding 'free and fair' elections to the state assembly in October.

The last election saw the National Conference come to power with less than fifteen per cent Kashmiris voting and something similar could happen again so the election is unlikely to be a solution. There can be no solution without a policy that outlines a clear road map. A solution to our domestic problem in Kashmir is needed more urgently than ever before.

It will not come through flying visits by the prime minister and ad hoc announcements of economic and other packages. If we concentrate on our internal problems in Kashmir and leave the Americans to deal with their favourite general we might find a way out of the frightening morass we are trapped in.

Meanwhile, to end on a happy note, it is nice to have the Fifth Column back in the newspaper where it began.

A DATE WITH PRESS AND PRESSURE

30 June 2002

That our politicians are duplicitous, dishonest and breathtakingly amoral I have long learned to accept but two speeches last week by Messrs Vajpayee and Advani surprised even cynical old me.

The event was the release of the home minister's latest literary work, *A Prisoner's Scrap Book*, in New Delhi, in which, as the title indicates, he dwells on the months he spent in jail during the Emergency whose anniversary (June 26) dictated the timing of the book's release.

At this event, according to a report in this newspaper, our home minister wiped tears from his eyes as he said, 'I get emotional whenever I think of the Emergency. I feel very strongly about it. It was painful and also exhilarating that we all came out stronger out of it. It was a win for democracy.'

When it came to the prime minister's turn to speak, he described Indira Gandhi's brief flirtation with dictatorship as a dark period in Indian history but added, 'I am sure people of the country will never allow it to happen. Even at that time people displayed maturity and threw out the government.'

This emotional rejection of dictatorship by these two titans of the Bharatiya Janata Party came on the very day that the Central Bureau of Investigation (CBI) raided the offices of Tehelka.com. But the irony escaped them or they may have waited a day before ordering the raid.

The relentless attack on Tehelka.com and its main financier

Shankar Sharma represents the most shaming assault on press freedom that we have seen in India in a long while. And in more ways than one it is more evil than the ham-fisted press censorship Mrs Gandhi imposed during the Emergency.

Mrs Gandhi's censorship was a crude, idiotic thing that harmed her more than it did the press. For those of us who worked in newspapers like the *Statesman* and the *Indian Express* it was, to use Advani's words, an 'exhilarating' experience, and democracy came out stronger because we fought it the whole way and were able to make it clear that we were fighting.

What has happened to Tehelka.com is a much more insidious, frightening thing and it saddens me that we of the fourth estate have paid it so little attention. What we have seen is a sophisticated, new form of press censorship which will undoubtedly be emulated by future governments because of its effectiveness.

Interestingly the Vajpayee government itself used it again only recently in the case of *Time* magazine reporter Alex Perry. His story on the prime minister's health upset the government but the normal response should have been to register a complaint with the magazine. This the prime minister's office did in the form of a letter that was duly published.

The matter should have ended there but it did not. The home ministry went into an astonishing overdrive to prove that Perry was not just a bad journalist but a criminal. Stories of his having more than one passport were leaked to the press and he was summoned to the foreigners registration office (an institution that should not even exist in a democracy) to see if his papers were in order.

It was a pathetic, ridiculous response to a story that basically said the same things that the Indian press has been saying for months. But I digress.

What happened to Perry was wrong but nothing compared to what has been done to Tehelka.com. From the day that Tehelka released its tapes showing Bangaru Laxman and Jaya Jaitly collecting 'party funds' from shady arms dealers, the

Vajpayee government's only concern has been to prove that the Tehelka exposé was not journalism but a sinister plot to destabilize India. Shades of Indira Gandhi?

So, instead of cleaning up the corruption so evident in the defence establishment that it almost does not even need an exposé, and instead of making a sincere effort to legalize political funding the government has spent its entire time trying to destroy Tehelka by ensuring that nobody dares fund it.

The method used was to first destroy Shankar Sharma who dared fund it in the first place. So he and his wife Devina Mehra, among our brightest, most successful entrepreneurs, have been raided more than twenty-five times. Shankar has been arrested and jailed despite no evidence of cheating on taxes, his bank accounts have been frozen and his life taken away.

Naturally Tehelka.com has found it impossible to raise more funds so it barely survives and has not paid salaries for five months. The latest raid, ostensibly under the Wildlife Protection Act, is only the one more attempt to prove that it is not a bona fide media organization but a den of criminals.

The message from the government is clear. Any journalist who dares expose corruption in defence deals, or even tries to point out that the prime minister's health is not as good as it should be, will be treated as a criminal if not as a traitor. Beat that for censorship. And at least spare us the prison reminiscences.

The prime minister likes poetry so he might appreciate this line from a poem by Majrooh Sultanpuri: *Hum kucha, kucha dekh rahey hain alam-e-zindan tumsey zyada.* In the streets (of our country) we learn more about the atmosphere of a prison cell than you ever will.

THE RASHTRIYA SWAYAM-SEVA SANGH

11 August 2002

Some months ago when the RSS was sending its propagandists door to door to persuade people of its noble, patriotic (alas, misunderstood) credentials a posse of persuaders turned up at my doorstep. Among them was M.G. Vaidya, who had just become RSS spokesman. He and the two gentlemen with him settled themselves in my drawing room and over tea and namkeen tried to persuade me they had a worthwhile political viewpoint.

When this endeavour failed we talked of other things and Vaidya expounded on his economic vision. We did not need to ape Western consumerism, he said, because Indians had no desire for consumer goods and other luxuries, Indians knew how to live without them. When I replied that I had never, in all my travels, met a single Indian villager who would not buy if he could a colour TV, a refrigerator and if possible even a car, he proudly announced that his son had chosen to live in a village on an income of Rs. 2500 a month. He could earn more, he added, but he is happy and so is his family.

Imagine then my surprise when, in the first list of names in the petrol pump scam, I should find the name of Vaidya's son. No sooner was he exposed than he graciously returned his petrol pump and gave a pontificating little speech about how his father had always told him not to use his name. He was even praised for this by some newspapers but praise is not called for. What Vaidya's son did is very much of a piece with the sort of hypocrisy that has become an essential part of the RSS approach to life.

For public display is their 'austerity and their simplicity' and for private consumption are petrol pumps and all the other fruits of power that have come the RSS way ever since a swayamsewak became prime minister. So pervasive is the RSS greed for the good things that taxpayers' money can provide that the word swayamsewak (self-helper) has acquired a whole new meaning.

In the list of those who self-helped themselves to petrol pumps for their kith and kin there are many who cut their teeth in the shakhas (units) of the RSS but this is not even the half of it.

If you probe even slightly the channels of patronage that the Vajpayee government has set in motion, you will find RSS men at the receiving end everywhere. And sadly the prime minister has taken an indulgent view so whenever RSS greed clashes with good governance or the interests of the people of India RSS greed has almost always won.

Do you remember when Vasundhara Raje had khadi taken away from her in the mini-cabinet reshuffle the prime minister effected last year? Ostensibly it was only to expand the ministry—provide more jobs for the boys—but behind this little change lies another tale of RSS greed. Vasundhara was a little too eager to 'clean up' the open loot of taxpayers' money that goes on in the name of helping India's poorest craftsmen and weavers. She noticed that more than Rs. 500 crore that had been given to the Khadi Village Industries Commission (KVIC) for disbursement to poor craftsmen and weavers was sitting in the bank. Who was collecting the interest? Why?

She also noticed during sixty surprise checks that the ministry conducted that large amounts of money were going as rebates to people who were not producing a single yard of khadi cloth. It was an intricate web of corruption set up by the Congress party in the name of Gandhiji, and she should have had total support when she tried to dismantle it but this did not happen.

The opposite did. The head of the KVIC, Mahesh Sharma, is a well-known swayamsewak and he objected to her trying to clean things up so Vasundhara lost her job even though one visit to the khadi shop in Delhi's Khan Market is proof that she was doing good work. And the spate of suicides by desperately poor weavers and craftsmen across the country is more than proof that the organization set up to help them is not doing its job.

The RSS appears to have understood very quickly that its supporters could benefit hugely from the powers of patronage that government inevitably brings so it ensured that the Congress system of patronage remained intact.

What makes this more sickening than it was in Congress times is the hypocrisy. The RSS is the mother ship that produces organizations like the Swadeshi Jagaran Manch and its spokesman's son and many of its other acolytes have no hesitation in helping themselves to petrol pumps that bring in an average income of Rs. 50,000 a month. Is the petrol they supply made in India? Is the idea of a petrol pump swadeshi?

The solution lies not in setting up a commission of inquiry to find out how many swayamsewaks have helped themselves at our expense but in reducing government's powers of patronage. Why should a petroleum minister have control over petroleum companies that dole out petrol pumps? Why are these companies not already in private hands? Meanwhile, would the RSS spokesman like to explain why his son wanted an income of Rs. 50,000 a month?

AFTER RAJIV, BEFORE MODI

15 December 2002

Some of the political commentary that the Gujarat election inspired left me as worried about secularist amnesia as I am about Narendra Modi's politics of hate. Let me say first as I have said before in this column that Modi's attempt to get the Hindus of Gujarat to vote on his pogroms was in my view despicable.

Civilized societies are built on certain principles that are self-evident, a priori, and not taking a vote on murder and rape has to be one of them. It should never be left to the people to decide if pogroms are a good idea and I have no doubt that this is what Modi offered—scarcely veiled behind all that talk of pride and nationalism—as his main attraction in the recent campaign. In doing so he succeeded in building a wall of hatred between Hindus and Muslims that Gujarat will continue to pay a very heavy price for.

My problem is that I do not believe that his winning the election (I write before the results are known) will be the end of India, the end of history or as one commentator in this newspaper put it that his campaign has forever 'changed the grammar and vocabulary of Indian politics'. There has, ever since the Gujarat election was announced, been so much of this kind of comment in the newspapers and on television that I have found myself wondering if these commentators were comatose, unborn or in some other country in 1984.

Have they forgotten that within a day of Indira Gandhi's

assassination by her two Sikh bodyguards every Sikh in India became a target? Have they forgotten the mobs that roamed the streets of Delhi with their cans of petrol and their burning rags? Have they forgotten that there was never a policeman in sight when Sikhs were burned alive in trucks and taxis and that the administration of India's capital city collapsed so shamefully that dogs ate the dead in Delhi's streets? The toll at the end of three days was more than 3000 Sikhs dead (not one Hindu) in Delhi alone.

That the violence was carefully organized was clear because the mobs knew exactly which house, shop or factory belonged to a Sikh, knowledge that could only have come from voter lists or administrative records. If the mobs in Ahmedabad and Vadodara worked with similar foreknowledge it was because they had a model to work from.

And if Modi then used hatred to consolidate the Hindu vote behind the Bharatiya Janata Party he also had a model to work from. Remember, please, that after the 1984 violence Rajiv Gandhi came to power with the largest majority in Indian parliamentary history because he openly espoused the politics of hate. Not only did he justify the massacre of the Sikhs in a speech that was to become famous ('When a big tree falls the earth shakes...') but his party ran a series of newspaper advertisements in which Sikhs were depicted as terrorists and enemies of India.

The trouble with using intercommunal hatred to win elections is that the price is always too heavy. So, largely as a result of what happened to Sikhs after Mrs Gandhi's assassination, terrorism spread across the cities and states of Northern India and young Sikh boys crossed the border into Pakistan to return trained for revenge. When they came back they killed major political leaders, planted bombs in crowded bazaars and attacked the authority of the state in whichever way they could.

In India because we have a strange disdain for history we forget easily so we have even forgotten that when the Babri Masjid was destroyed and violence spread across the country there were many who predicted then that it was the end of India. Hindus and Muslims would never live together in peace again, it was said, and we would have to reconcile ourselves to 'fascism' becoming part of our lives.

Well, the opposite happened, did it not? The nineties saw economic growth at a pace unknown before in India. Economic liberalization, however reluctantly it was introduced, brought new technology, modern ideas and modern systems of communication. One of the states that benefited most from all this was Gujarat and its real tragedy is that instead of continuing along the path of economic progress it has retreated into more primitive politics thanks to Modi.

What happened in Gujarat was terrible and Modi is a truly repellent creature to have in Indian public life but please let us not lose perspective and start believing that he is uniquely evil or that the violence we saw in Gujarat signals the end of India. It does not. But the lesson we can learn from Gujarat is that primitive politics usually leads to unspeakable barbarism and in these days when the world has become such a small place governments that allow the mob to rule do more damage to the image of India than anyone else.

The other lesson, of course, is that if the Congress party had not done it all before it could have fought Modi's repugnant politics with aggressive secularism. It might have helped also if its campaign in Gujarat had not been led by a man who himself cut his political teeth in a pair of khaki knickers.

YOUR LORDSHIP, SEVERAL POINTS OF ORDER

22 December 2002

Last week, a new chief justice of India took office. We have had four this year, so the change can hardly be described as momentous and I would have ignored all mention of it if I had not, while switching channels, caught Justice V.N. Khare's first interview as chief justice. The interviewer was an eager young reporter who wanted (naturally) to know what the new chief justice's priorities were going to be. After mulling awhile over this utterly simple question, our new chief upholder of the rule of law said something to the effect that 'there are so many things, so many challenges'.

If this were not banal enough he proceeded to elucidate in a way that gives banality a whole new meaning. Infrastructure needed to be improved, India had only 13.5 judges per 10 lakh people, other countries had 125 and every time there is a new law there is more pressure on the judiciary. It was as if he were taking charge of a judicial system in perfect condition instead of one so mired in stagnation that it will take an estimated three hundred years for it to deal with its accumulated cases.

Surely, a new chief justice should have more to say about why things never seem to improve? Surely we have a right to know why there are not enough judges? And why physical infrastructure is in such bad shape that in courtrooms in Mumbai and Delhi it is not unusual to trip over stray cats and dogs on your way in? Conditions in our lower courts are even more appalling and in places like Ujjain I have personally fought my way past cows who seemed strangely drawn to the courtroom I was due to appear in.

It was, interestingly, on account of my having made comments on the mess in the judiciary that I was summoned in a case that in any other country would not even have been admitted. There are hundreds of thousands of such cases in India, cases of no merit, cases that should be thrown out at a pre-trial hearing but in India they find their way into a judicial process that has stagnated so dangerously that more and more young Indians pick up a gun when they want justice.

A state that cannot deliver justice cannot deliver the rule of law. Or to use the words of Syed Abdul Rehman Geelani, sentenced last week to death, 'Peace comes with justice; if there is no justice there is no democracy. Democracy in India is under threat.'

Geelani, a former professor at Delhi University, has been convicted for being part of the conspiracy that brought about the December 13 attack on Parliament. He was arrested under POTA (Prevention of Terrorism Act), which does not allow bail so he has spent a year in jail despite a powerful campaign by his former colleagues, students and human rights groups to get him released. He has reason to be bitter about Indian justice because on the basis of the evidence the prosecution presented against him he would almost certainly not spend a day in jail in a country that recognizes the principle of a person being innocent till proved guilty.

A week before he was sentenced to death I spoke to his lawyer Seema Gulati who said the case against him was so weak that they were certain he would be acquitted. The case is that the Delhi police while routinely tapping the mobile telephones of Kashmiris taped a conversation between him and his brother in Baramulla a day after the attack on Parliament. They had this conversation translated by an illiterate vegetable seller who said Geelani had used the words *yeh to zaroori tha* to justify the attack. When his lawyers had the same tape recording translated by two other Kashmiris neither came up with these words but even if they had would it be enough to establish conspiracy?

What kind of justice system sentences a man with no previous criminal record to death in a year but allows the alleged mastermind of the plot, Masood Azhar, to remain under trial for five years? Masood was arrested for active involvement in acts of terrorism and was Pakistani and yet his case was allowed to drag on long enough for him to be released in exchange for the passengers of IC-814. What does that tell us about our justice system?

There are thousands of people in Indian jails, some barely out of their teens, who have spent years in prison simply because they cannot afford bail. I know of one case in which a young boy has spent six years in jail for stealing Rs. 100 because he could not afford the Rs. 5000 he was asked to pay as bail. This sort of thing happens only when there are serious flaws in the justice system.

If the new chief justice wants to make a difference he will need to go beyond banalities. We know there are too few judges, that our courtrooms in no way look like courtrooms should, that the system is clogged with cases that should never have come to court, that laws and legal procedures are outdated and obsolete. We know all this, what we want to know from the chief justice is how long it will take for things to improve. Months, years or decades?

ALL MAYA, JOSHI'S 'STRIDES' INVISIBLE

16 March 2003

A glossy propaganda pamphlet that the ministry of human resource development recently issued as testimony of its achievements inspired me to spend two days touring schools in Uttar Pradesh. The pamphlet, called 'Strides in Education', is reminiscent of propaganda of earlier socialist times when the assumption of those who ruled us was they could fool most of the people most of the time because the average Indian was too poor and illiterate to raise objections to taxpayers' money being wasted on expensive, useless pamphlets when it could have been better spent on schools.

On the pamphlet's cover we have a smiling Murli Manohar Joshi gazing joyfully at the prime minister whose benign gaze appears fixed on some distant future. On the inside cover are Atal Bihari Vajpayee's thoughts on education: 'The most valuable investment that we can make in India's future is to ensure that every child gets education. We have decided that by 2010, every Indian child will get education up to class eight. We have launched Sarva Shiksha Abhiyan (Education for All campaign) to achieve this goal.'

Then, follows a list of things that the NDA government claims to have achieved 'in partnership with states, local bodies and the community' in the last three years.

These are an expenditure of Rs. 7571 crore on the 'universalization' of elementary education; the setting up of 31,000 new primary and upper primary schools with 80,000 more teachers; 21,219 new school buildings, 23,490 new classrooms, 47,000 toilets and 24,000 drinking water facilities sanctioned for this year; 13 lakh teachers provided Rs. 500 grant for 'developing teaching learning material' annually for the past three years and another 22 lakh in the current year; 5 lakh primary teachers trained annually for the past three years and another 7.22 lakh this year; 4 lakh primary schools given Rs. 2000 for improving their facilities and another 6 lakh schools this year; over 15 lakh members of community organizations trained to ensure community participation in education with another 6.86 lakh up for training this year.

Finally, we have free textbooks for scheduled caste and tribe children and Rs. 5000 provided for school building upkeep under the Sarva Shiksha Abhiyan.

My reason for giving you the full list is because if you glance through it even casually the thing that should strike you is how thinly the HRD ministry spreads its money on the ground. The end result can only be tokenism and not a serious effort to ensure that all Indian children are literate by 2010. It is the same tokenism that you see in last month's budget which dismisses education in a single paragraph of high-minded eloquence.

'Education is the central vein of our "life-time concerns". Therefore, at the level of the citizen taxpayers, as a first step, education expenses up to Rs. 12,000 per child for two children will be made eligible for rebate under Section 88 of the Income Tax Act.'

When you remember that we need to double our education budget to even begin to deal with our problems you see how feeble this 'first step' is. It was with the idea of seeing how policies like the Sarva Shiksha Abhiyan translate into reality that I went on my tour of UP schools last week. My journey began in the village of Badalpur where Mayawati went to her first school and ended in the village of Saifayi where Mulayam Singh Yadav comes from and where he has now built two schools.

Badalpur is on the edge of suburban Delhi but remains a

village with the usual filthy drains, flies, uncollected garbage and narrow alleys. At the end of one of these alleys is a locked, blue-washed house which local people identify as the house in which Mayawati was born.

A man called Rajpal Singh, who said he was Mayawati's cousin, told us that nobody used the house any more and that the chief minister was building herself a big house on the outskirts of the village.

Although she was only two when her family moved to Delhi, Mayawati seems to feel enough of a connection with Badalpur to have bequeathed it the Kumari Mayawati Rajkiya Kanya Inter College, which she opened when she was chief minister in 1997. It now has 700 students to whom it provides free tuition.

But, because there is not enough money to maintain it, the building looks grubby and dank and teachers admit that they cannot dream of such things as computers and other teaching aids.

On its grounds is Badalpur 1, an elementary school which Mayawati is believed to have briefly attended.

The school now has 172 children on its rolls but that day there would have been no more than fifty in attendance. One of the two lady teachers said this was 'marriage season' when attendance always dropped low.

The older children sat on strips of gunny sack in the verandah and the smaller ones on the bare floor in the single classroom—a bleak, unfurnished space with unpainted walls. The only furniture in the whole school was a single table and chair at which the teacher sat and occasionally looked up from to take notice of what the children were doing.

'They've had their lesson,' she said, 'they are now revising it and I have to finish these voters' lists.'

Why was she finishing voters' lists during school hours? Because that is what the government told her to do. There was always something or the other they had to do which had nothing to do with school work, sometimes it was voters' lists and sometimes polio drops. What to do? They were employed by the government so they could hardly refuse to do these tasks. The teachers came from nearby Ghaziabad and seemed not just indifferent to the children in their charge but were almost contemptuous of them.

'These lower caste children,' one said, 'they hardly come to school and sometimes we have to go to their homes to bring them here. They are not interested in anything except collecting their scholarship money and the three kilos of wheat they get every month.'

The wheat is distributed as part of the midday meal scheme and the scholarships—Rs. 300 a year—are specifically for dalit and Muslim children.

There was not much of an atmosphere of learning at Mayawati's old school but by the time I ended my journey in Mulayam's village I had started thinking of it as one of the best schools in UP. The children had books and a roof over their heads and teachers, and by the standards of Uttar Pradesh, which is second only to Bihar in terms of illiteracy, that is a lot.

COME ON BUSH, STOP THIS MORALITY TALK

23 March 2003

The war on Iraq has begun and we are forced to take sides. George W. Bush, who sounds more and more like John Wayne in one of those black-and-white movies from the fifties, tells us we can either be with America or with the terrorists. Are the battle lines that clear? On which side do we count Pakistan? What of Saudi Arabia? As far as anyone knows there were no Iraqi hijackers on September 11 and no Iraqis fighting in any of the Islamic jehads we see from Kashmir and Kabul to Bali and Manila and yet it is Iraq that faces 'decisive force'.

Saddam Hussein may be a very bad man but he has always been a very bad man so why did he have America's support when he was murdering his opponents, using chemical weapons on Kurds and dragging Iran into a war in which more than a million people lost their lives? Did nobody notice then that he was trying to build weapons of mass destruction?

The problem with America's new Gulf War is that there are too many questions and too few people asking them. Last Thursday, when the first US strikes against Iraq began, I remained transfixed by CNN and BBC for several hours and except for one short BBC documentary which mentioned in passing that Saddam had been supported by the West in some of his more evil moments I heard almost not a single word of criticism.

The world's two leading Western news channels reported the war as if it were nothing more than some exciting new spectator sport. The word 'decapitation' was used to describe the objective of the early strikes and it took me a few moments to realize that it was a description of what they were trying to do to Saddam.

To prove that he was still 'un-decapitated' he appeared on Iraqi television shortly afterwards to make the war sound even more bizarre with his talk of using 'swords' to fight the 'criminal Zionists'. Swords? Evil will be defeated, he added, clearly unaware that he was supposed to be the evil one.

Not only are the lines blurred in this new Gulf War but the objectives seem murky as well. From the moment the Americans rediscovered Saddam shortly after the war on Afghanistan failed to 'decapitate' Osama there have been rumours of ulterior motives, rumours that this war is more about oil and reviving the American economy than terrorism.

Who will rebuild Iraq after it has been blown to bits by thousands of American bombs? The *New York Times* columnist, Bob Herbert, writing on the day the war began, had this to say.

'Do most Americans understand that even as we are launching one of the most devastating air assaults in the history of warfare, private companies are lining up to reap the riches of rebuilding the very structures we're in the process of destroying?' As he put it, companies like Halliburton, Schlumberger and the Bechtel Group understood the conflict much better than most of those who would fight in it—that there were billions of dollars to be made in Iraq.

When you remember that Vice President Dick Cheney used to be chief executive of Halliburton it makes the Bush administration's zeal to 'bring freedom' to the Iraqi people less than credible.

There are other problems with this war of which perhaps the biggest one is whether a country, even the most powerful country in the world, has the right to forcibly implement 'regime change' in another sovereign country.

Is this not colonization in another form? The colonialists also came with noble motives. They wanted to bring civilization and modernity to us savages, did they not? They wanted us to abandon our barbarous practices and pagan religions for Western ideas and Christianity and they were convinced that they were right in what they were trying to do. History judged them otherwise. History might judge this war otherwise too. It might not see it as the great battle between good and evil, right and wrong, that George Bush would have us believe it is. So the quicker he abandons his high moral stand the more credible he could end up sounding.

War is very rarely about morality. From the more immediate perspective of the present moment, though, what is frightening is the prospect that this second Gulf War will serve not to destroy militant Islam but to swell its ranks with new terrorists.

For us in India this is a terrifying prospect. In the past decade more than 30,000 people have lost their lives to Islamic terrorism in Kashmir alone and the attacks on Parliament and the Akshardham temple prove that the violence spreads. So, we should have been firmly on America's side in its war against terrorism if the lines had been more clear and the objectives more evident.

Meanwhile, we need to be grateful that the prime minister has not rushed off to Baghdad to hug Saddam and that the Congress party has not sent some emissary off to Moscow to stop the ground war, as happened last time. Let us hope that this is a sign that whatever stand the government takes on the war and its aftermath will be decided on the basis of India's interests and not some ideological mumbo-jumbo.

A CASE FOR THIRD PARTY MEDIATION IN KASHMIR

13 April 2003

For most of the course of this second Gulf War our politicians behaved with unusual circumspection and restraint. But this unusual behaviour was too good to last.

So even as Iraqis danced in the streets of Baghdad and celebrated the toppling of Saddam Hussein's statue last week, the Rajya Sabha unanimously 'deplored' the 'US-led war on Iraq'. Not good timing and irrelevant since the war is virtually over and it is time to discuss what this means for India as there will be consequences in the region that affect us directly.

Our members of Parliament were not totally unaware of this and it should comfort you to know that even as they discussed the resolution deploring the Iraq war there were those who remembered Kashmir. What should we do, they asked the external affairs minister, if Kashmir was next, as Colin Powell indicated when he said recently that after Iraq the US state department would concentrate on Kashmir.

Yashwant Sinha was nonchalant. 'We should ignore these sort of statements from Washington,' he said. 'We should not be too sensitive about these things. We are a confident nation, let them say what they are saying.' He added that India would never accept third party mediation in Kashmir and reiterated his view that if absence of democracy, sponsoring terrorism and building weapons of mass destruction were the criteria then Pakistan deserved a pre-emptive attack more than any other country.

This will be music to the ears of local hawks, fanatics and general loonies but will do nothing to bring peace to the Indian subcontinent. A commodity we desperately need if we are to ever provide our people with simple, basic necessities like water, electricity and a decent standard of living. It amused me to see Indian television commentators gasp breathlessly about living conditions in Iraq without noticing that they were pretty similar to living conditions in vast swathes of India.

Living conditions in rural Pakistan are not much better and one of the reasons why Akhand Bharat continues to rot in misery and degradation is because of our obsession with that political problem we call Kashmir. In fifty years of trying to solve it bilaterally we have failed so totally that distances between our respective viewpoints are further apart now than they were thirty years ago.

Also, thanks mainly to our own stupid mistakes, Kashmir is no longer a domestic problem that can be solved by a change of government. It is an international problem and the world sees it that way even if our own ministry of external affairs refuses to do so in the desperate hope that by some miracle, some mysterious metamorphosis, it will return one day to being the domestic problem it once was.

Well, it is the humble view of this humble columnist that Kashmir is never going to return to being a simple, domestic problem that can be solved by sending some new interlocutor there or by holding fair elections. It's too late for that now and the quicker we realize this the better.

It is also my humble view that India has a very good case when it comes to Kashmir and we are foolish to fear a peace process with an international mediator like, for example, Bill Clinton. When I have tried bringing up the subject in the exalted corridors of the ministry of external affairs I have met stubborn resistance on the grounds that whenever we have allowed foreigners to intervene as in Tashkent all those years ago we have been betrayed.

Surely, there is no chance of that if we are the confident country we like to think we are, but beneath our confidence lie our old fears of the East India Company.

The world has changed more than anyone could have imagined before September 11. Whether you approve of the war on Iraq or not there is a global war on terrorism and that terrorism is currently Islamic in nature. The epicentre, as our former external affairs minister Jaswant Singh memorably pointed out, is Pakistan.

By declaring himself an American ally after September 11, General Musharraf may have deflected the attack but must know that the Americans are not idiots and are aware of the support that terrorist groups in Kashmir continue to receive from Pakistan.

They are also aware that many of the Islamic fundamentalists who fled Afghanistan are currently ensconced in safe houses in Pakistani cities as are the killers who cross into Kashmir to kill innocent women and children.

When the American Taliban, John Walker Lindh, was interrogated he talked, according to a recent issue of the *New Yorker* magazine, of being trained in a training camp in the Himalayas, 'across the road from a Pakistani military base, and Pakistani intelligence officers regularly came to give instruction.' He was trained by the Hizbul Mujahideen to fight in the Kashmir jehad before he shifted base to Afghanistan.

So, if we ever allow international mediation and a peace process, Pakistan starts off with a blotted, blood-stained copybook. Another point in our favour is that it is by no means clear that the average Kashmiri wants to exchange Indian citizenship for Pakistani. There are other changes in the international climate that favour a solution in Kashmir that does not involve redrawing India's boundaries.

In a world that wants to see less Islamic fundamentalist countries rather than more, how much support is there going to be for yet another country being carved out of India in the name of Islam? We should welcome international mediation and if Parliament is so keen on discussing foreign affairs these days this could be the next subject of debate. It would be a lot more useful than debating whether to deplore or condemn a war that is almost over.

DRINKS ON THE HOUSE

10 August 2003

Sixty-one per cent of Indians do without clean drinking water, forty-four per cent have no electricity, ninety-one per cent do without telephones and thirty-eight per cent live in one-room hovels. And what do our elected representatives become passionate about? Coca-Cola.

So disturbed were they by reports of high pesticide levels in Coke and Pepsi that in typical, self-serving mode these drinks have been officially banned from Parliament as of last week. But, 'we the people' continue to have access to them just as we continue to have access to unclean contaminated drinking water. Does that make sense? Is it possible any more to take Parliament seriously?

It has been evident for some time that our elected representatives waste time on trivial pursuits instead of debating real issues. But this monsoon session has been such an endlessly silly season that it sets a new record. First, there was all that fuss about the prime minister's alleged flip-flop over Ayodhya.

Was there really a flip-flop? Does it matter anyway? That stopped only when the pesticide story broke and by the time you read this, there might be some other irrelevant thing that concentrates the energies (and vocal chords) of our MPs.

You would think with so much trivia causing so much uproar in Parliament that India was a wondrously wealthy country instead of one in which half the population lives without such basic necessities as clean drinking water and housing.

The sad part is that there is so much work to be done. With terrorism one of the terrible new realities we confront daily, you would think that at least one session of Parliament could have been spent debating why the police still functions under a penal code written in 1860 by Lord Macaulay.

We expect our security forces to deal with the horrors of new twenty-first century violence under laws so antiquated as to be a joke. When was the last time there was a walkout—or a debate—on this subject?

While on the subject of our ancient penal code it is worth mentioning yet again that the judiciary is another subject that needs an entire session devoted to it. Our justice system will remain ineffectual and unreliable as long as the backlog in our courts remains so overwhelming that it will take more than three hundred years to clear. The results of having a stagnant justice system are painfully evident. Last week saw a verdict in the Bali bombing case, which happened barely a year ago, but victims of the Mumbai bomb blasts continue ten years later to wait for justice to be done. We need urgent reform but Parliament has so far not found time to discuss the subject.

Just as it has not found time to discuss ways to modernize governance and elections. Speaking of which, another special session should be devoted to the vice-president's suggestion that we have fixed terms for governments and legislatures and a fixed date on which elections are held to Parliament and the state legislatures.

Whatever qualms Chief Election Commissioner J.M. Lyngdoh may have about the possibilities of 'cheating like hell', we need to discuss the subject because as things stand our politicians spend far too much time on politics and elections and far too little on governance and real issues. So, Bharat Mata's achievements are inclined to be largely negative—the largest number of illiterate, malnourished, destitute people in the world. These are problems that can only be solved by governance and by Parliament concentrating on the things that matter.

The way the government spends our money should matter

but when was the last time you heard a serious debate on the Finance Bill? The result? Idiotic ideas get included like the finance minister's attempt in this budget to tax expatriates living in India. Who is going to come to India or bring their money to India if they are going to be at the mercy of our income tax department? There are not that many foreigners who want to come here anyway so it's not as if vast amounts of money are going to be collected in taxes. But certainly it opens vast new possibilities for corrupt income tax officials.

Patently foolish ideas get passed because there is rarely a real debate on the budget. Had there been a real debate, would we not by now have some idea why successive governments have spent so little on primary education, healthcare and sanitation? And why we continue to spend so much on armies of officials and needless government machinery that far from delivering governance actually blocks it.

Having said this, it would be wrong if I did not admit that part of the blame lies with the media. Our newspapers and TV channels give trivia more importance than it deserves. There was a time when newspapers sent only their most experienced reporters to cover Parliament but with the arrival of private TV channels this has changed. Nearly every news channel I watch usually has some breathless young creature reporting from the Lok Sabha and the result is reportage that is almost as banal as the issues that excite our MPs.

So on the pesticides in Coke and Pepsi we had the sort of wall-to-wall detailed reportage that only a major political crisis deserves. Perhaps the media needs to grow up as well, perhaps we get the MPs we deserve.

One way or another, it's becoming increasingly difficult to take Parliament seriously.

THE MAYA BEHIND THE RAIDS

12 October 2003

What I like about Mayawati is her honesty. That may sound like a funny thing to say but I am being completely serious. I like her for never having made any attempt to hide her millions. Remember the diamonds she wore on her birthday party? Did she make any effort to hide them or that someone who could afford to spend lakhs on diamonds must have at least a few crores stashed away? And last week when the CBI (Central Bureau of Investigation) raided her, instead of apologizing for her enormous wealth or even trying to explain it, she went on national television to denounce all politicians.

How many politicians do you know who would dare admit publicly that everyone is naked in this hamam? Since she thought the prime minister was behind the raids, she singled his son-in-law out for personal attack. 'What was he in the past and what has he become today? Why doesn't the CBI take action against him?' Well, the answer to that one is easy. He has not tried, so far, to turn the Taj Mahal into a condominium. If he were trying as she was to do this or if, for instance, it caught his fancy to build a penthouse in the Qutab Minar he would certainly attract attention. But Mayawati has a point that should not be ignored if behind the public humiliation of a major political figure lies a serious effort to clean up public life.

If there is seriousness of purpose CBI raids are not the solution as they tend to be selective and too often politically motivated. Having personally witnessed the horror of an income tax raid may I add that raids of any kind are intrusive, barbaric and usually pointless because the only transfer of wealth that occurs is from the raided victim to the raiding officials. Then, if they do not share the booty someone in the income tax department snitches to the CBI and they conduct more selective raids and we read—like we did last week about Mayawati—that such and such official had crores in his many bank accounts and crores of rupees worth of properties that were beyond his means to buy. Then the matter goes to court and everyone lives happily ever after because the case goes on forever.

What happened to the cases against Narasimha Rao and Sukh Ram and what of the elusive Mr Quattrocchi? It would be worth asking if any of the CBI's cases against major public figures have ever resulted in convictions. So instead of wasting time and taxpayers' money on raids, and cases that will probably come to naught the CBI needs to spend its energy and our resources on doing more important things like finding out how much money the Mayawati government spent on public projects that remain unfinished.

While her personal wealth, as exposed by the CBI, amounts to less than Rs. 10 crore, the public money she may have squandered on unfinished projects could go into thousands of crores. If the CBI is serious about its attempts to clean up public life then it must extend its search beyond Uttar Pradesh and Mayawati.

It could discover that nearly every chief minister in the country is similarly guilty of squandering public money on dams that remain unfinished, canals that remain unlined, power plants that remain forever half-built and a thousand other utilities that nobody seems under pressure to complete. According to some estimates, there could be more than Rs. 30,000 crore locked up in unfinished projects. This is a criminal waste of public money but nobody is held to account because no sooner does a government change than it comes up with its own list of grandiose projects as it is from these that big money can be made. This is why so many big public works get announced whenever elections draw near.

If we are serious about cleaning up public life we must make chief ministers and ministers accountable for the money they waste. We also need to reduce their discretionary powers by introducing enough transparency for it to never be possible in future for a shopping mall to start being built near the Taj Mahal without even the prime minister's office getting a whiff of what was happening.

Transparency would serve a dual purpose as it would serve also to reduce the need for constant interference from the Central Vigilance Commission (CVC) and the CAG (Comptroller and Auditor General). As things stand, the fear of these two watchdogs often becomes the reason why big public projects take so long to move forward. With the best of intentions they have become more obstacles than watchdogs because officials prefer not to take a decision rather than take one that would come under CVC or CAG scrutiny. So in the case of one irrigation project, which is ready to bring water to an area of perpetual drought, the only thing blocking the way is an unlined canal which remains unlined because the state government cannot hand out a contract without going through a full tendering process.

What puzzles me is why the CVC and CAG spend so much time going through government accounts with a fine toothcomb and so little on holding governments to account for much more obvious waste of public money. All they need to do is order governments to submit an annual list of public projects and ask how many remain incomplete and why and we could have the beginning of real transparency. CBI raids on public figures like Mayawati create excitement and headlines but in the end all they amount to are fun and games. It is serious change that never seems to happen.

OUR TERROR, NOW THEIRS TOO

28 December 2003

The end of the year seems always to bring either war or peace between India and Pakistan. This time it is a hesitant, nervous sort of peace that appears to be breaking out. We talk of cross-border trains and flights instead of terrorism and hear words like 'bold and flexible' from the general across the border. Even hints that other words like 'plebiscite' should be dropped from the terms of dialogue. That was before the two attempts on Pervez Musharraf's life, which who knows could have been inspired by his ostensible (dare we hope) desire to end his Kashmir jehad. Clearly, even his own government was worried or his prime minister would not have had to deny his remarks almost instantly. How ironic that the general who has used terrorism as his main instrument of foreign policy on the subcontinent should now be in danger of becoming its victim.

India knows better than anyone the price of that foreign policy. Think of that other December, two years ago, when the attack on Parliament brought us to the verge of war and that Christmas just before the millennium changed when IC-814 was hijacked from Kathmandu to force the Indian government to release two of the most vicious terrorists known to mankind, Omar Sheikh and Masood Azhar. Sheikh went on to plan the inhuman, unforgivable murder of Daniel Pearl and Maulana Masood continues to spread the wickedest kind of terrorist Islam through organizations like Jaish-e-Mohammed. When Jaish and Lashkar get onto American state department terrorist lists they reincarnate themselves under new names that are announced on the internet. This would not happen if the general was serious about abandoning terrorism as an instrument of foreign policy and it would not happen if the United States understood that its policy on the Indian subcontinent needs to go beyond backing one shaky general. It needs to acknowledge that the said shaky general is fully aware that the Pakistan government, specifically the Pakistani army, is deeply involved with the promotion of terrorism and militant Islam.

It needs also to acknowledge that Abdul Qadeer Khan, the father of the Pakistani bomb, would not have been able to sell nuclear technology to Iran and North Korea without the sanction of the Pakistani government. But, Pakistani foreign ministry spokesman Masood Khan says, 'There are indications that certain individuals might have been motivated by personal ambition or greed,' and Musharraf continues to be counted a trustworthy ally.

We in India understand him better and understand better the nature of the Pakistani state but our problem is that it is becoming increasingly hard to tell where the state ends and what V.S. Naipaul called 'a criminal enterprise' begins. Where does the ISI (Inter-Services Intelligence) fit in? And, if Musharraf is the modern Islamic leader he would like the world to believe he is, then why were Sheikh and Masood not immediately jailed when they crossed from Afghanistan into Pakistan? Why is there such a strong nexus between the ISI and terrorist groups in Kashmir that it is sometimes difficult to distinguish between them?

The foreign policy experts who sit in South Block believe that democratic Pakistani leaders are better. Whenever Pakistan has a democratically elected prime minister in charge, they like to say, peace becomes more possible. Really? It happens that when Benazir Bhutto was in Delhi a couple of weeks ago, I came upon a clip of one of the speeches she made on Kashmir as prime minister. In a voice hysterical with hatred, she shouted abuse against India and urged her Islamic brethren to rally to the defence of Kashmir because the Kashmiris were Muslims 'like us' and like us descendants of those who fought in the Prophet's armies. It was a more racist speech than any Musharraf has made. Let us please remember that it was Benazir's Kashmir policy that caused such terrible violence in the valley, that more than 300,000 Kashmiri Hindus fled for their lives in the worst instance of ethnic cleansing the subcontinent has seen.

That these displaced people continue to live in makeshift camps in Jammu is disgraceful, and it is even more disgraceful that no human rights group in India takes up their cause. All those of you who have been so passionate in defence of Muslim victims in Gujarat, where are you when it comes to Kashmiri pandits? And Benazir, do you remember your speeches? Do you remember that it was under your government that the so-called Kashmir jehad began?

So if democracy in Pakistan will not bring peace either—what is the solution? Personally, I believe we need to make a distinction between the Pakistani people and the Pakistani state. We need to encourage ordinary Pakistanis to come to India because it is only when they come here that they realize that India is very different than the lies and propaganda they have been bred on. We need to encourage trade, even if we take unilateral measures, because it is another way of getting ordinary Pakistanis to travel to India and build up a vested interest in peace.

Peace with Pakistan was the first item on Atal Bihari Vajpayee's foreign policy agenda when he became prime minister. It remains there right at the top as he enters the last year of his government. It may not be possible to achieve in a year but what is possible is to lay the foundations for it by making it easier for Pakistani civil society to discover that it has much more in common with India than it has with its own military government. Unilaterally making the visa system easier would be a good first step.

BLAME CONGRESS FOR RISE OF HINDUTVA

25 April 2004

At about the exact moment the Congress party declared Sajjan Kumar its candidate in Outer Delhi, Sonia Gandhi declared that India would not survive without secularism. 'An India that is not secular will simply not survive. Secularism is our destiny,' she said loftily to a Delhi newspaper. She explained what she understood secularism to mean. 'Secularism in the sense of equal respect for all religions, in the sense of combating communalism of all kinds, in the sense of giving minorities safety, security and equality of opportunity.'

Secularism does not mean any of these things. It is a European word that relates to separating the church from the state and in that sense irrelevant in India since no Shankaracharya ever ruled or had an army, as the Vatican once did, but why quibble, let us take our Italian prime ministerial aspirant up on her own definition. Combating communalism of all kinds. Giving minorities safety and security. So how should we understand the rehabilitation of a man who was seen leading mobs that dragged innocent Sikhs out of their homes and burned them alive in front of their wives and children? Did the widows of the murdered men misunderstand his purpose for being present at the scene of the massacres? Was he really there only to 'combat communalism' and provide them security?

Can we please cut the crap? Can we acknowledge once and for all that it is because of the Congress party's twisted secularism that we saw the rise of Hindutva. You cannot justify the killing of Sikhs in Delhi and condemn what happened in Gujarat, you cannot condemn Narendra Modi if Sajjan Kumar is your man in Delhi. But Congress gets away with occupying the secular high ground because fifty years of propaganda have brainwashed most of our thinkers, academics and hacks into believing a lot of nonsense about communalism and secularism. On the ground this translates into many becoming partisans of Congress for supposedly secular reasons. So if you run into a secular hack you get one version of what this election is about and if you run into someone as communal as your columnist you get another version.

My communal viewpoint is that religion has played no role in this election and that if Muslims continue to fear the BJP they do so because they are the real victims of Congress secularism. This kind of secularism allowed the growth of an unattractive, unpleasant Islamism that was allowed to discriminate against women and promote hysterical religiosity of the kind I personally encountered at the Dar-ul-Uloom seminary in Deoband last week. This institution, incidentally, is where the Taliban got their inspiration from and has been allowed in our supposedly secular country to create a little patch of Saudi Arabia.

Don't believe me? Read on. I was in UP trying to get a sense of how Muslims would be voting and thought that the Dar-ul-Uloom would be a good place to visit. So, from Muzaffarabad I turned off the highway on to an impossibly bumpy broken ribbon of a road that took me to Deoband. A ramshackle town even by UP standards but get to the gates of the Dar-ul-Uloom and you see quite a different Deoband. Fine Islamic buildings, whitewashed and shining, and a mosque whose minarets rise so high they seem to touch the sky. Sadly for me my problems began at the gates. The chowkidar said I could not enter till he was instructed to let me in. So I waited and waited while he talked to someone on the telephone. When this conversation went on a little too long I took the phone myself and requested permission to meet the chief maulana of the seminary.

The person at the other end said he had no authority to allow me in and I must go back to Delhi and make an appointment. I assumed he was some lowly employee and asked to speak to someone higher up, at which point the chowkidar said, 'How dare you talk like that? You were speaking to the chief maulana.'

A passing student, in Islamic skull cap and beard, intervened here and told me that in any case the maulana would not see me because I was not in purdah. Unveiled women were banned, he said, and because this struck me as curious I did my own unpermitted tour of the Dar-ul-Uloom premises and saw only two women, both covered in black from nose to toes.

I also met students who told me they could speak only of the Quran and the hadith because that was all they were allowed to learn about at the seminary. Some were openly hostile and told me I had no right to talk to them and that my presence was offensive.

Tell me, please, oh fighters for secularism, how you would describe the Dar-ul-Uloom? Secular or communal? Tell me if the rigid, fundamentalist version of Islam that the students are being taught at this seminary is capable of producing anything but Taliban? Tell me how an institution that seals off not just the modern world but also women can deal with the issues that concern the international community ever since Osama bin Laden became the face of Islam?

Sonia Gandhi, for her part, needs to tell us if she believes it was wrong for the Congress party to encourage and defend the worst kind of minority communalism (Muslim Personal Law) in the hope of keeping the Muslim vote. She needs to recognize that the Hindutva lunatics with their *trishuls* and saffron bandanas are the direct result of Congress secularism.

WHY SIGNORA SONIA AS PM?

17 May 2004

You can count on the fingers of one hand columnists who have openly objected to India having an Italian prime minister. As one of them, may I make it clear that in my view the ascent of Sonia Gandhi is a matter of deep shame and not a tribute to our supposedly vibrant democracy. I am not the only Indian who feels this way. Those who believe that the question of her foreign origin is now a thing of the past are quite wrong. The questions will only now begin.

There have been attempts by some of my more sycophantic colleagues in the media to portray Sonia's victory as a massive mandate for the return of the Gandhi dynasty but the truth is that if Congress had not won those twenty-nine seats in Andhra Pradesh it would have not got many more seats than the 114 it got last time.

Indian newspapers are replete with hacks of 'secular' persuasion who have not stopped gushing about Rahul Gandhi's 'youthful sincerity' and Priyanka Vadra's 'gorgeous looks' and concluded that it was this dazzling combination that made the difference. One of our financial newspapers passed this off as political analysis. 'The gerontocracy did not stand a chance. Charisma works absolutely. Mix it with a liberal dose of Rahul Gandhi's youthful sincerity and Priyanka Gandhi's gorgeous fetching looks, and the choice was unambiguous.'

Alas, if you analyse the results in less obsequious mode you discover that the Gandhi children did not make much difference even in the four Hindi-belt states. Congress won nine seats in Uttar Pradesh, one in Bihar, four in Madhya Pradesh and four in Rajasthan. Not exactly a massive mandate, but you would not know it from reading editorials in the Indian newspapers last week. Kowtowing, a timeless feature of the Gandhi durbar, has returned with such sickening speed that a leading Hindi newspaper had a front page editorial saying Rahul Gandhi was the sort of person India needs in public life because he is 'polite'.

Personally, I have no objection to Mr Gandhi and Mrs Vadra. They are Indian and as entitled as any other son or daughter of a politician to inherit daddy's *jagir*. My problem is that as an Indian it offends me to be represented by an Italian woman. It arouses in me the worst kind of chauvinistic nationalism and there are millions of Indians who feel as I do and who believe that if Sonia had even minimum respect (forget love) for India she would not have humiliated us by putting herself forward as prime minister. With even former prime ministers like Chandra Shekhar and V.P. Singh assuring her that she is completely acceptable and surrounded as she is by a durbar, she may not notice in the euphoria of becoming the prime minister of the world's largest democracy that the reaction to her victory has mostly been shock. Even people who voted Congress now say they would not have if they had known she had half a chance of becoming the prime minister.

More dangerous still are the murmurings that you already hear from Hindutva nationalists. On the day of the election results, I happened to travel on a flight with a leading light of the Vishwa Hindu Parishad. When I asked how he reacted to India having an Italian prime minister he spat out the word democracy as if it was poison. 'This is what comes when you give illiterate, desperately poor people the vote.' And, from Pravin Togadia we already hear that it is because the BJP moved away from its Hindu nationalism that it was defeated.

Those who think having Sonia as prime minister is insurance against the sort of ugly nationalism that men like Togadia represent need to think again. When the backlash begins, and it will not take long, you will see violent nationalism of a kind we have never seen before. Already, people have started talking about how embarrassed they are that when talks are next held with Pakistan (somehow Pakistan gets mentioned more than China) India will be represented by Signora Sonia. She can wear saris, tie puja threads on her wrist and plaster her forehead with *tika* but as India's prime minister what will stand out more than ever before is her foreignness.

Her presence in Indian politics is dangerously divisive. During the campaign, wherever I travelled I asked people if they objected to having an Italian prime minister and everywhere there was a division on this issue so inflammatory that the question would invariably provoke a shouting match. Those who said it was Indian tradition for a *bahu* to consider her husband's country her own usually lost to those who shouted them down for being sycophants and traitors.

The divisions will grow not lessen with every decision she makes as prime minister because whatever she does will be questioned. Doubts about her motives and loyalties will become particularly unpleasant if there is a crisis like the Kargil war. Even peacetime decisions will be doubted and a wiser woman less surrounded by courtiers would have seen this a long time ago.

But, here she is now. India's first Italian prime minister exalted to this position by Marxists who have always put India after internationalism. Please remember that they found the Indian freedom movement distasteful because it was not in keeping with the internationalism of their revolution. They have a truly international prime minister now but should remember—as should the others who support her government—that history is unlikely to forgive them for humiliating India in this way. As for me, for the first time in my life I feel ashamed to be Indian.

AFTER POLL SLAUGHTER, SUICIDE BY BJP

20 June 2004

Having snatched defeat from the jaws of victory the BJP now appears to be in the mood for suicide. There can be no other explanation for why on a daily basis these days the party's senior leaders are going public with their assorted and extraordinarily idiotic reasons for the defeat.

Why can they not save their theories for when the party meets for one of those *chintan baithaks* in Mumbai next week? Especially since every new statement seems designed to convince Indian voters that they did the right thing by throwing the NDA (National Democratic Alliance) government out of power. I mean, for goodness sake, what were we doing with a government in which the prime minister and the deputy prime minister cannot agree on something as important as why their party lost an election that even their enemies did not think it was possible for them to lose.

The disagreement is not of degrees either but total. The former deputy prime minister fired the first shot. In those measured tones that always make you mistakenly think he has something profound to say, he pronounced before TV cameras that it was his considered view that the 'India Shining' campaign was the reason for the party's defeat.

Then it was our former prime minister's turn to give us his opinion, en passant, as he took off for summer holiday with family. The Gujarat violence had gone against them, he said, and this statement caused more damage to the party because it unleashed a fanatics feeding frenzy. How dare he, shrieked the VHP angrily. Tell him to shut up at once, said the RSS with cold fury. And from the Bajrang Dal, ever the most virulent, came a tirade of abuse against 'old men' needing to retire from politics.

The last thing we people need is a reminder that the old fools who control the Sangh Parivar are still in a position to control the BJP. If the BJP is to survive its humiliating defeat it is going to need to stay as far away from the Parivar as possible or suicide is certain.

You and I may know that the RSS consists mainly of a collection of toothless old fanatics who have not had a new idea since the 1920s, but to many Indians (Hindus included), the RSS remains a sinister organization that thrives on spreading hatred and poison.

If the BJP wants to remain a force it needs to continue the process so ably initiated by Atal Bihari Vajpayee of loosening its links with the RSS. The RSS for its part needs to stick to cultural matters like, for instance, modernizing its khaki knickers.

Since most of its cadres are spindly old men with spindly old legs they must opt for longer shorts or something. Perhaps, Gudda or Tarun or Ritu could help. What about saffron harem pants with one of those t-shirts of Vishnu or Shiva? Might attract young people.

The BJP, meanwhile, has more important things to think about. There needs to be serious analysis of the defeat. If there is, it will not take long for it to become clear that it had nothing to do with India Shining or Gujarat. Certainly, the violence in Gujarat was abhorrent and certainly it convinced Muslim voters to stay away from the BJP but they were convinced of this long before Narendra Modi came along.

The RSS and its ugly sister organizations have over the years played such a stellar role in this department that you will not find a Muslim wandering about in khaki knickers. So it was not the loss of the Muslim vote that caused the defeat.

Ditching the DMK in Tamil Nadu and teaming up with

Jayalalitha helped as did unwisely abandoning Mayawati in Uttar Pradesh. So, she was a bit 'tainted' and tried to turn the Taj into a shopping mall but is Jayalalitha not a little 'tainted' too?

This time the BJP needed her particularly badly because of that ghastly incident in Lucknow which made it clear that India could not be 'shining' if women in UP's capital city could stampede each other to death to get a free sari.

Serious analysis will reveal other reasons. As Shekhar Gupta pointed out to me during a recent afternoon of political punditry, sixty-five per cent of sitting MPs lost their seats. The BJP had more MPs in the last Lok Sabha and so ended up losing more seats.

Further analysis of this phenomenon will reveal that on account of an almost total collapse of local government the MP gets blamed for everything from dirty drains to a new airport not being built. If the MP is foolish enough to try pointing out that municipal problems and major infrastructure do not fall under him he gets dumped for being a shirker.

There is then much that the BJP's senior leaders should be mulling over, many things that need urgent change, but in the view of your humble columnist, the biggest mistake the party could make would be to revive Hindutva and rebuild its links with the RSS. The old men in it belong to yesterday even if they switch from khaki knickers to saffron harem pants.

WHY WE NEED TO INDIANIZE OUR EDUCATION SYSTEM

25 July 2004

Let me begin by saying that I think Arjun Singh's campaign to detoxify Indian education is more dangerous than Murli Manohar Joshi's pathetic attempts to Indianize it. Let me add that Indian education must be Indianized. It is pathetic that so many years after the Raj ended, our best schools remain colonial in their curriculum, their medium of instruction and their attitudes. The result is that they churn out Indians so deracinated they know nothing of their own country and culture and so much about Western culture that they spend their lives aspiring to become Xerox Westerners.

As a product of the haute end of Indian education let me tell you my own story as an illustration of the point I am making. Till I went to school the only language I spoke was Punjabi but by the time I left school the only language I spoke was English and I remember being slightly embarrassed by my relatives who persisted in speaking only Punjabi. Ditto my compatriots. Whether they were Maharashtrian, Gujarati, Tamil or Bengali they spoke, thought, dreamed in English and were more than a little embarrassed if they happened to have parents who only spoke a native tongue.

After leaving school it took strenuous efforts on my part to learn how to read and write in Hindi but most of my compatriots still speak only English and their children speak only English and are even more deracinated than we were.

Most never read an Indian book unless it is written in English, most would not be able to identify a single Indian poet and what they know about Indian civilization would fit on a postage stamp.

If this disdain for India were confined to the so-called English speaking elite it would not be a problem. Our tragedy is that the problem is much more serious in lesser private schools and state schools because the children that they send out into the world are usually unable to communicate properly in either English or any Indian language. They may be functionally literate at the end of their school days but by no stretch of the imagination could they be described as educated and, extraordinarily, they tend to be as deracinated as their more privileged brethren. The reason for this is that there is nothing in their curriculum that teaches them about India or its civilization. The odd slogan of the *Mera Bharat Mahaan* kind might creep in but beyond the slogans there is nothing because 'secular' education meant not mentioning the word Hindu except pejoratively.

The problem is that Indian civilization, at the height of its glory, was Hindu civilization. It was that Hindu civilization that gave the world the numerals that came to be wrongly described as Arabic and it was that civilization from which came the Vedas and the Upanishads and religious traditions that are sophisticated and tolerant when compared with those that have come out of the Middle East. But to say that in India is to risk being labelled anti-Muslim and to praise India's ancient civilization is to risk being called a 'saffronite' so let me quote the American author Henry Thoreau instead.

'Whenever I have read any part of the Vedas, I have felt that some unearthly and unknown light illuminated me. In the great teaching of the Vedas, there is no touch of sectarianism. It is of all ages, climes and nationalities and is the royal road for the attainment of the Great Knowledge. When I read it, I feel that I am under the spangled heavens of a summer night.'

When will we allow Indian children to learn about a heritage that is theirs by right? When will we get ourselves an education minister educated enough to understand that learning is something that goes beyond the tired cliches of secularism and communalism?

The answer to both those questions is: not for a while. The 'secular' philosophy of the new government as articulated by Shri Arjun Singh is that anything to do with the word Hindu is necessarily 'saffron', necessarily 'toxic'.

When our new HRD minister conducts his 'weeding out' he might find that there is very little to be done because Murli Manohar Joshi spent more time making a noise than making changes in history textbooks. In all the pamphlets that have been published about the 'saffronization' he supposedly instilled you will find more rhetoric and hysteria than examples of changed historical texts.

If Arjun Singh was wiser, better educated, he would have understood that instead of wasting his time on stupidities of this kind he could make a much greater contribution by finding out what can be done to Indianize our education. Indian children need to learn not just about ancient India but about modern India as well. They need to read poetry written by Indian poets and literature written by Indian writers in native tongues. That all our most celebrated modern writers are those who write in English speaks for itself.

When I last wrote about education in this column, the former Maharaja of Dhrangadhra sent me a copy of a speech made by Lord Curzon at Rajkot's Rajkumar College on 5 November 1900. In his speech, Curzon urges the Indian princes he is addressing to be Indian. 'Though educated in a Western curriculum, they should still remain Indians, true to their own beliefs, their own traditions, and their own people.' How sad that a British viceroy could see a hundred years ago what our HRD ministers cannot see even now.

TO WIN THE WAR, FIRST IDENTIFY THE ENEMY

12 September 2004

Last night I lit a candle in my window in memory of the children who died in Beslan. It was a rite of mourning that millions of people all over the world were urged to participate in and participate though I did, I believe the time for candlelight vigils and symbolic gestures is gone. It is time to face the horrible truth, in the week of the third anniversary of 9/11, that Islamic terrorists are winning the global war against terrorism because the countries who are its victims have not had the courage to look evil in the face and call it evil or dared to admit that we are up against malevolent forces the like of which the world has not seen since Nazi Germany.

They cannot be fought unless the world comes together to fight with a common strategy and without double standards. You cannot condemn acts of terrorism in New York and Madrid but justify them in Beslan because you think the Chechens have a political cause. You cannot justify them in New Delhi and Mumbai because you think the Kashmiris have a political cause.

For me if there was anything more sickening than the horror of those tiny hostages in the Beslan school, it was the justification of the horror by liberal commentators across the world including in our own country. Ah, the poor Chechens! Who can blame them for being angry when Russia treats them so badly, when it rigs elections and refuses to negotiate? I do not support President Putin's policy in Chechnya but believe he was right to respond by asking why Osama bin Laden was not being invited to the White House for talks. Bin Laden also has a political cause. He believes the West is the enemy of Islam and must be defeated, and that America as the most successful symbol of Western civilization must be destroyed first. He holds the Americans directly responsible for what is happening in Palestine, and that is as political a cause as Chechnya or Kashmir.

After Beslan the least we can do is not desecrate the memory of those children who died such terrible deaths by talking about political causes in the same breath as terrorism. No political cause justifies taking small children hostage and starving and torturing them for two days before shooting them in the back when they tried to flee. No political cause justifies asking a mother to choose between her two tiny children before allowing her to leave with only one. What kind of men and women are capable of such unspeakable horror? What kind of religion permits the killing of small children and since the religion of the killers in the Beslan school was Islam why are the mullahs silent? So vocal as they always are when it comes to the West's so-called atrocities against Muslim countries why is it we hear no word of condemnation against the monsters who took hundreds of children hostage in Beslan and forced them to survive without a drop of water for two days? Where are Islam's moderate voices?

Something terrible has happened to Islam in the past twenty years and nobody needs to admit this more than the Muslims themselves. From being a religion that had learned to live in relative peace with the world it has become a religion that seems unable to live in peace with anybody. Not with us infidels and not even with the Christians and Jews they once considered brothers for being *ahl-e-kitab*, people of the Book. The isolation of Islam, its current pariah status, comes from the radicalization that the religion has undergone since Ayatullah Khomeini brought about his Islamic revolution in Iran in the late 1970s.

In India, you see this radicalized new Islam everywhere. I have seen villages in Rajasthan where every woman is veiled, every child in a madarsa and every man bearded and dressed in a way that distinguishes him from his Hindu brethren. Twenty years ago it would have been hard to tell a Rajasthani Hindu from a Muslim. In Tamil Nadu and Maharashtra I now meet Muslims who try to speak Urdu and wear salwar-kameez in some mistaken belief that Islam comes from northern India and in Deoband recently in the famed Dar-ul-Uloom, I discovered a world so blinkered and medieval it was hard to believe I was not in Saudi Arabia.

When we speak of Saudi Arabia we come close to the crux of why the free world appears to be losing the war against terrorism. Saudi Arabia as everyone knows is largely responsible for this radicalized new Islam. It is Saudi money that builds mosques and madarsas in Indian villages and it is Saudi money that funds Islamic militancy in the rest of the world. The men who hijacked the planes on 9/11 were nearly all from Saudi Arabia and yet Saudi Arabia remains a valued ally of the United States in the war on terrorism. It is not possible to win a war in which you cannot identify the enemy.

If the Americans are guilty of not doing this because of a vested interest called oil our own political leaders are guilty of not identifying the enemy because of a vested interest called the Muslim vote bank. Our governments fund madarsas and other Islamic institutions without admitting that even the most moderate teach the difference between believers and infidels. When a child grows up believing in this difference it does not take long for radical preachers to convince him that in the holy war that good Muslims are now fighting to 'save Islam' killing infidel children is alright. If anything proves that we need our own jehad against radical Islam Beslan does.

JUNGLE LAW: LAND FOR VOTES?

15 May 2005

It is the view of this column that the proposal to give adivasis land rights in what remains of our forests is probably the most dangerous act of any Indian government since 1947. There have been bad policies in the past that have caused the poisoning of our rivers, the pollution of the air we breathe and the denudation of the Himalayas but if this latest bill goes through it is likely to be more destructive than anything we have seen so far. I say this after having listened at length to the government's side of the story.

What is their side of their story? That the Scheduled Tribes (Recognition of Forest Rights) Draft Bill is an attempt to rectify the historical wrong done to the adivasis (the word means original inhabitant) by taking away their lands and not allowing them to preserve their traditional way of life. The government's side is that 'not an inch' of forest will be destroyed by giving each adivasi family the right to own 2.5 hectares of forest land because they are occupying the land already. The government's side of the story is that since adivasis already cultivate the land they occupy, all that is happening is that they will now have land records establishing their ownership of the land. Should they not have the same rights as you and I? This is about equal rights, said the official in the prime minister's office who explained the government's view.

When I asked if the land could be sold, he said that tribals were not allowed to sell their land to non-tribals and that once they owned it they would become part of the process of conserving the forest. Had I not heard of 'sacred groves' that existed in tribal lore, had I not noticed that the forests have been destroyed by corrupt officials and timber mafias and not by the poor old adivasis. 'Nothing is going to happen that will further damage the forests,' he said. 'Those who are saying that fifty million hectares of forest land will be given to the tribals are lying. They will have to eat crow when the bill is posted on the web which the prime minister has asked us to do.'

Look out for it please and write to the prime minister damning his bill because the government's side of the story leaves me totally unconvinced. If the adivasis are already living happily in the forest why do they need ownership rights? Why should politicians and officials who have not bothered to bring even minimal development to the adivasis suddenly become so caring that they are prepared to allow them to own forest land? If the motive is not political it is hard to think what it is.

Now let me tell you why I believe the proposed law is dangerous and must be fought. To start with, it is a retrograde measure. When countries develop and prosper people usually move off the land into urban centres, so in supposedly booming twenty-first century India why are we making it attractive for adivasis to continue living their miserable, subsistence existence? The answer is that government policies have failed so totally to improve their lives that giving them 2.5 hectares of land for 'livelihood' uses is a sop of the most cynical kind.

The solution is not to encourage them to continue living as noble savages but to offer them the benefits of modern education and ideas so that they can at least have a choice between the twenty-first century and the stone age. At the moment they do not. The officials that draft laws in Delhi have little experience of living conditions in the adivasi villages or their traditional way of life or they would have known that it is a lifestyle in which babies die routinely of starvation, in which whole families live in tiny mud huts in conditions that should be considered unfit for human habitation, in which the women are lucky to have one piece of cloth to cover their bodies. It is not a standard of living that is worth preserving and if the tribals were asked whether they would like to trade it for a comfortable apartment with running water, electricity and colour television they would trade in a minute.

In giving them the 2.5 hectare sop this government, possibly under pressure from its loony Left friends, is taking the risk of destroying the twenty per cent forest cover we have managed to hang on to after the depredations of corrupt officials and poachers. It is a risk we cannot allow this government to take. If it wants to help the adivasis lead better lives then it must build the schools, hospitals, roads and electricity that would help them transform their lives and if after that they want to continue living their traditional way of life then of course they can.

Meanwhile, we need to ensure that nobody is trying to create a political vote bank in the name of helping the adivasis. Please let us remember that in the name of protecting the rights of Muslims and harijans, certain political parties kept them poor and illiterate for decades and certain other political parties now play that same game. Maybe I am a cynic—it's hard not to be if you cover Indian politics—but the way I see it is that the adivasis have become the latest plaything of the Congress party which needs to build a political base but has given up on the possibility of Muslims and harijans coming back to be the building blocks. Every political party has the right to build a political base but it cannot do it by doing permanent damage to India.

BLAST FROM THE PAST: BIG PLANS, LITTLE ACTION

26 June 2005

There is something about this government's grandiose schemes to guarantee employment and improve rural India that bring back, at least for me, memories of central planning and Nehruvian socialism. These memories are nearly all depressing because of the second-rate, shoddy quality that nearly everything had. Roads were bad, telephones looked like relics, airports and airlines had the dead hand of government stamped all over them, electricity and water came and went at their own sweet will, shops stocked goods of such shoddy quality that the average Indian was crazy about all things foreign and everything was always in short supply. People waited decades for a telephone connection, and as for domestic gas almost the only people who got it were those who knew an MP. The reason for this sad state of affairs was central planning and big government, and something about the Sonia-Manmohan approach to governance has a worrying reek of the past.

Last week, one of the financial newspapers reported that the ambitious Bharat Nirman programme was going to cost another Rs. 70,000 crore. The five-year plan to build rural infrastructure already has a bill of Rs. 174,000 crore and the plan is to spend this money on irrigation, roads, water, electricity, telecommunications and housing. Sounds wonderful? Only on paper.

This is the sort of grandiose plan that used to routinely

emanate from the Planning Commission in those bad old days of yore. Highly educated mandarins would gather together and pore over maps of rural India planning which villages would get electricity, which ones would be blessed with roads, which deserved a bit of drinking water and which ones needed telephones. Allocations would be made and then the Planning Commission with its permanent air of smug satisfaction would go on to devise yet another grandiose scheme.

If all these schemes had worked, India would have been a developed country long ago. Sadly they never did work then and they are unlikely to work now because rural India's ground realities have proved stubbornly resistant to central planning.

Remember that it was the Planning Commission itself that gloomily concluded under the last government that the best way to help those living below the poverty line was to send each family a cheque of Rs. 8000 instead of spending thousands of crores on more grandiose planning.

The reason why central planning does not work is because the central planners are usually oblivious to the degree to which the delivery system has collapsed, become corrupt or antiquated. So the money that Delhi so generously pours into rural development nearly always ends up in the wrong hands. In states like Uttar Pradesh and Bihar where rural poverty is at its grimmest, I have seen villages in which money meant for dalit housing has been distributed by upper caste sarpanches to brahmin families. I have seen illiterate dalits being forced to put their thumb impressions on papers giving them loans that they never get and as for BPL (Below Poverty Line) cards they get used as prizes to be distributed only to those BPL families who cooperate and do not protest.

If Bharat Nirman is not going to be as easy to implement as its very grand name implies, then the Employment Guarantee Scheme is going to be even harder to implement. Who is going to ensure that the 'employment' goes to those who are really below the poverty line? The short answer is nobody.

If our Planning Commission mandarins travelled incognito

into the wilds of rural India they would discover that the officials they entrust with their grand schemes rarely bother to step out of district headquarters. The collector usually lives in the largest house in the best part of town and when he travels in his car with its flashing red light it is generally not to some backward village. It is usually to meet the chief minister or some minister in order to pay court and ensure that he is not transferred to some punishment post.

Instead of more grandiose schemes, what we need from the Planning Commission—if we need a Planning Commission—is a comprehensive plan of radical administrative reform. Why do we continue to have collectors? It was a colonial post that should have been abolished when the British left.

It is not just one post but the entire administrative structure that needs change, but all that has changed so far is that government offices in rural India have become more and more impressive and forbidding so that nobody living below the poverty line would dare enter their portals.

This is not to say that change is not coming to the villages. There is change but it is coming not through grandiose government schemes but through the arrival of modern technology—mobile phones, television—and here credit can be given to government, the ubiquitous STD-ISD booths, these are the instruments through which the twenty-first century is slowly beginning to arrive in the villages. Sadly, those who live below the poverty line continue to be deprived of these things and something must be done to help them rise out of their poverty but massive schemes are not going to solve the problem unless radical administrative reform comes first. Meanwhile, just as we need to think seriously about abolishing collectors we need to think seriously about abolishing the Planning Commission. It is an institution that is a relic of central planning times and as long as it exists governments of 'socialist' bent will continue to be tempted to plan centrally.

HOW ABOUT A FATWA AGAINST THE IMRANA FATWA

3 July 2005

For once I find myself in total agreement with the Communist Party of India (Marxist). So much in agreement that I am tempted at least for this week to forgive them for following economic policies that appear to be designed to keep as many Indians in poverty for as long as possible. Understandable, if you think about it, because if poverty disappears where will Marxists get their political constituency from.

My generous mood arises from CPM general secretary Prakash Karat's strong reaction against the outrageous fatwa from the mullahs of Deoband in the Imrana rape case. 'If the personal law of any community infringes upon the genuine rights of women, the law of the land should take centre stage and impart justice,' he said. Three cheers for you Mr Karat and a big fat kick in the butt to Mulayam Singh Yadav for supporting the fatwa that in effect punishes Imrana for daring to admit that she was raped by her father-in-law.

On account of this admission, according to the wise men of the Dar-ul-Uloom, she has become *haram* for her husband and can no longer live with him but the husband must continue to support his five children. This is the same seminary, please remember, whose interpretation of Islam inspired the Taliban so their contempt for women should not surprise us. What should surprise and sicken us is the support the fatwa got from the chief minister of Uttar Pradesh.

Correct me if I am wrong but did he not take an oath to uphold the Constitution of India? Is it not his responsibility to uphold the law of the land or has Uttar Pradesh officially become an Islamic republic? I was recently on a flight with Mulayam Singh's right-hand man Amar Singh, who complained about the English press always being 'anti-Mulayam'. Personally I am amazed that he even dares to expect support for a man who is so ready to put political considerations above law, justice and simple decency.

Can we hope that Sonia Gandhi or the prime minister will have the courage to come forward and announce publicly that no religious seminary has the right to interfere with the law? They would be doing India a huge service if they went a step further and added that panchayats that believe they have the right to dispense justice will be instantly disbanded and fresh elections ordered.

Trust me when I tell you that this is all it will take for our semi-literate, socially backward sarpanches to stop dispensing barbarism in the name of justice. They routinely order women to be gang-raped, they routinely murder young lovers who have broken caste taboos, they routinely strip women naked and parade them through villages. And the only reason why they continue to do this is because they get away with it.

The police does not interfere just as it does not interfere in cases of sati and child marriage because most chief ministers take the view that these are social problems that will end when society improves. My view is that they will disappear tomorrow if the police is ordered to implement the laws of India. Whenever the police turns up in a village and takes preventive action the panchayat always backs down. I have personally seen this happen not once but many times. The minute the police does its job or the courts intervene and declare panchayat actions illegal the peasants who sit in these village councils quietly let the matter drop.

Last year in Haryana's Assanda village there was the case of Rampal and Sonia. The couple fell in love and got married and romantic love is something that Indian society disapproves of, it is not in our 'culture', so Raathi caste leaders called a special gathering and pronounced that Rampal would have to declare his pregnant wife his sister because she was of the same caste. Sonia decided she was not going to accept any such decision—especially as she did not believe she was of the same sub-caste as her husband—and when she protested she was beaten up by one of the caste crusaders who had gathered at her doorstep. These upholders of Indian social standards then pulled her dupatta off to humiliate her and threw her out of the village.

Luckily she came from a family that was modern enough to take the matter to court. Luckily for her Haryana is not far from Delhi and it was easy for TV networks to cover the story in detail so the Raathi caste panchayat quickly realized that it was time for discretion not valour and backed down. But, when I met Sonia she was in Rohtak hospital in danger of losing her baby because of the actions of her barbarian caste leaders.

The fatwa of the mullahs of Deoband is barbaric. And, it has no place in India. Rajiv Gandhi may have, misguidedly inspired by the same political considerations as Mulayam, given Muslims the right to their own personal law, but this does not apply in criminal cases. Islamic punishments have not been allowed. Rape is a crime under Indian law and rapists must be punished according to the law. If we had an elected prime minister (instead of an appointed one), and if he was a real leader he would have had the mullahs who pronounced this fatwa arrested and tried.

Alas, we do not have many real leaders around but can we at least hope that the mullahs are warned that obstruction of justice is a criminal offence and they would do well to withdraw their shameful fatwa.

RED STAR OVER INDIRA'S INDIA

25 September 2005

The only surprising thing about the latest revelations from Vasili Mitrokhin's archives is that we should be surprised at all. It's understandable that the Congress and the two Communist parties should try desperately to deny that they were in the pay of the KGB but for those of us who lived in the time of Indira's India the revelations come as no surprise. For the benefit of those of you who were not around in those long ago days when Stalin and Mao were still heroes and only the Left was right, allow me to share some reminiscences.

My career as a journalist in Delhi began a month before Indira Gandhi declared her Emergency and imposed press censorship. From a personal point of view, nothing better could have happened because it made me realize immediately that political journalism was where the action was even if it stood temporarily suspended by our Soviet-style Press Information Bureau. Everything was Soviet style in those days—from the cumbersome procedures we followed at our airports to the shoddy technology and consumer goods we made do with, as I was to discover when I visited the Soviet Union in its period of 'glasnost'.

To return, though, to the Emergency and censorship, what intrigued me was the number of journalists who were not upset by either censorship or the Emergency. They defended both on the grounds that Indira Gandhi was being opposed by rightists who were all creatures of the CIA. Never having been of ideological bent I found this analysis puzzling and even more puzzling that nearly every journalist I knew was Marxist, semi-Marxist or at least socialist. Their worldview was clear not just in the articles they wrote but in the conversations we had in those endless months of Emergency when journalism was just a joke.

On foreign policy they opposed everything American and supported everything Soviet. So Palestine and not Israel in the Middle East and Algeria not Morocco in the Western Sahara and naturally the Soviet Union and not the United States in the Cold War. These were the unwritten rules under which we worked.

If you took hospitality and freebies from the Soviet government or countries in the Soviet bloc it was fine but if you went to Washington you were instantly suspect. Now that we know from Mitrokhin's archives that at least ten major Indian newspapers, and many journalists, were on the KGB payroll it is for me a little like pieces of a puzzle falling into place.

On the political front as well. It's now clear that it was no coincidence that every politician and aide in Indira Gandhi's inner circle was Marxist or ex-Marxist. It makes sense that the Communist Party of India (CPI) supported her even when she became a dictator. In those bad old days the CPI was open about its closeness to the Soviet Union and the CPI(M) made no secret of its proximity to China. So why should we be surprised that *The Mitrokhin Archive II* reveals that the KGB funneled 10.6 million roubles into Indira's India. Christopher Andrew, the Cambridge University professor who has written *The Mitrokhin Archive II*, talks of 'suitcases' filled with money being sent to Congress party leaders and may I remind you that in those days at election time ordinary people in the bazaars of Delhi used to talk of 'suitcases' of money coming from the Soviet Union.

The book also talks of how the Soviets went out of their way to convince Indira Gandhi that the CIA was bent on destabilizing India. That they more than succeeded can be seen from Mrs Gandhi's paranoia about the 'foreign hand'. The Russians were foreign too but everyone knew that they were not the 'foreign hand'.

How quickly we have forgotten that until economic liberalization began in the nineties India was so totally in the Soviet bloc that nearly all our defence purchases were from the Soviets and nearly all our exports were to that country.

My faith in Mitrokhin's revelations comes not just from having cut my teeth in political journalism in the times when India was Indira but also because I happen to be reading the new biography of Mao Tse-Tung, *Mao: The Unknown Story* by Jung Chang and Jon Halliday. They reveal that the Soviet Union poured millions into China to help Mao create the Chinese Communist Party.

They back this allegation with facts and figures and even if you do not read the book please at least look at the pictures where you will find evidence of these payments in the form of a receipt signed by Mao for US$ 300,000 (worth about US$ 4 million in 2005) received from the Russians on 28 April 1938.

I am only halfway through the book and already convinced that if it had not been for Soviet money and arms there would have been no communist revolution in China and that poor country would not have been forced to suffer decades under Mao's monstrous rule. In his twenty-seven-year rule more than seventy million Chinese died on account of his policies but he remains a hero to our homegrown commies.

Funny how they get away with it. Funny how the Congress party manages to brazen its way out of the Mitrokhin revelations by simply stating that they are 'vague' and 'sensationalist'. Vasili Mitrokhin has made serious charges, the Congress party and its Marxist friends must come up with serious answers.

GOOD RIDDANCE, BUT ROAD ALL UPHILL AHEAD

27 November 2005

Last week provided us with a rare moment of hope in politics—the defeat of Mr and Mrs Laloo Yadav. No defeat was more deserved, more reassuring for those of us who remain recklessly optimistic about the future of Bharat Mata despite the abysmal quality of our political class. But even abysmal has degrees of abysmal-ness and if we looked for its nadir we would find nestled at rock-bottom Mr and Mrs Laloo. They are perfect examples of the kind of politicians India does not need. Their politics reminds us of a time when divisions of caste and creed were so much our only reality that even our better political leaders were forced to use these divisions to get elected. The Congress party still does as we saw from the list printed in this newspaper of their Bihar candidates. Not only were they identified by caste but by their sub-castes. Shame, shame, Soniaji. But, whatever the flaws of the Congress party, and there are many, they pale when compared with those of Laloo and Rabri.

Bihar was far from perfect in pre-Laloo times but there were norms of public behaviour, aspirations to ethical standards, accountability at least in some measure. The most obvious example of how things changed under Laloo is Rabri herself. It would have been impossible in earlier times for a chief minister charged with corruption to hand his job over to his semi-literate wife and openly rule on her behalf. Impossible for him to continue winning elections despite this outrage but Laloo manipulated caste and 'commnal phorces' better than anyone else and managed to keep Muslims and other backward castes fooled a lot longer than they should have been fooled.

So what now? Bihar's institutions of governance, law and order, education, healthcare and development are in such a state of ruin that Nitish Kumar is going to need more than good intentions to bring about change. The only glimmer of hope in the ruined state he inherits is that he can initiate radical changes more easily than if the structures had been intact.

He has mentioned law and order as his first priority and it should be if you keep in mind that nearly half the state's districts are in the grip of Naxalite terrorist groups. If he is serious about changing this terrible state of affairs he would need first to tour the police stations in these districts and personally examine the conditions in which policemen work. Once he has finished this tour he needs to appoint somebody like K.P.S. Gill to create a special anti-terrorist force to deal with the problem. If he thinks that the average Bihari policeman can do the job he will be making the same mistake Laloo Yadav did for fifteen years as Leftist and casteist terrorism grew and grew.

He has talked of infrastructure development as one of his top priorities and again it should be but the task before him is monumental. Other states have bad roads but as someone who travels much in the wilds of rural India may I say that I have seen no other state in which there is almost not a single proper road. Laloo Yadav did not build any because he believed that roads were only for rich people. It is a convenient Leftist lie because the truth is that what you really achieve by not building roads is forcing wretchedly poor people to continue living in wretched poverty.

On the electricity front the situation is so bad that enterprising jobless young men in Bihar's smaller towns make a living out of alternative power supply. They buy generators and use them to supply bazaars and other consumers with electricity. Again, Nitish Kumar needs to innovate and seriously start decentralizing generation and distribution so that towns and villages find ways of generating their own supplies. Without privatization it is hard to think how the state can meet the demand.

If he manages to deal with basic infrastructure problems it would still only be a beginning. He would then have to get down to building schools—Bihar's literacy rates are half the national average—and building the state's non-existent public health services. Then there are the jobs that Biharis need so desperately that they travel to distant states in search of the most menial work.

So, although the defeat of Mr and Mrs Laloo is a moment of hope it is only a small hope. Because if Nitish Kumar's government fails to make radical changes we will be back to questions of caste and creed and if that happens Bihar has had it. The rest of India will find it increasingly hard to wait for it to catch up.

INDIA'S KILLING FIELDS

8 January 2006

The first politician I met in 2006 was Sharad Pawar. It was a fortuitous meeting because this column now has a new cause. Agriculture. Boring? Yes, it is but listen to what our agriculture minister had to say and you might not find it so boring after all.

I confess that even I, a farmer's daughter, have found it hard to be passionately interested in agriculture. There is such a dreary quality about the sound of the word and it invokes all those depressing images of the 'real' India...flies, open drains, squalid hovels and the stench of cow dung and human waste. The sad thing is that it does not have to be this way and as long as it is this way we can forget about India becoming an economic superpower or even just a developed country. This affects us all and if for no reason than that we need to show more interest in agriculture.

It has become fashionable these days for politicians to talk of agricultural reform. Only last week the prime minister called for a second green revolution. Addressing the 93rd Indian Science Congress in Hyderabad, he said: 'Let me focus attention on the three challenges that science and technology must address to promote development. First, we need to increase agricultural productivity... We need to increase factor productivity (whatever that means) and develop technologies that conserve energy and water...and finally, to generate employment in rural areas.'

Ad nauseam we hear talk about the need for agricultural reform without anyone explaining what this means exactly and ever since I became a political columnist I have heard politicians hold forth on increasing the 'purchasing power' of farmers. But it was only when I met Mr Pawar on New Year's Day in a Maharashtrian village by the sea did I understand why we seem to get nowhere when it comes to improving the lot of those who depend on agriculture for their livelihood and their way of life—seventy per cent of India's population, and that is a problem in itself because, as Mr Pawar pointed out that New Year morning, the rich countries are those in which less than five per cent of people depend on agriculture.

I think the conversation began by my asking him what sort of reform was needed in agriculture and what he was doing about it as agriculture minister. He gave me the sort of withering look experts reserve for non-experts who ask cheeky questions and then held forth. He is passionate about agriculture.

Did I know that under the government of Shri Atal Bihari Vajpayee investment in agriculture came down to less than one per cent of GDP? Did I know that investment in irrigation was less than a half per cent of GDP? I admitted that I did not and tried not to look too shocked by the statistics he was giving me. Is it any wonder that Vajpayee's government was booted out?

We cannot begin to talk of agricultural reform until we recognize that the first requirement is a massive increase in investment, especially in irrigation. Since the Sonia-Manmohan coalition took power there has been a slight increase in agricultural investment and Mr Pawar is trying to ease the controls that prevent our farmers from selling their produce where they like but the change will make only marginal difference.

To expect farmers to produce crops without irrigation is like expecting Infosys to produce software without computers. Yet we spend less than half per cent of GDP on irrigation. What is wrong with our planners and policymakers?

Most countries with vast populations dependent on agriculture for a living make sure that what farmers produce does not go waste. Brazil processes more than eighty per cent of its farm produce, and we how do we compare? India processes less than twenty per cent of farm produce and there are no signs yet that the government has understood the importance of food processing.

Our political leaders fight angry battles in the forums of the world about agricultural subsidies in developed Western countries. How will our poor farmers compete, they cry, and those hypocritical lefties are forever railing against the duplicitous ways of the WTO (World Trade Organization) but nobody bothers to notice that without cold storages, refrigerated trucks, good roads and other infrastructure our farmers cannot get their produce to our own airports leave alone to international markets.

Our farmers are so mired in desperate poverty that in supposedly rich states like Punjab and Maharashtra we hear of farmers routinely killing themselves as the only escape. Nothing will change until we see massive investment in agriculture. Governments need to find the money to do this and one way would be privatization but here the Marxists come in the way because for them a few thousand workers are more important than hundreds of thousands of peasants. What sense does that make?

ON THIS ONE, FOLLOW THE GENERAL

29 January 2006

It has been a while since you read about Kashmir in this space. This is because I have been too bored with the subject to write about it. Terrorism has wiped out the rage people like me once felt about human rights violations in the Kashmir valley and if truth be told I have not had much faith in the peace process. It has seemed to me to be in a rut caused by India's belief that peace can only come after terrorism ends and Pakistan's belief that a peace process has to come before its 'freedom fighters' stop killing innocent people.

If I write about Kashmir this week it is because I met General Pervez Musharraf a few moments before I sat down to write this piece and got a chance to ask him the question I have wanted to ask for a long time. What does he mean by the 'out-of-the-box' solution that he bangs on about?

I met the general in Davos at a press meet attended mostly by Western journalists who were not as interested in Kashmir as in the Hamas victory in Palestine, Iran's nuclear ambitions and the American air strike that may or may not have killed Osama's chief lieutenant, Ayman al-Zawahiri. We were a small group but these issues so dominated that it was only at the very end that I was able to slip in my question. What is the solution in Kashmir?

I am going to give you the general's answer as fully as I remember it because I believe he is saying something new and important and if we trust him enough to go forward we might finally have a solution to a problem on which we have already wasted too much time, money and innocent lives. The general is neither liked nor trusted by Indians (including this one) because we blame him for the Kargil war. But people and times change and by one of history's ironies it could fall to the villain of Kargil to deliver peace on the subcontinent.

This is the solution he believes would be acceptable to Indians, Pakistanis and Kashmiris. First, we identify which regions constitute Kashmir, then we demilitarize and set up a group of experts to work out a model of self-governance. This would not mean autonomy or independence or redrawing the borders, said the general, but 'self-governance' for Kashmir with security guaranteed by a managing council that would consist of Indians, Pakistanis and Kashmiris. 'It will mean a stepping back for everyone. India will have to step back from its position that Kashmir is an internal matter. Kashmir will have to step back from its demand for independence and Pakistan will have to step back from its demand for a plebiscite. We are ready to do this but will not do it unilaterally.'

Let me explain why the general's offer is worth considering. Thanks to the political ineptitude and mistaken policies of successive governments in Delhi, Kashmir is no longer a domestic problem. Not only did these governments succeed in reviving the historical problem in Kashmir, they succeeded in giving it a new modern dimension. The insistence on a military solution to a political problem caused more than 50,000 people to be killed in the past fifteen years. It is time the bloodshed stopped.

Our Kashmir policy now is to wait it out and hope that miraculously one day peace and Bollywood filmmakers will return to the valley. It is not going to happen and it harms India's future and the hopes and aspirations of yet another generation of Indians if we allow the problem to last for a few more decades. There is also always the possibility of another war if General Musharraf is replaced by a more hardline jehadi military dictator. It is a dreadful possibility now that both countries have nuclear weapons.

What sense does it make to fight over people who hate us anyway? A self-governed Kashmir only threatens India if it turns into the next Islamic republic of Al Qaeda. If the joint security council that General Musharraf is suggesting includes Indians then we can ensure that this does not happen.

This is a good moment to get General Musharraf to put his money where his mouth is because he appears to have discovered that 'the economy is the basis of any nation's progress'. He reminded us that when he seized power in 1999 Pakistan was considered a failed state. Today its economy is growing at 8.4 per cent a year which makes it the second fastest growing country in Asia after China.

Pakistan seems to have discovered that it can either grow and prosper economically or spend its resources on the Kashmir jehad. Let us seize the moment—who knows how long it will last?

THE LAND OF ELECTED CRIMINALS

26 February 2006

When I heard this week that the man charged with killing Jessica Lall had been acquitted by a Delhi court, it made me sick. Not just because it is evil when murder goes unpunished but because this particular murder offers us a mirror of modern India and the reflection that we see is repugnant. It shows us a country in which you can get away with the most horrible crimes if you know the right people and if your pockets are deep enough.

Manu Sharma and his eight accomplices were acquitted for want of evidence. There were more than a hundred people at the restaurant in which he allegedly fired a shot at Jessica because she said the bar was closed and she could not give him a whisky. As the spoilt son of a politician he was unused to taking no for an answer. Three people said they saw him fire the shot, many others saw him run from the restaurant after he shot Jessica, some chased him and others informed the police that his car was still parked outside the Tamarind Court. The police were so unconcerned that the car was left standing long enough for his friends to come and drive it away.

In those first days after the night of the shooting (30 April 1999), nobody had any doubt about the identity of the killer. He must have been aware of his own guilt or why would he have gone into hiding but our criminal justice system moves with arthritic slowness. And as the years went by powerful influences came into play and crucial witnesses discovered that they had seen nothing. One even denied he had been at the restaurant that night and by October 2004, Manu Sharma made bail. It should have been a sign of things to come but as someone with a naive belief that good always triumphs over evil I remained convinced that justice would be done. I was wrong.

We live in a country in which you can and will get away with murder if your daddy is a powerful politician. One of Sharma's accomplices, Vikas Yadav, also the son of a powerful politician, was so sure of this he was charged with killing his sister's boyfriend three years later. When they found Nitish Katara's body it was so badly burned his mother found it hard to recognize him. She has fought a long lonely battle for justice but she may as well give up. Vikas Yadav will probably be a free man soon just like his friend Manu Sharma and before we know it they could both be sitting in Parliament.

That is where the sickness begins. We have allowed our politicians to believe that they and their ghastly children are above the law and because of this the worst kind of scum have come to see the Lok Sabha as the ultimate absolution. You can be a murderer, smuggler, rapist or thief but if you can find some rotten borough that will elect you—or that you can intimidate into electing you—then the cases against you become irrelevant. The very policemen who have been hunting you are forced to give you protection.

Scum produces scum and the progeny of our elected representatives are usually worse than their parents. They grow up at taxpayers' expense to a life of unimaginable luxury and privilege. Mostly, this renders them unemployable so daddyji is obliged to either set them up in business of some kind or offer them his seat in Parliament. Our political parties do not have any system that would bring into their ranks good people so party bosses find it convenient to accommodate these sons and heirs. Some turn out all right, most are ghastly. And, of course, those of criminal bent are more welcome than others because they have no scruples about using any means possible to get elected.

It is a terrible business and proud as we are of our democracy this is one aspect we should be ashamed of. But if this is the land of elected criminals it is also the land of karma and I believe Jessica's killer will pay according to those mystic laws of cause and effect that are the foundation of Indian philosophy. Those who helped him walk free will pay too and for my part I wish only that in this life not the next one they suffer even half the pain Jessica's family has suffered. May they live with the terrible unrelenting grief of seeing someone they love die for no reason at all.

BUSH AND THE BUSHMEN

5 March 2006

Even as someone who has difficulties with many aspects of President Bush's policies I found myself on his side last week when the streets of Delhi and Mumbai filled up with the people who oppose him. They were a motley crew. A melange of Marxists, Islamists and well-meaning loonies of activist genre and if they should ever be in a position to create the world of their dreams it would be a totalitarian, Marxist, Islamist theocracy. How scary is that? Give me the US of A any old time. It is a free society like our own and we would like to keep India the way it is. This is not what the protesters against President Bush want.

While President Bush and our prime minister were signing the 'historic' nuclear agreement, anti-American protesters used television to enunciate their worldview. It is a simple one. Everything American is bad and George Bush is the 'biggest terrorist' and mass murderer. Pretty rich coming from Marxists and Islamists. On the mass murder front how does Bush compare with Chairman Mao and Comrade Stalin? Osama bin Laden? Saddam Hussein?

Arundhati Roy, who has the unique ability to approach politics through fiction instead of reality made the amazing claim that she and the Marxists she marched with represented popular Indian sentiment while Bush was speaking only 'to a few caged rich people in the Delhi zoo'. She uses words so imaginatively she must go back to writing fiction. Politics and economics are not her forte or she would not have blamed the American president for India's 'new economic order', which in her view is 'garroting' the poor. It has escaped her notice that in the days before India opted for a new economic order there were twice as many garroted poor people than there are today.

At least she was not carrying a placard supporting Ayatullah Khomeini. This was left to more Islamist protesters who appeared to have confused the American president with the Danish cartoonist. The largely Muslim rally in Mumbai came together mainly to express rage against the cartoons apparently without noticing that they have nothing to do with Bush. TV anchors had a hard time explaining the situation to their viewers.

The protesters had a cartoon quality and a serious one. The serious aspect is that Indian Muslims who have so far stayed away from the Islamist war against the West now seem to be joining in. When was the last time Muslims came out in such large numbers to protest against anything? In doing so they showed that they were at odds with the general sentiment of the country. Recent polls indicate that most Indians feel no resentment against the United States and many think of it as the promised land. The largest number of foreign students in American universities come from India and in the global war against terrorism most Indians think we are on the same side as America.

As for Dr Manmohan Singh's Marxist supporters, it is time that he asked them whether they seriously believe that Iran going nuclear is good for India but India coming to an agreement with the United States on nuclear energy is bad. What kind of twisted logic is that? Not only was last week's nuclear agreement very much in India's interest but, as the prime minister said, 'we made history'. More is the shame that he could not persuade his commie friends to be more dignified in their protests. It is extremely bad behaviour to call a visiting head of state a 'mass murderer' and considering how well our prime minister was received in Washington last July it is unfortunate that leftist bullying tactics prevented President Bush from addressing Parliament.

How would we have reacted if our prime minister was invited to a foreign capital city and called a 'mass murderer' on account of the situation in the Kashmir valley? How would we have reacted if our prime minister was prevented from addressing the American Congress because a small group of badly behaved Congressmen shouted and screamed? If the protests in the streets were bad the behaviour of Marxist MPs at the doorstep of Parliament was disgusting and should not have been permitted. 'He is the biggest killer of humanity,' shrieked one CPI(M) MP, 'and we will not let him spread his tentacles on our soil.'

Let us not pretend either that this is acceptable democratic protest, because it is not. In all the years I have covered politics in Delhi I have never seen a foreign head of state called a 'mass murderer', and in the bad old days when Moscow dictated India's 'non-aligned' foreign policy there were many visiting dictators for whom that term could have been appropriately used.

HIGH GROUND VS GROUND REALITY

2 April 2006

First let me say that I was deeply impressed by Sonia Gandhi's speech in Rae Bareli last week. Her Hindi is much better now, which helps, but what really blew me away was her mimicry of Indira Gandhi on the warpath. It was an Oscar-winning performance.

Overwhelmed TV anchors went into raptures over her resemblance to the late Mrs Gandhi, hinting that this was an indication that her daughter-in-law had now grown into the role, thereby becoming a formidable political force. As for me I loved the melodrama as much as the mimicry. The way she called herself the *dushman number one* of those who opposed the Congress and the brilliant job she did of transforming herself from villain to victim, manipulator to martyr. Indira Gandhi failed so totally to do this over the Allahabad High Court judgement that found her guilty of electoral malpractices that she had to declare an Emergency to save her skin.

Her daughter-in-law needed no such drastic measures. One speech did the trick. By the time I listened to it for the tenth time, switching news channels, I had quite forgotten that she resigned as an MP because of the danger of imminent disqualification. So mesmerized was I by the sycophantic tributes she inspired among her followers in Rae Bareli (someone compared her to Mother Teresa) I almost forgot how she had tried to manipulate the government to bring an ordinance to prevent herself from being disqualified. Really, it is no wonder that all she needed to do to defeat our tallest political leaders was learn a bit of Hindi.

She is a consummate politician and deserves her remarkable rise to political power and glory. Never in the history of democratic India has anyone been able to place themselves in such a unique position of power without responsibility. Who wants to be the prime minister when you can be Sonia Gandhi? This is why I was a little disappointed that she should take such a vicious stance against her opponents. The Rae Bareli speech was a declaration of war against those who targeted 'Indiraji, Rajivji and now me'. If there is a hailstorm they blame Sonia Gandhi, she said angrily, whatever happens I get blamed. But I am not the one to retreat, I am no loser, she added, with a hint of menace in her voice.

That is for sure, but Madame appears not to have grasped that the reason why she gets targeted by our desperately seeking Opposition parties is because despite her 'sacrifice' of the prime minister's job everyone knows that she is India's super prime minister. You would have to be blind and deaf or deluded in Delhi's corridors of power not to know this. And Sonia's own website says it best. Plastered against the colours of the Indian flag you see two large pictures of Madame and in a fold of her sari there is a tiny icon-sized picture of our prime minister with instructions to 'Click here for Dr Manmohan Singh'. What more is there to say?

Sonia's complaint that the Nehru-Gandhi family gets targeted is unfair. Our Opposition leaders may be political pygmies but it has not escaped their notice that the dynasty is much bigger than the Congress party and that at the present moment Sonia is the party. Instead of declaring war on the Opposition by appointing herself their *dushman number one*, what Madameji needs to worry about is whether the Gandhi name will be enough to win back Uttar Pradesh and Bihar. Unless this becomes a possibility, Rahul Gandhi's future remains on hold. The Congress has more sycophants and family retainers than normal politicians but they are very good at blaming the Gandhis when defeat comes their way. Already if you listen carefully you hear murmurs of discontent. She can attract crowds in Rae Bareli, they say, but can she win back Uttar Pradesh and Bihar?

The problem with reducing a political party to an adjunct of a family is that it stops being a force by itself and relies on the family name to win elections. This is the condition of the Congress today. It depends on Sonia Gandhi as it once did on Indira Gandhi. The late Mrs Gandhi liked it this way and proved more than once that it was not she who needed the party but the party that needed her. This is the test Sonia Gandhi faces. She is going to need to be more than a mimic of Mrs Gandhi.

EYES CLOSED, THIS ARJUN SHOOTS FROM THE HIP

9 April 2006

Right. Enough is enough. It's time for Arjun Singh to go before he implements his insane plan to reserve half the seats in institutions of higher education for the lower castes. If the prime minister and Sonia Gandhi are not prepared to sack the minister of human resource development for his irresponsible populism, it is time for us to appeal to the Supreme Court to stop the minister before he takes one more step towards destroying our institutes of higher learning at a time when India needs thousands more.

The pressure on universities and technical colleges is so severe that it is easier for Indian students to find placement in colleges abroad than here. The largest number of foreign students in American universities last year came from India. Arjun Singh's mad plan will ensure that our best students are forced out of the country to be replaced by those whose only qualification for college will be caste. The result will not be better educated lower caste Indians, the result will be the replacement of excellence by mediocrity in institutions like the IITs and IIMs.

As these are virtually our only colleges that compare with the best in the world we must fight Arjun Singh. He cannot be allowed to go ahead with reserving twenty-seven per cent of seats in central universities, IITs and IIMs for the OBCs. When this is added to the twenty-two per cent of seats already reserved for SCs and STs you almost end up needing reserved seats for those who qualify on merit and not caste.

This column once described Murli Manohar Joshi as a lousy HRD minister. I take it back. He achieved little in terms of giving us better quality education because he spent most of his time meddling in trivia and raising secularist hackles, but when compared to Arjun Singh he shines like a beacon of enlightenment. Arjun Singh is the worst HRD minister this country has ever had. He began his tenure with a drive to 'detoxify' textbooks that he claimed had been made toxic by BJP rule. The truth is that nobody has come up with more than a handful of examples of this so-called toxicity. If Joshi had been a good HRD minister he would have decolonized Indian education by introducing subjects that made Indian children understand their own culture and civilization better. Instead, he meddled with history books and made silly changes. There was no need for 'detoxification' but Arjun Singh needed to distract attention from his inability to give us an education policy that would improve the abysmal quality of our state schools.

Had he been able to do this we would not have needed reservations in higher education because low caste children would be able to compete on merit with those from the upper castes. As things stand, dalit and adivasi children start off handicapped by the dreadful quality of the state schools they are forced to go to since they cannot afford private education.

This is not true for OBC children. If Arjun Singh bothered to spend time in rural India, he would notice that the OBCs are far from being backward when it comes to education. Upper castes like the Rajputs are more backward because of their reluctance to educate their daughters. He might also notice that the OBCs have almost taken over the powers that the upper castes once exercised. To think Yadavs and Jats are underprivileged is almost too ludicrous to discuss.

But Arjun Singh is not motivated by concern for the educational backwardness of our so-called backward castes. He makes his reservations with a cynical eye on luring the backward castes of Uttar Pradesh and Bihar. This can be the only explanation for why he has been able to go ahead with announcing his second set of reserved sops.

Earlier he gave us the 104th constitutional amendment to ensure reservations for the educationally backward in private schools and colleges. It will serve mainly to enhance the powers of petty officials and provide them with a new channel of corruption. But clearly the move had the support of the prime minister and his boss or it would not have happened.

The most dangerous aspect of what Arjun Singh is doing is its irreversibility. No political party can afford to oppose a move that ostensibly seeks the upliftment of the poor and the low of caste. If there is to be a fight it will have to be fought by you and I. It's time to stand up and be counted, time to demand an end to all caste-based reservations. Let us demand good schools instead now that education is a fundamental right.

BEYOND DYNASTY, TOWARD COMPETENCE

22 April 2007

It surprises me that it continues to surprise us every time one of our elected representatives is caught indulging in criminal activity. We reacted with the usual shock and horror last week when the honourable MP from Dahod, Gujarat, Babubhai Katara of the BJP, was caught trafficking in humans. He tried smuggling a woman out on his wife's passport and after he was arrested the police discovered that he was a serial offender and probably part of a trafficking syndicate.

So? What's the big deal? Human trafficking is a white-collar crime, compared to murder, rape, armed robbery and kidnapping, and we know that across our unfortunate land we are increasingly being forced to elect people who have been charged with one or the other of these crimes.

Often the choice that Indian voters face is between two criminals, and in such situations, they usually select the better criminal, as a wise old man once explained to me in D.P. Yadav's constituency. During an earlier election in Uttar Pradesh, I stopped at a teashop in Yadav's constituency to ask why people voted for a man infamous for his illicit activities and the old man said, 'Because the man who is standing against him is also a criminal, so we may as well vote for a stronger and better criminal.'

Yadav's son Vikas went on to be implicated in the murders of Jessica Lall and Nitish Katara and continues to take so active an interest in politics that he wants to contest the election from jail. He is not D.P. Yadav's only heir in our unique system of hereditary democracy. The mother of Vikas has abandoned hearth and home for 'public service' and is contesting in the UP elections along with other relatives of Big Daddy Yadav.

Indian politics is truly the last refuge of scoundrels. And heirs. When we are not choosing between two criminals, we are these days increasingly offered a choice between two heirs. Nearly every major political leader in the country has started his own baby dynasty, his personal experiment in hereditary democracy. The BJP, which at one point fought a strident battle against the Congress party's dynastic politics, now participates fully in dynasty making, so that in Uttar Pradesh we have the heirs of Rajnath Singh, Kalyan Singh, and Lalji Tandon all fighting to keep the family business intact.

Rumour has it that the BJP's holier-than-thou national leaders are encouraging this trend because they have themselves discovered the benefits of hereditary democracy.

But who can cast the first stone when this is an all-party, all-India political trend. In the recent Punjab election, nearly every new face was an heir, whichever party's list you wanted to examine. The new Punjab government is almost a Badal family affair. The most outrageous example of 'public service' as family business remains the Rabri Devi story, in which our union minister for railways had handed the chief ministership of Bihar to his semi-literate wife when he faced a jail term for alleged corruption.

The contempt our political class has for India shows every time some so-called 'leader' dumps an heir on us, and this contempt is evident in our most refined and educated politicians.

Are we going to waste a decade or so acquiescing or has the time come to start thinking about a correction in our system of democracy? Has the time come to demand a referendum on the kind of political system we want?

One of the letters I received in response to last week's column came from a former chief justice of Himachal Pradesh, who suggested that we begin a public debate on why we should not switch to a presidential system of government. This column supports the idea from the bottom of its Fifth Columnist heart.

The two most obvious benefits of directly electing a president are that he (or she) would need to prove that he had the support of the whole country, and the second is that he could choose his cabinet from outside the ranks of our elected representatives.

Governance in the twenty-first century requires administrators who are technically competent to handle their jobs, not men who are there just because they are the people's choice. One of the reasons why Indian infrastructure is being built at bullock-cart pace despite lagging so much behind the rest of the world is that our ministers for power, transport, urban development and, for instance, telecommunications, are often men without any knowledge of the subject they are in charge of.

We can no longer afford on-the-job training. If the Indian economy is doing better today than ever before, it is despite the government, not because of it. But think how much faster things would happen if we had good governance? It's time to talk of change.

UTTAR PRADESH READY FOR TAKEOVER

13 May 2007

Having grown up in the dark ages of Indian politics, when India was the private property of not just one party but one family, it thrills me every time an incumbent government bites the dust. It is my view that one of the reasons why our ancient land progressed at bullock cart pace in the first forty years of becoming a nation state is because we suffered a peculiarly Indian form of ballot-box totalitarianism caused by the absence of choices at election time.

Chacha Nehru, we learned in nursery school, was the 'tallest leader' in the country so how could we think of voting for anyone other than his party. It was an unhealthy situation that took decades to change and has not yet changed enough. We currently have a prime minister urging us to return to our days of demagogues and subservience by pronouncing during the Uttar Pradesh election that Rahul Gandhi was our 'future'. And the little 'laat sahib' modestly agreed. His family had broken up Pakistan, he declared proudly, and would have saved the Babri Masjid had we continued to allow India to be treated as their private estate.

So every time an incumbent government is thrown out I send up three cheers. But the ousting of Mulayam Singh's government last week pleased me particularly. Not because I have anything personal against him but because we cannot afford to have our largest, most populous state growing so slowly that it drags the country down. Mulayam Singh's government, despite Amitabh Bachchan's certificates of good character, did nothing to stop the state's decline into lawlessness and chaos. Things are so bad now that it is this column's considered opinion that Uttar Pradesh is the worst-governed state in the country. In the reign of Mr and Mrs Laloo Yadav this honour went to Bihar, but while things have improved for Biharis there has been no sign of improvement in Uttar Pradesh.

The only people who have done well are the politicians. Amazingly well. They own vast properties, their children go to fine universities in foreign lands, their cars are bigger than the cars of businessmen (though mysteriously they never own them) and they rarely need to fly commercial any more. If someone counted how many private planes and helicopters were used in the Uttar Pradesh election, it could make an interesting document of economic change.

Nobody paid for them personally, you will hear, it was the party. To which we should ask, where are the parties getting so much money from these days? Frankly, though, corruption is now endemic in Indian politics. It cannot be eradicated. The only solution is for us to teach our politicians to make money out of doing some good for the country instead of making it out of bad things like trying to turn the Taj Mahal into a shopping mall, as Mayawati tried to do when she was the chief minister last time.

From all accounts she is now older and wiser and there is no point in spoiling her magnificent victory by dredging up bad memories, so in a spirit of goodwill I offer some humble suggestions on how Uttar Pradesh can be transformed within the next five years.

As the state that has the Taj Mahal and Varanasi, the new government should consider the economic possibilities of tourism. The potential is enormous if you consider that more foreign tourists visit the Taj than any other Indian monument, and Varanasi is increasingly the ancient Hindu city every visitor wants to see.

If millions of tourists are not already flocking to Uttar

Pradesh, it is because the roads are bad, power supply unreliable, means of transport dodgy and municipal government so abysmal that beautiful old Moghul single-trade towns like Ferozabad, Khurja and Kannauj today resemble garbage dumps.

Agra and Varanasi are not much better off where this is concerned, but private enterprise has stepped in and made a little difference. What private enterprise cannot do is build the heavy infrastructure or take charge of cleaning up the cities. This has to be taken up by the government. The benefits of using tourism as a vehicle of economic change is that the infrastructure the tourism industry needs is the exact infrastructure that ordinary people need—electricity, sanitary living conditions, roads and the rule of law.

Mayawati has proved that when it comes to social engineering and caste she is the most adept of all Uttar Pradesh politicians. She now has a chance to prove that on the economic front she can do more than build Ambedkar Parks. She inherits a state that is in a state of disrepair and will need the best help in the world to put it together again. Meanwhile, let's raise a toast to incumbent governments continuing to bite the dust.

DOCTOR, HEAL THY GOVERNMENT

27 May 2007

The most intriguing aspect of the prime minister's ten commandments to businessmen last week was that if he made the same speech to his ministers and coalition partners it would make such a difference.

We might hope for real change, and the first sign of good governance in the remaining two years of the United Progressive Alliance's rule, if the prime minister's colleagues listened to his advice. 'India has made us,' the prime minister said, 'we must make Bharat.' Nobody needs to be reminded of this more than Dr Manmohan Singh's government.

Speaking to the CII (Confederation of Indian Industries) in Delhi last week, the prime minister said, 'The time has come for the better off sections of our society to understand the need to make our growth process more inclusive; to eschew conspicuous consumption; to save more and waste less; to care for those who are less privileged and less well-off; to be role models of probity, moderation and charity.'

If I had been invited to the dinner party that celebrated the UPA government's third anniversary last week and asked to explain the drubbing the Congress party and its allies have taken in recent assembly elections I would have said the same thing in those very words.

What annoys the *aam aadmi* is not whether Ratan Tata or Mukesh Ambani fly around in private planes or whether Vijay Mallya likes buying fleets of yatchs. What annoys him is when he sees the man he elects to Parliament suddenly become a vulgar, conspicuous consumer with no known source of income. Barely does he enter the hallowed portals of the Lok Sabha that MP sahib begins to live like a tycoon.

Expensive cars appear, the ancestral home gets bigger, interior decorators descend, the wife starts sparkling with jewels and the children go off to foreign universities. This bothers the *aam aadmi* because he sees no change at all in his own life. He asks for very little. Regular supplies of electricity for which he would gladly pay, clean water, minimal public healthcare, a decent school for his children, reliable public transport and a road that does not disappear when the rains come.

It is when none of these things happen that the *aam aadmi* begins plotting to throw his MP and government out. As an economist does the prime minister not see this? Does he not see that because of his inability to effect administrative reforms his government's wondrous schemes to provide jobs and homes to the poor continue to fail. We now hear that the Public Distribution System (PDS) will include more items of food because the poor are being hit by rising prices.

What is the point if the Planning Commission itself admits that sixty per cent of the food is stolen and sold in the black market. Ila Patnaik analysed the Planning Commission study in this newspaper (24 May 2007) and provided this scary statistic the day before the prime minister made his speech: 'Of the estimated 45.41 million Below Poverty Line (BPL) households in India in 2001, just fifty-seven per cent are covered by the PDS.'

Why has the prime minister been able to do nothing to give us a less leaky PDS? What has stopped him from stepping up the pace at which roads are built? Why has it slowed down under his government? Why has he done nothing about reforms in the power sector? Why do we see no cuts in government spending on itself? Why do his ministers live in houses in Delhi that only the richest Indians can afford? Why has he done nothing to cut their fringe benefits like free travel and subsidized electricity and water?

Instead of worrying about how much CEOs are paid, something decided by the market, why does he not worry about how much the Indian taxpayer pays to keep ministers and MPs living in a style that does not match their 'socialist' ideals.

Among the prime minister's ten commandments was advice on ending corruption and concern for the environment. Would he like to tell us where the Congress Party got its funds from for the recent elections in Uttar Pradesh? Whose private aeroplanes did party leaders fly around in? Who paid? As for the environment, can his government explain why it has failed so abysmally to protect the last of our tigers? Could he tell us why the Ganga and the Yamuna remain polluted despite hundreds of crores having been spent on cleaning them?

Industry must do its bit for building Bharat but it will make little difference as long as government continues to fail us on every front time and time again. So spare us the moral science lectures please, prime minister, and concentrate on putting your own government in order.

THE JEHAD AT OUR DOOR

15 July 2007

As someone who spent years reporting on the events that led to Operation Bluestar and the decade of terrorism that followed in its aftermath I watched the siege of Islamabad's Lal Masjid with deep interest. Last week when it ended with one of the two head mullahs, Abdul Rashid Ghazi, and many of his holy warriors dead, General Pervez Musharraf received kudos from his friends in the West. And condemnation from Ayman al-Zawahiri that amounted to a character certificate in the eyes of the West and us infidels on this side of the border. Urging the Muslims of Pakistan to join the jehad Osama bin Laden's lieutenant said, 'Musharraf and his hunting dogs have rubbed your honour in the dirt in the service of the crusaders and the Jews.' This resulted in more praise for the general with the American president publicly patting him on the back. But I fear that Operation Silence could turn out to be as much of a disaster as Operation Bluestar.

If you covered Punjab in the eighties as closely as I did you would not need to be told that Sant Jarnail Singh Bhindranwale could have been stopped without blowing up the Akal Takht and killing hundreds of people in the battle of the Golden Temple. You would not need to be told either that Punjab's decade of terrorism began as a result of that botched attack, and who knows Indira Gandhi may still have been alive. Bhindranwale moved into the Golden Temple with a handful of armed followers in 1982. Between then and the summer of

1984 there must have been a hundred opportunities to persuade him to desist from his violent ways. But for reasons that remain a mystery these opportunities were never taken.

While watching the armed assault on the Lal Masjid last week I could not suppress a sense of deja vu. Was this not the same thing happening in a different way? The Lal Masjid is in the heart of Islamabad, yards away from ISI headquarters and the seat of Pakistan's government. So how is it that the general did not know that it was a nest of fanatical jehadis? The two Ghazi brothers gave interviews on television explaining their Islamist philosophy and days before the final battle of the Lal Masjid, Abdul Aziz Ghazi, the one caught escaping in a burqa and high heels, admitted on a Pakistani television channel that his relationship with terrorist groups like the Lashkar-e-Tayyaba and Hizbul Mujahideen was one of love. 'Mohabbat ka rishta hai' he said poetically. Well? Did General Musharraf not know this?

Did the Pakistani government not itself have a 'mohabbat ka rishta' with horrible monsters like Daniel Pearl's killer Omar Sheikh, and his fellow traveller, Maulana Masood Azhar? When these two gentlemen were graciously released by our external affairs minister in Kandahar in exchange for the passengers of IC-814 did they not flee instantly across the border into Pakistan and were they not honoured guests of the ISI until Daniel Pearl was murdered?

As a proud infidel, resident in our very vulnerable Dar-ul-Harb, I worry about the consequences of the Lal Masjid siege for us. If Al Qaeda is training its radar on Pakistan and urging all Muslims to rise up and join the jehad we are unlikely to remain unaffected. The jehad will almost certainly spill over and Al Qaeda may notice that if instead of concentrating on the West they had tried to make the Indian subcontinent the new Dar-ul-Islam they may well have succeeded.

We have a government that has done nothing to indicate that it can protect us from the jehad. There have been a series of jehadi attacks on Indian soil since Manmohan Singh became prime minister and not once have they resulted in his government evolving a strategy to deal with the global jehad. Not once have the killers been caught. All we have got so far are suspects picked up after the event in dubious circumstances.

Lal Krishna Advani has been very vocal in his criticism of this lately without noting that he did no better when he was home minister. And he a Hindu nationalist bred on Hindutva ideology! What excuse does he have for doing so little to protect Bharat Mata? Meanwhile, jehad notches up success after success. Formerly peaceful Bangladesh is now pulsating with jehadi sentiment and many of those who kill on Indian soil find shelter in that country.

Jehadi ideology finds sympathizers here as well, as can be seen from the rise of mullah political parties. These exist in Uttar Pradesh and Assam and the municipal election in Malegaon was recently won by a party of maulvis. How long before we have our own Lal Masjid?

CAN WE STILL CALL IT JUSTICE?

5 August 2007

Such a pity that the sentencing of Sanjay Dutt hogged all headlines last week, or we may have noticed that it was a great week to observe the worrying pace at which the law takes its course in India. It moves with such geriatric slowness that we need to ask once more why chief justices come and chief justices go, committees come and committees go, and the Indian justice system continues to work at a pace that defeats the idea of justice.

Some of the most important cases in Indian criminal history reached a climax last week and the shortest time it took for justice to be done in any of them was nine years. This was the case of the Coimbatore bombers who tried to bump off L.K. Advani on 14 February 1998. He was not the only target, and the nineteen bombs that went off in synchronized blasts killed fifty-eight people and left two hundred injured.

A special court was set up to try the case based on a report by a special investigation team that was 17,000 pages long. Why should any report be that long? If it takes that long to say something there has to be a problem in articulation, and there is.

The language of the Indian justice system is a mixture of Victorian English and Indian officialese. It has nothing to do with modern English and has so many hithertos, therebys and henceforwards thrown in that it would not surprise me if a competent sub-editor succeeded in reducing 17,000 pages to seven hundred or even seventy.

So the first problem is language. If the justice system cannot start functioning in comprehensible, concise English, then let it try doing so in Indian languages. Then should begin the process of tackling procedures. In these days of computers and digitalization why should a judge need six months to deliver his judgement, as happened in the Bombay bomb blasts case?

Has anything been done to modernize these archaic procedures? We need to know.

Another case that was decided last week was that of the assassination of the chief minister of Punjab, Beant Singh, who was killed on 31 August 1995 by a suicide bomber named Dilawar Singh. Twelve years later, Jagtar Singh Hawara and Balwant Singh have been sentenced to death for criminal conspiracy and murder. Can we stop here for a moment and think about the implications of it taking this long to sentence the killers of a major politician?

If you or I or one of our loved ones was murdered in relative obscurity, how long would that case take? Forever?

May I mention here that twenty years ago I registered a case against a DTC bus that rammed into the back of my humble Maruti 800 near the Hyatt Regency hotel in Delhi. I was shaken up but unhurt, so off I trotted to the nearest police station and registered a case. I have not heard a word about it so far. Around the same time my tiny office was broken into by some municipal thugs who started smashing it up before my eyes. It turned out they had no legal right to do this and were merely carrying out someone's vendetta against my landlord. I registered a case but have heard nothing about it since.

Why should I expect to, when it takes twenty years for justice to begin to happen in the massacre of dalits? Last week, a special court in Andhra Pradesh finally pronounced judgement in the massacre of dalits in the village of Tsundur in Guntur district in 1991. Fifty-six upper caste killers were found guilty of murder and conspiracy. Great, but who remembers the case except the relatives of those who died?

We have recently seen much melodrama about the supposed

violation of Mohammad Haneef's human rights by the Australian government. Haneef was so exalted by the support he received from the Indian media that he returned to a hero's welcome with TV crews camping outside his Bangalore home to give us a detailed coverage of his homecoming. Senior anchors went into hysterics over the violation of his fundamental rights, only to discover later that he may have known about his cousins' jehadi activities.

He needs to praise Allah that he was arrested in Australia and not India. He could have spent years in jail before being allowed to hold a press conference, if you consider that nearly eighty per cent of those incarcerated in Indian jails are still under trial. Some are adolescents who remain in jail only because they are unable to pay Rs. 500 for bail in cases of petty thefts. What hope can ordinary people have when it takes fifteen-twenty years for terrorists to be punished? Is it not time that the chief justice of India gave us some answers?

CONGRESS AND THE COMMISSAR

26 August 2007

As I watched Commissar Karat and his fellow commies charge the prime minister with bartering away India's 'sovereignty' in exchange for the nuclear deal, I wondered if they were suffering from historical amnesia. Or do they just choose not to remember our Soviet era in the hope that nobody else will either.

Well, having become politically conscious in those bleak decades, I remember all too well. I remember that all our weapons came from the Soviet Union and all the shoddy consumer goods we produced were exported to that country in a form of commerce that was more barter than trade. I remember what a shabby hopeless country India was on account of this restricted engagement with the world. I remember how India's foreign policy was so dictated by the USSR that we did not even dare condemn the invasion of Afghanistan? How is it that the comrades did not see any threat to our sovereignty in those bad old days?

If our sovereignty was strong enough to survive when all anyone talked about when they discussed India was 'our starving millions', then it is more than likely to survive now when the economy is growing at nearly ten per cent and we are considered an 'emerging economy'.

As a proud Indian who relishes the fact that we no longer wander the world with a begging bowl in our hands, it disgusts me when people talk of our 'sovereignty' as if it were so fragile that it could be destroyed by a single treaty. But it is not about a single treaty, is it?

What bothers our lefties is our growing closeness to the United States. In the words of a statement that arrived in my mailbox from Medha Patkar and a couple of her NGO pals, 'This deal is part of a successful attempt by the United States to build a strategic relationship with India, in confronting the rising capitalist challenge from China, where India will be used as its client in the region.'

Thank you Ms Patkar for spelling it out. China is indeed a capitalist country today and it does not want India to begin to compete, so it uses our communists and muddle-headed activists like Medha Patkar as a fifth column. Well, it's time that the prime minister took them on, even if it means sacrificing his government. Let him state clearly that a closer strategic and commercial relationship with the United States is in India's national interest and if the Marxists and sundry other political parties think otherwise, then let them put their case before voters in the next election and see what happens.

As every poll indicates, the average Indian thinks friendship with the United States is a good thing and a very large number think the nuclear deal is in India's national interest. On my travels these days, I constantly run into people who harangue me for not writing strongly enough against those 'Chinese agents'. And it delights me to inform you that the Hindi press is currently filled with articles that revile Commissar Karat and his comrades for their inordinate fondness for China. The sense I get of the public mood is that our communist parties are not going to get enough seats to bully whichever government comes to power after the next general election.

May I happily predict that the party that is going to suffer most over its cussed and incomprehensible opposition to the nuclear deal is the Bharatiya Janata Party. Last week, its ally, the Shiv Sena, broke ranks on the issue, and if the BJP bothers to conduct its own poll, it is likely to find that its voters are no longer sure that the national interest is safe in BJP hands.

Where it was looking quite strong a few months ago, it

now looks like it is going to be in no position to lead a coalition government, leave alone win even the seats it currently has in the Lok Sabha. Good. Another spell on the Opposition benches may restore some sense of reality.

The real beneficiary of the prime minister standing up to the commissar will be the Congress. There are optimistic murmurings from party headquarters even over the possibility that the government may fall as soon as next month. As for the prime minister, he has not looked more prime ministerial since he took the job. As someone who has been critical of many of the things he has done and failed to do in the past three years, may I say that over the nuclear deal, he has behaved like a statesman. It would be a terrible shame if he is forced to back down now by those pressures the Left is so adept at exerting over the Congress party's crypto-Marxists.